D0379207

Books by Irving Chernev

PRACTICAL CHESS ENDINGS

LOGICAL CHESS, MOVE BY MOVE

1000 BEST SHORT GAMES OF CHESS

COMBINATIONS: THE HEART OF CHESS

AN INVITATION TO CHESS
(with Kenneth Harkness)

WINNING CHESS
(with Fred Reinfeld)

THE FIRESIDE BOOK OF CHESS
(with Fred Reinfeld)

WINNING CHESS TRAPS

THE BRIGHT SIDE OF CHESS

CHESSBOARD MAGIC!

THE RUSSIANS PLAY CHESS

CHESS STRATEGY AND TACTICS
(with Fred Reinfeld)

PRACTICAL
Chess Endings

A BASIC GUIDE TO ENDGAME STRATEGY FOR THE BEGINNER AND THE MORE ADVANCED CHESS PLAYER

BY *Irving Chernev*

DOVER PUBLICATIONS, INC.

NEW YORK

Published in Canada by General Publishing Company, Ltd., 30 Lesmill Road, Don Mills, Toronto, Ontario.
Published in the United Kingdom by Constable and Company, Ltd., 10 Orange Street, London WC 2.

This Dover edition, first published in 1969, is an unabridged and unaltered republication of the work originally published in 1961 by Simon and Schuster, Inc.

Standard Book Number: 486-22208-X
Library of Congress Catalog Card Number: 69-15362

Manufactured in the United States of America
Dover Publications, Inc.
180 Varick Street
New York, N. Y. 10014

For Aimée and Mel

CONTENTS

Introduction

THE BASIC object in the endgame is to promote a Pawn, and get a new Queen. An extra Queen on the board gives a player a superiority in material which is usually decisive.

A good part of this book is devoted to King and Pawn endings, where the win is achieved by turning a Pawn into a Queen. I agree with Purdy, who says, "Without knowing something of the ending King and Pawn against King, one cannot call oneself a chess player."

Other sections of the book feature the Knight, the Bishop, the Rook, and the Queen in important roles, either in helping a Pawn become a Queen, or in themselves engineering mating combinations.

The terms in all positions are "White to play and win." The purpose is to maintain uniformity, so that White's Pawns move up the board in all cases.

The book is designed to improve the skill of the practical player who is interested in winning the ending clearly, simply and efficiently. The dilettante, though, who revels in artistry in an ending, has not been neglected. Many fine compositions whose chief purpose is to entertain have also been included. Thus, the author hopes, all needs will be served.

The Pawn

FASCINATED by the subtle strategy to be found in Pawn endings, I have included enough to satisfy the most avid student or the most ardent connoisseur. The latter will revel especially in the splendid endings by Grigoriev.

If there is one thing to be learned in Pawn play, it is that the King is a powerful piece. *The King must be used aggressively.*

No. 3 is a basic position in King and Pawn against King. The winning idea is easy enough, *but it must be understood.*

Simple Opposition is illustrated in Positions No. 3 through 10, No. 13, No. 15 and No. 33. Incidentally, No. 9 and No. 10 show a couple of interesting King wanderings.

Distant Opposition (where one King's influence on the other is felt the length of the chessboard) is beautifully demonstrated by Grigoriev in No. 66.

Delightful finesses in King and Pawn against King and Pawn endings are found in positions by Moravec No. 19, De Feijter No. 21, Grigoriev No. 23,

Duras No. 24 and Grigoriev No. 26.

Surprising key moves are those in Dedrle No. 16, Maiselis No. 18, Mandler No. 25, Grigoriev No. 27, Ebersz No. 47, Crum No. 50, Moravec No. 58, and Chekhover No. 68.

Impressive enough to qualify as masterpieces are the compositions of Chéron No. 44, Grigoriev Nos. 46, No. 53, No. 62, No. 63, No. 69, No. 78, De Feijter No. 93, and Isenegger No. 94.

Piquant play marks the Grigoriev No. 10, Grigoriev No. 59, Rey No. 61, Grigoriev No. 64, Kupczewski No. 67 and Fontana No. 73.

Amusing ideas abound in Grigoriev No. 51, Moravec No. 58, Sackmann No. 82, Horwitz No. 84, Troitzky No. 85, Rinck No. 88, Lapin No. 89, Neumann No. 90, Rinck No. 92 and Moravec No. 97.

The theme of Triangulation is neatly illustrated in Nos. 40 and 41.

Saavedra No. 101 is of course an old favorite, and could hardly be omitted from an endgame anthology.

NO. *1*

WHITE
to play
and win

PROMOTING the Pawn will win easily for White. With King and Queen against King, the process of forcing mate is elementary.

Can the Pawn advance at once, or will it be caught by Black? Let's try moving the Pawn and see:

1 P-R4	K-B5
2 P-R5	K-Q4
3 P-R6	K-K3
4 P-R7	K-B2
5 P-R8(Q)	

White wins

We can thus play out the moves (mentally, of course) or get the answer by a simple count. The latter method tells us that after four moves the Pawn will stand at R7, and Black's pursuing King at his B2—too late to stop the Pawn from Queening.

NO. 2

WHITE
to play
and win

CHERNEV 1960

WHITE cannot win by merely advancing the Pawn. A little preparation is needed.

A simple count shows that the Pawn can reach R7 in four moves, but that the pursuing King, rushing back along the diagonal, will head it off at Kt2.

The play would be: *1* P-R4, K-K5 *2* P-R5, K-Q4 *3* P-R6, K-B3 *4* P-R7, K-Kt2 and the Pawn is lost. White must try other means:

1 K-B5!

This prevents Black from moving along the diagonal to stop the Pawn, and threatens to win by *2* P-R4, *3* P-R5 etc.

1 . . . K-K6

Black seizes a new diagonal and is ready for this continuation: *2* P-R4, K-Q5 *3* P-R5, K-B4 *4* P-R6, K-Kt3, and he wins the Pawn.

2 K-K5!

Interferes with that little idea, and once again threatens to win by pushing the Pawn.

2 . . . K-Q6

Now if *3* P-R4, K-B5 *4* P-R5, K-Kt4 and Black draws.

3 K-Q5!

Cuts Black off a third time from pursuing the Pawn.

3 . . . K-B6

This gives White a last chance to start the Pawn prematurely. If now *4* P-R4, K-Kt5 nails the Pawn down.

4 K-B5!

This is decisive! Black's King is shut out completely. The continuation (regardless of anything Black does) will be *5* P-R4, *6* P-R5, *7* P-R6, *8* P-R7 and *9* P-R8(Q).

White wins.

NO. *3*

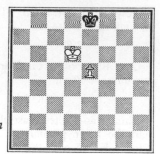

WHITE
to play
and win

THE key to the win:

Move the King, not the Pawn!

The King must clear a way for the Pawn to come through. He does this by taking the opposition: he moves to a face to face position with Black's King, and forces Black to give way. White can then seize control of K8, the square on which the Pawn promotes to a Queen.

Without this preparation, advancing the Pawn does not work. For instance: *1* P-K6, K-Q1 *2* P-K7ch, K-K1 *3* K-K6, (to protect the Pawn) and Black draws by stalemate.

The proper technique:

1 K-K6!

The Kings face each other, and White having the opposition, forces Black to give way. The King that can compel the other to yield ground either by retreating or stepping aside, is said to have the opposition.

This is now for White the ideal position in King and Pawn endings. He wins no matter whose move it is.

1 . . .   K-Q1

Or *1* . . . K-B1 *2* K-Q7, K-B2 *3* P-K6ch, K-B1 *4* P-K7ch, and wins.

2 K-B7

From this square, the King not only controls K8 (the square on which the Pawn becomes a Queen) but is also in position to escort the Pawn on its way up.

2 . . .	K-Q2
3 P-K6ch	K-Q1
4 P-K7ch	K-Q2
5 P-K8(Q)ch	

White wins

NO. 4

WHITE
to play
and win

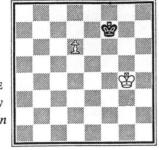

WHITE wins this ending by getting the opposition, *and maintaining it.*

1 K-B5

Strong, but obviously forced, as his Pawn was in danger.

The Kings face each other with one square between them. White has the opposition, since his opponent must give ground by retreating or stepping to one side.

1 . . .	K-B1
2 K-B6!	

Best, since it maintains the opposition. White must resist the temptation to move closer to the Pawn. This would be the consequence: 2 K-K6, K-K1 3 P-Q7ch, K-Q1 4 K-Q6, and Black draws by stalemate. Note in this and similar positions that the Pawn must reach the seventh rank *without checking* in order to win.

2 . . .	K-K1
3 K-K6	K-Q1
4 P-Q7	K-B2
5 K-K7	

White wins

NO. 5

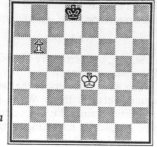

WHITE

to play
and win

ANOTHER song to the same tune. White uses the force of the opposition to help his Pawn reach the Queening square.

| *1* K-Q5 | K-Q2 |
| *2* K-B5 | |

If Black could meet this by *2 . . . K-B2, he* would have the opposition. This being impossible, he sets a little trap.

| *2 . . .* | K-Q1 |

He hopes that White will play the obvious *3* K-B6 (moving closer to the Pawn) whereupon *3 . . .* K-B1 *4* P-Kt7ch, K-Kt1 *5* K-Kt6 draws.

3 K-Q6!

This gives White the opposition and assures the win, since the Pawn will now reach the seventh rank without checking.

3 . . .	K-B1
4 K-B6	K-Kt1
5 P-Kt7	K-R2
6 K-B7	

White wins, as the Pawn will Queen.

NO. 6

WHITE
*to play
and win*

WHITE wins this ending by using his King aggressively. The King heads for QB6, an ideal King and Pawn position, since it wins with or without the move.

1 K-Kt6!

The only move to win. Moving *1* P-B5 instead allows *1* . . . K-B2 *2* K-Kt5, K-K3 and Black will win the Pawn.

After the actual move, White has the opposition and by maintaining it makes the winning process child's play.

1 . . .	K-B1
2 K-B6	K-K1
3 K-K6	K-Q1
4 K-Q6	

Black never gets a chance to approach the Pawn.

4 . . .	K-B1
5 K-B6	

An endgame position worth remembering, since *White wins no matter whose turn it is to move.*

5 . . .	K-Kt1

If instead *5* . . . K-Q1 *6* K-Kt7, (seizing control of the Pawn's Queening square) K-K2 *7* P-B5, and the Pawn cannot be stopped.

6 K-Q7	K-Kt2
7 P-B5	K-Kt1
8 P-B6	K-R2
9 P-B7	

White wins

NO. 7

WHITE
*to play
and win*

WHITE plays to get his King in front of the Pawn. The position is then a win, *no matter whose move it is.*

1 K-B7!

There is no win after *1* P-Kt6ch, K-R1 *2* P-Kt7ch (*2* K-B7 stalemates Black) K-Kt1 *3* K-Kt6, and Black is stalemated. Notice that the Pawn check at the seventh rank does not win unless White controls the Queening square.

1 . . .	K-R1
2 K-Kt6!	K-Kt1
3 K-R6	K-R1
4 P-Kt6	K-Kt1
5 P-Kt7	

The winning idea. The Pawn reaches the seventh rank *without checking.*

5 . . .	K-B2
6 K-R7	

Seizes control of Kt8, the Pawn's Queening square.

6 . . .	K-K2
7 P-Kt8(Q)	

White wins

NO. *8*

WHITE
*to play
and win*

WHITE plays to get the opposition. This will place his King in a dominating position, force Black to retreat, and clear a way for the Pawn to come through.

  1 K-K4 K-K3

White's position is ideal. His King is in front of the Pawn with one square between them. In cases such as this, where he does not have the opposition, he can wrest it from Black by gaining a tempo with a Pawn move.

    2 P-K3!

Shows the value of having a square between King and Pawn. The spare move leaves the position of the Kings unchanged—but it is Black's move and he must give way!

  2 . . . K-Q3
  3 K-B5 K-K2

If instead *3* . . . K-Q4, the procedure is *4* P-K4ch, K-Q3 *5* K-B6!, K-Q2 *6* P-K5, K-K1 *7* K-K6, and White wins.

    4 K-K5

Seizes the opposition. Black must retreat or step aside.

  4 . . . K-Q2
  5 K-B6 K-K1

Or *5* . . . K-Q3 *6* P-K4, K-Q2 *7* P-K5, K-Q1 (*7* . . . K-K1 *8* K-K6) *8* K-B7 and White wins.

    6 K-K6

The simplest, as White has a forced win no matter whose move it is, and no matter whether his Pawn stands on K2, K3, K4 or K5.

  6 . . . K-B1
  7 P-K4 K-K1
  8 P-K5 K-B1
  9 K-Q7 K-B2
  10 P-K6ch K-B1
  11 P-K7ch

White wins

NO. 9

WHITE
to play
and win

TO CLEAR a path for the Pawn, White must maneuver his King to a dominating position in front of the Pawn. He does so interestingly enough by having the King take a walk along the diagonal!

1 K-B2	K-Kt3
2 K-K3	K-B4
3 K-Q4!	K-K3
4 K-B5	K-Q2

If instead *4* . . . K-K4 *5* P-Q4ch, K-K3 *6* K-B6 (but not *6* P-Q5ch, K-Q2 *7* P-Q6, K-Q1 *8* K-B6, K-B1 *9* P-Q7ch, K-Q1 and Black draws) K-K2 *7* P-Q5, K-Q1 *8* K-Q6 and we have a familiar win.

5 K-Q5	K-K2

White could now ruin things by *6* P-Q4, K-Q2, and Black has the opposition and draws.

6 K-B6	K-K3

Or *6* . . . K-Q1 *7* K-Q6 and White wins.

7 P-Q4	K-K2
8 P-Q5	K-Q1

On *8* . . . K-K1 *9* K-B7 ends it.

9 K-Q6	

White wins

NO. *10*

WHITE
to play
and win

GRIGORIEV

WITHOUT the aid of the King, who makes a little trip, White's Pawn could never get to the Queening square.

1 K-Kt3

If instead *1* P-Kt4 (starting out unescorted) K-B4 *2* P-Kt5, K-Q4 *3* P-Kt6, K-K3, and the Pawn is lost.

| *1* . . . | K-B4 |
| *2* K-B3 | |

Here too, and for the next few moves, advancing the Pawn permits Black to capture it and draw.

2 . . .	K-Q4
3 K-Q3	K-K4
4 K-K3	K-B4
5 K-B3	K-Kt4
6 K-Kt3	

Sometimes the way to ensure the Pawn's progress is to get right in its way!

6 . . .	K-B4
7 K-R4	K-B3
8 K-R5	K-Kt2

Or *8* . . . K-B4 *9* P-Kt4ch, K-B3 *10* K-R6, K-B2 *11* P-Kt5, K-Kt1 (*11* . . . K-B1 *12* K-R7) *12* K-Kt6 and White wins.

| *9* K-Kt5 | K-B2 |
| *10* K-R6 | K-Kt1 |

If *10* . . . K-B3 *11* P-Kt4, K-B2 *12* P-Kt5 as in the previous note.

11 K-Kt6

White wins

NO. *11*

WHITE
*to play
and win*

IN ORDER to win (and this applies to all endings where the passed Pawn is on the Rook file) White must prevent Black's King from getting in front of the Pawn, since that always ends in a draw. He must also (this may seem strange!) guard against having his own King boxed in!

These are the drawing possibilities:

A] *1* K-Kt6, K-B1 *2* P-R4, K-Kt1 *3* P-R5, K-R1 *4* P-R6, K-Kt1 *5* P-R7ch, (nothing else is any better) K-R1 *6* K-R6 and Black is stalemated.

B] *1* K-Kt6, K-B1 *2* K-R7, (to prevent *2* . . . K-Kt1) K-B2 *3* P-R4, K-B1 *4* P-R5, K-B2 *5* P-R6, K-B1 *6* K-R8, K-B2 *7* P-R7, K-B1, and White is stalemated.

The way to win is to use the King aggressively—keep Black out of B1 (and any drawing chances) completely.

1 K-Kt7!

After this move, Black has no play at all.

1 . . .	K-Q2
2 P-R4	K-Q3
3 P-R5	K-B4
4 P-R6	

White wins. The Pawn marches gaily up to become a Queen.

NO. *12*

WHITE
to play
and win

PONZIANI 1769

THIS looks like an easy win, since the connected Pawns are never in danger. If the rear Pawn is captured, the other one advances. However there remains the danger of stalemating Black.

White solves the problem by remembering that *one* Pawn ahead is enough to win.

1 K-B4	K-Kt2
2 K-B5	K-R1
3 K-Kt5	

If White tries *3* K-K6, then after *3* . . . K-Kt2 *4* K-K7, K-R1, his King must not come any closer.

3 . . .	K-Kt2
4 P-R8(Q)ch!	KxQ
5 K-B6	K-Kt1
6 P-Kt7	K-R2
7 K-B7	

White wins

NO. *13*

WHITE
to play
and win

HORWITZ 1851

DOUBLED Pawns are often an advantage in the endgame if only for the fact that one of the Pawns may give up his life for the other!

1 P-Kt7	K-R2

Careful, now! If White moves 2 K-B7 he allows a draw by stalemate, while 2 P-Kt6ch, K-Kt1 lets the win slip forever.

2 P-Kt8(Q)ch!	KxQ
3 K-Kt6	

To get the opposition.

3 . . .	K-R1

Or 3 . . . K-B1 4 K-R7 and White wins.

4 K-B7	K-R2
5 P-Kt6ch	K-R1
6 P-Kt7ch	

White wins

NO. *14*

WHITE
to play
and win

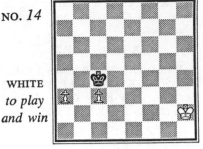

ALLGAIER 1795

THE isolated Pawns *look* weak and helpless. They are perfectly safe. An attack on either Pawn is parried by advancing the other!

1 P-R4!

Now if Black plays *1* . . . KxP the reply is *2* P-R5, and the Pawn cannot be overtaken.

1 . . .	K-B4
2 K-Kt3	

But not *2* P-B4, KxP nor *2* P-R5, K-Kt4. It is important not to advance the Pawns prematurely.

2 . . .   K-Kt3

Here too against *2* . . . K-B5, the Pawns stay put while the King moves closer by *3* K-B3.

3 P-B4   K-R4

The reply to *3* . . . K-B4 would be *4* P-R5.

4 P-B5	K-R3
5 K-B3	K-Kt2
6 P-R5	K-B3
7 P-R6	K-B2
8 K-K4	K-B3
9 K-K5	K-B2
10 K-Q5	K-Kt1
11 P-B6	K-B2

If *11* . . . K-R2 *12* P-B7 wins.

12 P-R7

White wins

NO. *15*

WHITE
to play
and win

PROKES 1946

THERE is a lesson in this ending for those who "take first and think it over later."

  1 K-B4   K-R2

If instead *1* . . . P-Kt4ch *2* K-B5, P-Kt5 *3* K-K6, P-Kt6 *4* P-B7, K-Kt2 (on *4* . . . P-Kt7, White Queens with check) *5* K-K7 and White wins.

  2 K-Kt5   K-R1
  3 K-R6!

Taking the opposition wins; taking the Pawn does not.

  3 . . .   K-Kt1

Or *3* . . . P-Kt4 *4* P-B7 followed by mate.

  4 KxP   K-R1
  5 K-B7   K-R2
  6 K-K8

White wins

NO. *16*

WHITE
to play
and win

DEDRLE 1921

1 K-Kt1!

A CURIOUS way to go after the Pawn! The obvious move *1* K-B3 lets Black escape. For example *1* K-B3, P-R6! *2* P-Kt4 (or *3* PxP, K-K3, and Black scurrying over to QR1 draws easily against a Pawn on the Rook file) K-K4 *3* K-Kt3, K-Q4 *4* KxP, K-B3 *5* K-R4, K-Kt3 *6* P-Kt5, K-Kt2 *7* K-R5, K-R2 *8* P-Kt6ch, K-Kt2 *9* K-Kt5, K-Kt1 *10* K-B6, K-B1, and White cannot avoid the draw.

  1 . . . P-R6

On *1* . . . K-K4 *2* K-R2, K-Q4 *3* K-R3, K-B4 *4* KxP, K-Kt3 *5* K-Kt4, and White having the opposition wins.

  2 P-Kt3! K-K4
  3 K-R2   K-Q4
  4 KxP   K-B3
  5 K-R4!

Certainly not *5* K-Kt4, K-Kt3, and all White's earlier strategy has been wasted since Black has the opposition and draws.

  5 . . . K-Kt3
  6 K-Kt4

White wins

WHITE
to play
and win

BERGER 1916

BLACK is double-crossed by his own Pawn! Without the Pawn on the board, Black's King simply heads for the magic square QR1, after which no power on earth can force a win.

1 P-R4	K-K5
2 P-R5	K-Q4
3 P-R6	K-Q3

Black's own Pawn stands in his way. His King is unable to move to the vital square QB3.

4 P-R7   K-B2

Too late.

5 P-R8(Q)

White wins

NO. *18*

WHITE
*to play
and win*

MAISELIS 1921

A STRAIGHT line is not the shortest distance between two points.

If White moves across the board to capture the Pawn, he wins the Pawn but not the game.

This is what would happen: *1* K-K7, K-B6 *2* K-Q7, K-Q5 *3* K-B7, K-B4 *4* K-Kt7, K-Q3 *5* KxP, K-B2 *6* K-R1, K-B1, and Black gets a draw.

Suppose he meanders down the board and then up again?

1 K-K6	K-B6
2 K-Q5!	

This is the point. Black is kept out of his Q5 square.

2 . . .	K-Kt5
3 K-B6	K-B5
4 K-Kt7	K-Kt4
5 KxP	K-B3
6 K-Kt8	

White wins

NO. *19*

WHITE
to play
and win

MORAVEC 1952

WHITE'S King must take a devious route to help his Pawn become a Queen.

1 P-Kt5   K-K4

There is no hope in *1* . . . P-R5 *2* P-Kt6, P-R6 *3* P-Kt7, P-R7 *4* P-Kt8(Q)ch.

2 P-Kt6!

If *2* K-B5 (trying to exclude Black's King) K-K3 *3* K-B6 (*3* P-Kt6, K-Q2 is a draw) P-R5 *4* P-Kt6, P-R6   *5* P-Kt7, P-R7   *6* P-Kt8(Q), P-R8(Q) and the position is a draw.

2 . . .   K-Q3
3 K-Kt5   P-R5

If *3* . . . K-Q2 *4* K-R6, K-B1 *5* K-R7 wins.

4 K-R6

Of course not *4* P-Kt7, K-B2 *5* K-R6, K-Kt1 and White loses.

4 . . .	P-R6
5 P-Kt7	K-B2
6 K-R7	P-R7
7 P-Kt8(Q)ch	

White wins

NO. 20

WHITE
*to play
and win*

THE race to Queen a Pawn is also a race to see who can check first, and perhaps win the other Queen.

> *1* P-K6   K-B3

Black loses quickly after *1* . . . P-Kt6 *2* P-K7, P-Kt7 *3* P-K8(Q), P-Kt8(Q) *4* Q-Kt8ch, and his Queen comes off the board.

> *2* K-Q6   P-Kt6
> *3* P-K7   P-Kt7

If *3* . . . K-B2 *4* K-Q7, and the threat of Queening with check wins for White.

> *4* P-K8(Q)   P-Kt8(Q)
> *5* Q-B8ch   K-Kt4
> *6* Q-Kt8ch

White wins the Queen and the game

NO. 21

WHITE
to play
and win

DE FEIJTER 1939

WHITE'S timing has to be precise in order to Queen his Pawn with a check.

1 K-Kt5	P-Kt4
2 K-B4	

To stop Black's Pawn. The alternative *2* P-R5, P-Kt5 leads to both Pawns Queening—and a draw.

2 . . .	K-K7

Naturally, if *2* . . . P-Kt5 *3* K-K4 will catch the Pawn.

3 K-K4	K-Q7

Here too *3* . . . P-Kt5 loses the Pawn.

4 K-Q4	K-B7

Now if White play *5* P-R5, Black draws by *5* . . . P-Kt5 *6* P-R6, P-Kt6 *7* P-R7, P-Kt7 *8* P-R8(Q), P-Kt8(Q).

5 K-B5	K-B6

Ready to meet *6* KxP with *6* . . . K-Q5 *7* P-R5, K-K4, winning White's Pawn in return.

6 P-R5	P-Kt5
7 P-R6	P-Kt6
8 P-R7	P-Kt7
9 P-R8(Q)ch	K-B7
10 Q-R2ch	K-B8
11 Q-B4ch	K-B7
12 Q-B4ch	K-Q7
13 Q-Kt3	K-B8
14 Q-B3ch	K-Kt8
15 K-B4	K-R7
16 Q-R5ch	K-Kt8
17 K-Kt3	K-B8
18 Q-K1 mate	

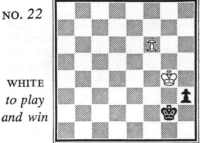

WHITE
to play
and win

WHERE both sides Queen their Pawns, the one who first gives check has an advantage that is often decisive.

1 P-B7	P-R7
2 P-B8(Q)	P-R8(Q)
3 Q-B3ch	K-Kt8

Forced, as *3* . . . K-R7 allows *4* Q-Kt3 mate.

4 Q-K3ch	K-B8
5 Q-B1ch	K-Kt7
6 Q-Q2ch	K-B8
7 Q-Q1ch	K-Kt7
8 Q-K2ch	K-Kt8
9 K-Kt3!	

White wins. Black is curiously helpless to prevent mate.

NO. *23*

WHITE
to play
and win

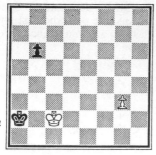

GRIGORIEV 1928

1 K-B3!

THE straightforward *1* P-Kt4 leads to *1* . . . P-Kt4 *2* P-Kt5, P-Kt5 *3* P-Kt6, P-Kt6ch *4* K-B3, P-Kt7 *5* P-Kt7, P-Kt8(Q) *6* P-Kt8(Q)ch, K-R1, and a draw.

1 . . .	K-R6

To escort the Pawn through. If instead *1* . . . P-Kt4 *2* K-Kt4, K-Kt7 *3* P-Kt4 wins easily.

2 K-B4	K-R5
3 P-Kt4	P-Kt4ch
4 K-Q3!	K-R6

The King must lose a move as *4* . . . P-Kt5 *5* K-B2, K-R6 *6* K-Kt1 is hopeless.

5 P-Kt5	P-Kt5
6 P-Kt6	P-Kt6
7 P-Kt7	P-Kt7
8 K-B2!	

Forcing Black into line for a check.

8 . . .	K-R7
9 P-Kt8(Q)ch	K-R8

Or *9* . . . K-R6 *10* Q-QKt3 mate.

10 Q-R8 mate	

♟ 34

NO. *24*

WHITE
to play
and win

DURAS 1905

1 K-B5!

THE star move to help his own pawn while making it difficult for Black's to advance.

1 . . .　　P-Kt4

If *1* . . . K-Kt3 (to cope with White's Pawn) *2* P-Kt4, K-B2 *3* P-Kt5, K-K2 *4* K-B6, K-Q1 *5* K-Kt7, P-Kt4 *6* P-Kt6, P-Kt5 *7* K-R7, P-Kt6 *8* P-Kt7, P-Kt7 *9* P-Kt8(Q)ch wins for White.

2 P-Kt4	P-Kt5
3 K-Q4	P-Kt6
4 K-K3	K-Kt4

To rescue his Pawn, as chasing after White's is useless.

5 P-Kt5

But not *5* K-B3 (to which Black would not meekly oblige with *5* . . . K-R5 *6* K-Kt2 and it's all over) K-B4 *6* KxP, K-K5 and Black captures the Pawn and draws.

5 . . .	K-Kt5
6 P-Kt6	K-R6

If *6* . . . P-Kt7 *7* K-B2, K-R6 *8* K-Kt1 wins.

7 P-Kt7	P-Kt7
8 K-B2	K-R7
9 P-Kt8(Q)ch	

White mates next move

35

NO. 25

WHITE
to play
and win

MANDLER 1938

THE natural move does not always win, even in the most innocent-looking position.

Two ideas suggest themselves to White: capturing Black's Pawn or advancing his own. Neither of them works!

If *1* KxP, K-Kt6 *2* K-B6 (*2* P-B4, K-B5 *3* P-B5, K-Q4 loses the Pawn) K-B5 *3* K-Q6, K-Q5 *4* P-B4, K-K5 and Black wins the Pawn.

If *1* P-B4, P-Kt4 *2* P-B5, P-Kt5, and both sides Queen with a drawn result.

1 K-Q6!	K-R6

Or *1* . . . P-Kt4 *2* K-B5, K-Kt6 *3* KxP, K-B6 *4* K-B5, K-Q6 *5* K-Q5, and the Pawn is safe.

2 K-B5	K-R5
3 P-B4	P-Kt4
4 P-B5	P-Kt5
5 K-B4!	

Necessary, as *5* P-B6, P-Kt6 *6* P-B7, P-Kt7 *7* P-B8(Q), P-Kt8(Q) *8* Q-R8ch, K-Kt6 *9* Q-Kt7ch, K-B7 is only a draw.

5 . . .	P-Kt6
6 K-B3!	K-R6
7 P-B6	P-Kt7
8 P-B7	P-Kt8(Q)
9 P-B8(Q)ch	K-R5

If *9* . . . K-R7 *10* Q-R8 is mate.

10 Q-R8ch	K-Kt4
11 Q-Kt7ch	

White wins the Queen and the game

♟ 36

NO. 26

WHITE
*to play
and win*

GRIGORIEV 1932

1 K-B5!

STARTING the Pawn instead would be premature: *1* P-R4, K-K5 *2* P-R5, K-Q4, and Black catches the Pawn.

1 . . .   K-K6

If *1* . . . P-B4 *2* K-K5, K-K6 *3* K-Q5, K-Q6 *4* KxP wins for White.

2 K-K5   P-B3

Playing for *3* K-Q6, K-Q5 *4* KxP, K-B5 and Black draws. There was no chance in *2* . . . K-Q6 *3* K-Q5, P-B3ch *4* K-B5, K-B6 *5* P-R4, and White wins.

3 P-R4   K-Q6
4 P-R5

Here too, attacking the Pawn by *4* K-Q6 allows *4* . . . K-B5 and Black saves himself.

4 . . .	P-B4
5 P-R6	P-B5
6 P-R7	P-B6
7 P-R8(Q)	P-B7

White must play carefully now. For example if *8* Q-K4ch, K-Q7 *9* Q-Q4ch, K-K7 *10* Q-B3, K-Q8 *11* Q-Q3ch, K-B8 *12* K-Q4, K-Kt7 *13* Q-K2 (with the last hope of a win by *13* . . . K-Kt8 *14* K-B3, P-B8[Q]ch *15* K-Kt3, and Black will be mated) K-R1! *14* QxP (nothing else is any better) and Black is stalemated.

8 Q-Q5ch!   K-K7

If Black tries *8* . . . K-B6 the following occurs: *9* Q-Q4ch, K-Kt6 *10* Q-R1, K-B5 *11* K-K4, and the Pawn falls.

Or if *8* . . . K-K6 *9* Q-Kt2, K-Q6 (*9* . . . P-B8[Q] *10* Q-Kt5ch winning the Queen) *10* Q-Kt5 followed by *11* Q-B1 is decisive.

9 Q-R2!	K-Q8
10 K-Q4	P-B8(Q)
11 K-Q3	

White mates or wins the Queen

NO. *27*

WHITE
to play
and win

GRIGORIEV 1931

THE obvious attack on Black's Pawns would lead to the following: *1* K-B7, P-Kt4 *2* K-Kt7, K-Kt6 *3* KxP, K-B5 *4* K-Kt6, P-Kt5 *5* K-B5, K-Q4 *6* KxP, K-K3 *7* K-Kt5, K-B2 and Black reaches R1 with an automatic draw against the Rook Pawn.

1 P-R4!   P-R4

If *1* . . . P-R3 *2* P-R5, K-Kt6 *3* K-B7 wins at once, or if *1* . . . K-Kt6 *2* K-B7, K-B5 *3* KxP, P-R4 *4* K-Kt6, K-Q4 *5* KxP, K-K3 *6* K-Kt6, K-K2 *7* K-Kt7 keeps the King at arm's length and wins.

Now comes the point of the position. The natural continuation *2* K-B7 allows *2* . . . P-Kt4 *3* PxP, P-R5 *4* P-Kt6, P-R6 and both sides Queen with a drawn result.

2 K-B8!

This move keeps Kt8 open so that after *2* . . . P-Kt4 *3* PxP White's Pawn will Queen with check.

2 . . .   P-Kt3
3 K-K7!

Here too if *3* K-B7 or *3* K-Kt7, the reply *3* . . . P-Kt4 *4* PxP, P-R5 leads to a draw. The move actually made keeps the square Kt8 open for White's Pawn to Queen with check.

3 . . .   P-Kt4

Or *3* . . . K-Kt6 *4* K-B6 and White captures both Pawns and wins.

4 PxP	P-R5
5 P-Kt6	P-R6
6 P-Kt7	P-R7
7 P-Kt8(Q)ch	K-R6
8 Q-Kt2	

White wins

♟ 38

NO. 28

WHITE
to play
and win

WHITE abandons his passed Pawn. Capturing it will keep Black busy on one side of the board, while White gets time to win on the other.

1 . . .   K-R3

The Pawn must be removed. If Black tries to defend the Knight Pawn, then after *1* . . . K-B2 *2* K-K5, K-K2 *3* K-Q5, K-Q2 *4* P-R6 makes him regret it.

2 K-K5	KxP
3 K-Q5	K-Kt3
4 K-B6	K-B3
5 KxP	K-K2
6 K-B7	

White wins
Another way to win is this:

1 P-R6ch	K-R2
2 K-R5	K-R1
3 K-Kt6	K-Kt1
4 P-R7ch	K-R1
5 K-R6	P-Kt4
6 P-R5	P-Kt5
7 P-R6	P-Kt6
8 P-R7	P-Kt7
9 P-R8(Q) mate	

WHITE
to play
and win

TRYING to win by promoting the Bishop Pawn does not work. For example, if *1* P-B5, K-B2 *2* K-K5, K-K2 *3* P-B6ch, K-B2 *4* K-B5, K-B1 *5* K-K6, K-K1 *6* P-B7ch, K-B1 *7* K-Q6 (too late, but the alternative 7 K-B6 draws by stalemate) KxP *8* K-B6, K-K2 *9* K-Kt6, K-Q2 *10* KxP, K-B2 *11* K-Kt5 (or R6) K-Kt1, and Black draws against the Rook Pawn.

The way to win is to abandon the Bishop Pawn, keep Black occupied in capturing it, and win on the other side of the board.

1 K-Q5	K-B4
2 K-B5	KxP
3 K-Kt5	K-K4
4 KxP	K-Q3
5 K-Kt6	K-Q2
6 K-Kt7	

Shuts the King out, after which the Pawn has clear sailing.

6 . . .	K-Q1
7 P-R5	

White wins

NO. *30*

WHITE
to play
and win

TO WIN this, the King forces his way in behind Black's Pawn and attacks from the rear.

1 K-Q5!

Of course not *1* K-B5, K-Q3 *2* K-B6, K-B4 *3* K-K6, KxP *4* K-Q5, K-Kt3 and White loses both Pawns!

1 . . .   K-Q1

Black must stay near his Pawn. If he makes some such move as *1* . . . K-B2 *2* P-Kt6 wins instantly.

2 K-K6   K-B1

If *2* . . . K-K1 *3* P-Kt6, PxP (or *3* . . . K-Q1 *4* P-Kt7 and mate next move) *4* P-B7 wins.

3 K-K7	K-Kt1
4 K-Q8	K-R2
5 KxP	K-R1
6 K-Q8	

White wins

NO. *31*

WHITE
*to play
and win*

1 K-B5   K-Kt1

BLACK has two other replies we should look at:

If *1* . . . P-Kt3ch *2* K-B6 (not *2* PxPch, K-Kt2 and Black draws) PxP *3* K-B7, P-R5 *4* P-Kt6ch, K-R3 *5* P-Kt7, P-R6   *6* P-Kt8(Q)   and White wins.

If *1* . . . K-R1 *2* K-Kt6, K-Kt1 *3* P-R6, PxP   (or   *3* . . . K-R1 *4* PxPch, K-Kt1 *5* K-R6, K-B2 *6* K-R7) *4* KxP!, K-R1 *5* P-Kt6, and wins.

2 K-Kt6	K-R1
3 K-B7	K-R2
4 P-R6	

One advantage in being a Pawn ahead is that you may sacrifice one Pawn for the sake of the other.

4 . . .	PxP
5 P-Kt6ch	K-R1
6 P-Kt7ch	K-R2
7 P-Kt8(Q) mate	

♟ 4²

NO. *32*

WHITE
*to play
and win*

WHITE has two ways of winning. One is to sacrifice the passed Pawn, get the opposition, capture Black's Pawn and march the Queen Pawn through. This is how it's done:

1 P-B6ch   K-B1!

Better than *1* . . . K-B2 *2* K-B5, K-B1 *3* K-K6 and it's all over.

2 P-B7!   KxP

If he refuses the Pawn by *2* . . . K-K2, then *3* P-B8(Q)ch forces *3* . . . KxQ when *4* K-B6, K-K1 *5* K-K6, K-Q1 *6* KxP, K-K1 *7* K-B7 wins.

3 K-B5	K-K2
4 K-Kt6	K-Q1
5 K-B6	K-Q2
6 K-B7	K-Q1
7 K-K6	K-B2
8 K-K7	K-B1
9 KxP	K-Q1

This wins for White no matter whose move it is. If it were Black's move, he would have to allow White's King to penetrate at his K7 or QB7. Since it is White's move now, he can advance the Pawn to the seventh without checking and win.

10 K-B6	K-B1

Or *10* . . . K-K2 *11* K-B7 and the Pawn has a clear road.

11 P-Q6	K-Q1
12 P-Q7	K-K2
13 K-B7 and wins	

The second method is by triangulation:

1 P-B6ch   K-B1!

If *1* . . . K-B2 *2* K-B5 followed by *3* K-K6 is immediately decisive.

2 K-B4!

Not at once *2* K-B5 as after *2* . . . K-B2 White must return to Kt5.

2 . . .	K-Kt1
3 K-Kt4!	

White's King circles about, avoiding the square B5 except in reply to . . . K-B2.

3 . . .	K-B1
4 K-Kt5	K-Kt1
5 K-Kt6	K-B1
6 P-B7	K-K2
7 K-Kt7	

White wins

43

NO. *33*

WHITE
to play
and win

THE key to the win is for White to give up his passed Pawn, force his way to Q6, capture Black's Pawn and then promote the remaining Pawn.

| 1 K-B6 | K-Q1! |

On *1* . . . K-K1 *2* K-K6, K-Q1 *3* P-Q7, K-B2 *4* K-K7 wins.

| 2 P-Q7! | KxP |
| 3 K-B7! | |

White now has the opposition, and will regain the Pawn he sacrificed.

3 . . .	K-Q1
4 K-K6	K-B2
5 K-K7	K-B1
6 K-Q6	K-Kt2
7 K-Q7	K-Kt1
8 KxP	K-B1
9 K-Q6	K-Q1
10 P-B6	K-B1
11 P-B7	

The Pawn reaches the seventh rank *without checking.*

| *11* . . . | K-Kt2 |
| *12* K-Q7 | |

White wins

♟ 44

NO. *34*

WHITE
to play
and win

AN EXCHANGE of Pawns, after suitable preparation, wins for White. The preparation consists in getting his King behind Black's Pawn, into a dominating position.

1 K-Q7

The immediate exchange is premature, as after *1* P-Q5, PxP *2* KxP, K-Kt3 *3* K-B4, K-B3 *4* P-Kt5ch, K-Kt3, the position is a familiar draw.

1 . . .	K-Kt3
2 K-B8	K-R3
3 K-B7	K-Kt4
4 K-Kt7	KxP
5 KxP	K-B5
6 P-Q5	

White wins

NO. 35

WHITE
to play
and win

THE method here is to crowd Black into a corner, sacrifice one Pawn and break through with the other.

1 K-Q6	K-Q1
2 K-K6	K-B1

The alternative loses at once: 2 . . . K-K1 3 P-B6, K-Q1 (or 3 . . . PxP 4 P-Kt7) 4 PxP, K-K1 5 P-Kt8(Q) mate.

3 K-K7	K-Kt1
4 K-Q7	K-R1
5 P-B6	

Clearly, not 5 K-B7 stalemating Black.

5 . . .	PxP
6 K-B7	P-B4
7 P-Kt7ch	K-R2
8 P-Kt8(Q)ch	K-R3
9 Q-Kt6 mate	

NO. *36*

WHITE
to play
and win

1 K-Q7!

A STRANGE-LOOKING move! From this square though, the King has two wins prepared, depending on which of two possible first moves Black selects.

1 . . .   K-Kt2

Against the alternative *1* . . . K-R2 White seizes the opposition, gets behind the Pawn and wins this way: *2* K-B7, K-R3 *3* K-Kt8, K-R4 *4* K-Kt7, KxP *5* KxP followed by *6* P-B5.

2 P-R5!   PxP

If *2* . . . K-R3 instead, then *3* PxP, KxP *4* K-Q6, K-Kt2 *5* P-B5, K-B1 *6* K-B6 and we have a familiar winning position.

3 P-B5	P-R5
4 P-B6ch	K-Kt3
5 P-B7	P-R6
6 P-B8(Q)	P-R7
7 Q-QR8	

White wins

NO. *37*

WHITE
*to play
and win*

IT IS obvious that giving up the Queen Pawn will clear the way for the Knight Pawn to come through, but the sacrifice must be prepared properly. The King must assume a most aggressive position—behind Black's Pawn in fact!

1 K-Kt7

If at once *1* P-Q6, K-B1 *2* P-Q7ch (or *2* P-Kt6, PxQP *3* KxP, K-Kt2 drawing easily) K-Q1 *3* K-Kt7, KxP *4* K-Kt8, K-Q3 and Black draws.

1 . . .	K-Q2
2 K-Kt8	K-Q1

Or *2* . . . K-Q3 *3* K-B8, KxP *4* KxP.

3 P-Q6!	PxP
4 P-Kt6	P-Q4
5 K-R7	P-Q5
6 P-Kt7	P-Q6
7 P-Kt8(Q)ch	K-Q2
8 Q-Kt5ch	

White wins

NO. *38*

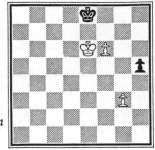

WHITE
to play
and win

WHITE can win easily by going after
Black's miserable Pawn thus: *1* K-
B5, K-B2 (*1* . . . K-B1 *2* K-Kt6)
2 K-Kt5, K-B1 *3* KxP etc.

Or, he can indulge in a bit of re-
fined cruelty by allowing Black to get
a Queen before being mated.

1 P-B7ch	K-B1
2 K-B6	P-R5
3 P-Kt4	P-R6
4 P-Kt5	P-R7
5 P-Kt6	P-R8(Q)
6 P-Kt7 mate	

NO. 39

WHITE
*to play
and win*

SHOULD White begin with *1* P-Kt3 or *1* P-Kt4? The Pawn must reach Kt7 without giving check, that is to say when the opposing King stands at his Kt1 square.

The right move is then. . . .

1 P-Kt3!

The aggressive *1* P-Kt4 leads to *1* . . . K-R1 *2* P-Kt5, K-Kt1 *3* P-Kt6, PxP *4* PxP (if *4* KxP, K-R1, and Black draws automatically against the Rook Pawn) K-R1 *5* P-Kt7ch and a draw.

1 . . .	K-R1
2 P-Kt4	K-Kt1
3 P-Kt5	K-R1
4 P-Kt6	PxP

Or *4* . . . K-Kt1 *5* P-Kt7, K-B2 *6* KxP and White wins.

5 PxP	K-Kt1
6 P-Kt7	K-B2
7 K-R7	

White wins

♟ 50

WHITE
*to play
and win*

BLACK is faced with the task of defending his Pawn, while restraining White's from advancing.

The difficulties would increase, if it were Black's turn to move.

White therefore plays to bring about the position in the diagram, with Black to move. This he does by the process of triangulation.

>   *1* K-B2   K-Kt3

On *1 . . .* K-K4 *2* P-Kt6, K-B3 *3* P-R5, K-K3 *4* P-Kt7, K-B2 *5* P-R6, and it is clear that Black's King cannot be all over the board at the same time.

2 K-K2	K-B4
3 K-K3	K-K4
4 P-Kt6	K-B3
5 P-R5	K-Kt2
6 KxP	

White wins

WHITE
to play
and win

FAHRNI

TO WIN this White must bring about the position in the diagram, with Black to move. He does this by triangulation.

1 K-Q5	K-B1
2 K-Q4!	

White is now ready to meet *2 . . .* K-B2 with *3* K-B5, and follow it up with *4* K-Kt6.

2 . . .	K-Q1
3 K-B4	

Still waiting for *3 . . .* K-B2.

3 . . .	K-B1
4 K-Q5	K-B2

The alternative is *4 . . .* K-Q1 *5* K-Q6, K-B1 *6* P-B7, K-Kt2 *7* K-Q7, K-R2 *8* K-B6 (but not *8* P-B8(Q) stalemate) K-R1 *9* P-B8(Q)ch and mate next.

5 K-B5

Now we have the position in the diagram—but it is Black to play. The rest is easy.

5 . . .	K-B1
6 K-Kt6	K-Kt1
7 KxP	K-B2
8 K-Kt5	K-B1
9 K-Kt6	K-Kt1
10 P-B7ch	K-B1
11 P-R6	K-Q2
12 K-Kt7	

White wins

NO. *42*

WHITE
to play
and win

THE problem for White is to force an exchange of Pawns. This would transform his two Pawns against one, to one Pawn against none.

| 1 P-B5 | K-B1 |

If *1* . . . P-Kt3 *2* P-B6, K-B1 *3* KxP and it's all over.

| 2 K-Kt6 | K-Kt1 |
| 3 P-B6 | K-R1 |

Hoping for *4* P-B7 stalemate. If instead *3* . . . K-B1 *4* P-B7, K-Q2 *5* KxP wins, or if *3* . . . PxP *4* KxP, K-B1 *5* K-Kt6, K-Kt1 *6* P-Kt5, K-B1 *7* K-R7 wins.

White can now win by *4* PxPch, K-Kt1 *5* K-R6, or by the following:

4 K-B7	PxP
5 KxP	K-R2
6 P-Kt5	K-Kt1
7 K-Kt6	

Definitely not *7* P-Kt6, K-B1 and Black escapes with a draw.

7 . . .	K-R1
8 K-B7	K-R2
9 P-Kt6ch	

White wins

NO. *43*

WHITE
to play
and win

WHITE'S strategy is simple: he forces an exchange of Pawns, (at the right time of course) moves his King to a dominating position, and wins.

1 P-Kt3

Not at once *1* P-B3ch as after *1* . . . PxPch *2* PxPch, K-B5, Black has a draw.

1 . . .   K-Q5

On *1* . . . K-K4, White goes after the Knight Pawn as follows: *2* K-K3, K-B4 *3* K-Q4, K-B3 *4* K-K4, K-Kt4 *5* K-K5, K-Kt3 *6* K-B4, K-R4 *7* K-B5, K-R3 *8* KxP and wins.

2 P-B3   PxPch

If *2* . . . K-K4, White demonstrates the Queening of a doubled Pawn by this: *3* PxP, K-K5 *4* K-B2, K-K4 *5* K-K3, K-K3 *6* K-B4, K-B3 *7* P-Kt5ch, K-Kt3 *8* K-Kt4, K-Kt2 *9* K-B5, K-B2 *10* P-Kt6ch, K-Kt2 *11* K-Kt5, K-Kt1 *12* K-B6, K-B1 *13* P-Kt7ch, K-Kt1 *14* P-Kt4, K-R2 *15* K-B7 and wins.

  3 KxP   K-K4
  4 K-Kt4!

The King must be aggressive. There is no win if the Pawn moves prematurely.

  4 . . .   K-B3
  5 K-R5   K-B4

Or *5* . . . K-Kt2 *6* K-Kt5, K-B2 *7* K-R6 etc.

  6 P-Kt4ch K-B3
  7 K-R6   K-B2
  8 P-Kt5   K-Kt1
  9 K-Kt6

White wins

WHITE

to play

and win

CHÉRON 1950

WHITE wins this by beautiful timing of moves.

1 K-Kt3

With the very first move White can go wrong. For instance, if *1* K-Kt4, P-B4ch *2* PxPch, K-B3 *3* K-Kt3, KxP and the position is a draw. Now if *1* . . . P-B4, White can reply *2* P-Q5 avoiding the exchange of Pawns.

1 . . .	K-B2
2 K-B3	K-Q3
3 K-Q3	K-Q2
4 K-K4	K-K3
5 P-B5	K-B3

If *5* . . . K-B2 *6* K-B5, K-K2 *7* K-K5, K-Q2 *8* K-B6, K-Q1 *9* K-K6, K-B2 *10* K-K7, K-B1 *11* K-Q6, K-Kt2 *12* K-Q7 and Black's Pawn falls.

6 P-Q5! K-K2

On *6* . . . PxPch *7* KxP, K-K2 *8* K-B6, K-Q1 *9* K-Kt7 assures the Pawn's future.

7 P-Q6ch

After *7* PxP, K-Q1 *8* K-K5, K-B2 *9* K-Q5, K-B1 *10* K-Q6, K-Q1 *11* P-

B7ch, K-B1 and Black has a draw.

7 . . .	K-Q2
8 K-K5	K-Q1
9 P-Q7!	

The point of the previous maneuvering.

9 . . . KxP

Avoiding the capture loses faster: *9* . . . K-K2 *10* P-Q8(Q)ch, KxQ *11* K-Q6, K-B1 *12* KxP, and we have a standard winning position.

10 K-B6

The King circles about to get behind the Pawn.

10 . . .	K-Q1
11 K-K6	K-B2
12 K-K7	K-B1
13 K-Q6	K-Kt2
14 K-Q7	K-Kt1
15 KxP	K-B1
16 K-Q6	K-Q1
17 P-B6	K-B1
18 P-B7	

Advances to the seventh without check, rendering the win certain.

| *18* . . . | K-Kt2 |
| *19* K-Q7 | |

White wins

WHITE
*to play
and win*

CRUM 1913

1 K-B1	K-Q5
2 K-B2	K-B4
3 P-K4!	

THIS diverts Black from pursuing the Rook Pawn. If now *3* . . . K-Kt3 *4* P-K5, KxP *5* P-K6 and White's Pawn cannot be caught.

3 . . .	K-Q5
4 K-B3	K-K4
5 K-K3	K-K3
6 K-Q4	K-Q3
7 P-K5ch	K-K3
8 K-K4	K-K2
9 K-Q5	K-Q2
10 P-K6ch	K-K2
11 K-K5	

The tempting *11* K-B6 (going after the Rook Pawn) is premature as Black takes the King Pawn *without loss of time.* The continuation would be *11* . . . KxP *12* K-Kt7, K-Q2 *13* KxP, K-B2 *14* K-R8, K-B1 and White cannot extricate his King.

11 . . .	K-K1
12 K-Q6	K-Q1
13 K-B6	

Now it will take Black two moves to capture the Pawn.

13 . . .	K-K2

Or quick suicide by *13* . . . K-B1 *14* P-K7 and mate next move.

14 K-Kt7	KxP
15 KxP	K-Q2
16 K-Kt7	

White wins

NO. *46*

WHITE
*to play
and win*

GRIGORIEV 1936

1 K-B6	K-K2
2 K-Q5	

THE first step. White prevents 2 . . . P-B3, after which the play would be *3* P-K6, K-K1 (on *3* . . . P-B4 *4* K-K5 wins the Pawn) *4* K-Q6, K-Q1 *5* P-K7ch, K-K1 *6* P-Kt4, K-B2 *7* K-Q7 and White wins.

2 . . .	K-Q2
3 K-Q4!	

Not at once *3* K-K4 as after *3* . . . K-K3 *4* K-B4, P-B3 *5* PxP, KxP *6* K-Kt4, K-Kt3, Black has the opposition and draws.

White is triangulating in order to move his King to K4 *after* Black plays . . . K-K3.

3 . . .	K-K2
4 K-K3	K-Q2
5 K-B4	

Threatening to invade at B5.

5 . . .	K-K3
6 K-K4	

This is the position White was angling for: his King at K4, Black's at K3—with Black to move.

6 . . .	K-Q2

This time if *6* . . . P-B3 *7* PxP, KxP *8* K-B4, K-Kt3 *9* K-Kt4 (White has the opposition) K-B3 *10* K-R5 and wins.

7 K-B5	K-K2
8 P-Kt4	K-K1!
9 K-B6!	

White does not fall for the attractive *9* P-K6 after which *9* . . . K-K2 *10* PxP, KxP *11* K-Kt5, K-Kt2 gives Black the opposition and a draw.

9 . . .	K-B1
10 P-Kt5	

Here too *10* P-K6 is premature, as the continuation *10* . . . PxP *11* KxP, K-Kt2 *12* K-B5, K-B2 lets Black draw easily.

10 . . .	K-K1
11 K-Kt7!	

Last chance for White to misplay it! If *11* P-K6, K-B1 *12* P-K7ch, K-K1 and White must concede the draw.

11 . . .	K-K2
12 K-Kt8	K-K1

If *12* . . . K-K3 *13* K-B8, KxP *14* KxP and White wins.

13 P-K6!

The point of the King's tour from QKt7 away over to KKt8.

13 . . .	PxP
14 P-Kt6	P-K4
15 P-Kt7	P-K5
16 K-R7	P-K6
17 P-Kt8(Q)ch	

White wins. An exquisite ending even for Grigoriev, who created so many masterpieces of beautifully-timed play.

NO. 47

WHITE
to play
and win

EBERSZ 1942

IT IS clear that White must capture the Knight Pawn in order to win. But how does he do so? The obvious *1* K-Kt4, K-B7 *2* K-Kt5, K-B6 *3* K-Kt6, KxP leads to a draw.

| *1* P-B6! | PxP |
| *2* P-B5 | |

Fixing the target. Now the King circles about and picks off the helpless victim.

2 . . .	K-R7
3 K-Kt4	K-Kt7
4 K-R5	K-B6
5 K-Kt6	K-Kt5
6 KxP	K-R4
7 K-Kt7	

White wins

♙ 58

NO. 48

WHITE
to play
and win

SELESNIEV 1914

1 K-Kt5	K-B6
2 K-B5	K-Q6
3 K-Q5	K-K6
4 K-K5	K-B6
5 K-B5	K-Kt6

AND now, White does not play 6 K-Kt6 which allows 6 . . . KxP and a draw, but. . . .

6 P-R6!	PxP
7 P-R5	K-R5
8 K-Kt6	K-Kt5
9 KxP	K-B4
10 K-Kt7	

White wins

NO. *49*

WHITE
to play
and win

GRIGORIEV 1935

THE natural line of play would seem to be to go after the Knight Pawn by way of B5 and Kt6. Here is what would happen: *1* K-B5, K-B6 *2* K-Kt6, K-Kt6 *3* P-R5, K-R5 *4* KxP (there is nothing better) KxP(R4) with a draw as result.

The winning idea is for White's King to reach Kt6 in a roundabout way—moving to K6, B7, and then Kt6!

1 K-K6!	K-B5
2 K-B7	K-Kt6

The desperate *2* . . . P-Kt4 leads to an easy White win after *3* P-R5, K-Kt6 *4* K-Kt6.

3 P-R5	K-R5
4 K-Kt6!	

Now we have the position after Black's third move in the first paragraph—but this time with Black to play.

4 . . .	KxP(R6)
5 KxP	

White wins

NO. 50

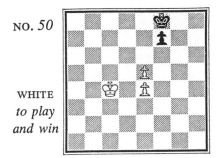

WHITE
*to play
and win*

CRUM 1913

TO WIN this White must sacrifice—and at once, or he never gets another chance to do so.

1 P-K6!

Against any other move Black's reply of *1 . . .* K-K2 assures him of a draw.

1 . . .   PxP

Black might refuse to capture, with this result: *1 . . .* K-K2 *2* PxP, KxP *3* K-Q5, K-K2 *4* K-K5 and White with the opposition wins. Or if *1 . . .* P-B3 *2* K-B5, K-K2 *3* K-Q5, K-K1 *4* K-Q6, K-Q1 *5* P-K7ch, K-K1 *6* K-K6, P-B4 *7* KxP, KxP *8* K-K5, and again the force of the opposition wins.

2 P-K5!

Fixes the Pawn. Now the King plays to get behind the Pawn.

2 . . .	K-K2
3 K-B5	K-Q2
4 K-Kt6	K-Q1
5 K-B6	K-K2
6 K-B7	K-K1
7 K-Q6	K-B2
8 K-Q7	K-B1
9 KxP	K-K1
10 K-B6	K-B1
11 P-K6	K-K1
12 P-K7	

White wins

NO. *51*

WHITE
to play
and win

GRIGORIEV 1935

THE doubled Pawns find a unique means of keeping the King at bay.

1 P-R5	K-B4
2 P-R4	K-Q3

Thwarted, the King tries coming around in front of the Pawns.

3 K-Q8	P-B4
4 P-R6	K-B3
5 P-R5	

Once again the Pawns set up a barricade.

5 . . .	P-B5
6 K-B1	P-B6
7 P-R7	P-B7
8 P-R8(Q)ch	K-Q3
9 Q-R1	

White wins

NO. *52*

WHITE
to play
and win

GRIGORIEV 1935

THE doubled Pawns hold their own against the King until help arrives.

1 K-B1	K-B6
2 K-K2	K-Q5
3 P-Kt4	K-K5
4 P-Kt3	K-Q5
5 P-Kt5	K-K4

Black must stop the passed Pawn even at the cost of deserting his own Pawn.

6 P-Kt4

Prevents the King from coming closer.

6 . . .	K-K3
7 KxP	K-B2
8 K-K4	

Not at once *8* K-B4 as the reply *8* . . . K-Kt3 costs a Pawn and gives Black an easy draw.

8 . . .	K-Kt3

Or *8* . . . K-K3 *9* K-B4 followed by *10* K-B5.

9 K-B4	K-B2
10 K-B5	K-Kt2
11 P-Kt6	K-Kt1

If *11* . . . K-R3 *12* P-Kt7 (certainly not *12* K-B6 stalemating Black) KxP *13* K-Kt5, and White having the opposition wins.

12 K-B6	K-B1
13 P-Kt7ch	K-Kt1
14 P-Kt5	K-R2
15 P-Kt8(Q)ch	

Here too, the hasty *15* K-B7 stalemating Black, deprives White of the win.

15 . . .	KxQ
16 K-Kt6	

White wins

NO. 53

WHITE
*to play
and win*

GRIGORIEV 1932

1 K-Kt3!

THIS apparent loss of time is the only way to a win. If instead *1* K-Kt5, K-B6 *2* P-R4, K-Kt7 *3* P-R5, K-R6! *4* K-Kt6, K-Kt5! (not *4* . . . K-R5 *5* P-R3, KxP *6* KxP and White wins) *5* P-R3ch, K-R5 *6* KxP, KxP(R4) and Black draws. Or if *1* K-Kt4, K-B7 *2* P-R4, K-Kt7 *3* P-R3, P-Kt3 *4* K-Kt5, KxP, and the position is drawn.

> *1* . . .   K-K6

If *1* . . . K-B8 *2* P-R4, P-Kt3 (or *2* . . . K-K7 *3* P-R5, K-K6 *4* P-R4, K-K5 *5* K-Kt4, K-K6 *6* K-B5, K-B6 *7* P-R6, PxP *8* P-R5 and White wins) *3* K-B4!, K-Kt7 *4* P-R5!, PxP *5* P-R4 and White wins.

> *2* P-R4   K-K5
> *3* K-Kt4   K-K4
> *4* K-Kt5   K-K5
> *5* P-R5   K-B6
> *6* K-B5!

Not at once *6* K-Kt6 when *6* . . . K-Kt5 *7* P-R3ch, K-R5 ends in a draw.

White's actual move forces Black's King to retreat.

> *6* . . .   K-Kt7
> *7* K-Kt6

White wins the Pawn and the game.

NO. 54

WHITE
to play
and win

WHITE has a great advantage in his outside passed Pawn. Its threat to march up the board keeps Black's King occupied, since he must eventually chase after it. Meanwhile White has time to pick off the abandoned Black Pawns.

1 P-R5	K-B3
2 P-R6	K-Kt3
3 P-R7	KxP
4 KxP	K-Kt2
5 K-Q6	K-B1
6 K-K6	K-Q1
7 KxP	K-K2
8 K-Kt6	K-K3

If 8 . . . K-B1 9 K-B6 is a win with or without the move.

9 P-B5ch	K-K2
10 K-Kt7	

White wins

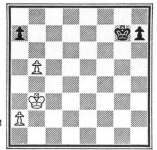

NO. 55

WHITE
*to play
and win*

IT IS important to Queen a Pawn on the right square, if there is a choice. Promoting on the wrong square might let the opponent get away with a draw when he should have lost.

    1 P-R4   P-KR4

The alternative *1* . . . K-B2, trying to head off White's Pawns, is too slow, viz: *2* P-R5, K-K2 *3* P-Kt6, PxP (*3* . . . K-Q2 *4* PxP) *4* P-R6!, and White wins.

        2 P-R5   P-R5
        3 P-Kt6   PxP
        4 P-R6!

If *4* PxP, P-R6 *5* P-Kt7, P-R7 *6* P-Kt8(Q), P-R8(Q) and the position is a draw.

        4 . . .   P-R6
        5 P-R7   P-R7
        6 P-R8(Q)

White wins

NO. *56*

WHITE
to play
and win

HORWITZ AND KLING 1851

WHITE'S strategy is based on the fact that his Pawns are safe from capture, while Black's will both be lost if either of them makes a move.

1 K-B4   K-Kt3

The Pawns must not move. If for example *1* . . . P-R4 *2* K-Kt5, K-Kt3 (or *2* . . . P-Q4 *3* KxP, P-Q5 *4* K-Kt4, P-Q6 *5* K-B3 and White overtakes the Pawn) *3* KxP, K-B2 *4* K-Kt5, K-Kt3 *5* K-B5, K-B2 *6* K-K6, and the second Pawn goes.

2 K-B5   K-B2
3 K-B6   K-Kt3

Here too if *3* . . . P-R4 *4* K-Kt5 or if *3* . . . P-Q4 *4* K-K5 and White will be in time to catch the second Pawn.

4 K-K6   K-B2

If *4* . . . P-R4 *5* KxP, P-R5 *6* P-B7, P-R6 *7* P-B8(Q), P-R7 *8* Q-R6 mate.

5 K-Q5   P-R4
6 P-Kt6ch   KxP
7 KxP   P-R5
8 P-B7   K-Kt2
9 K-Q7

White wins

WHITE
to play
and win

TEED 1885

1 K-B7!   P-R4

ON *1* . . . K-R1 instead, *2* K-Kt6 wins both of Black's Pawns.

2 P-R4!

The key move to break through. White cannot win with *2* K-B6 as *2* . . . PxP *3* PxP, K-R1 *4* KxP, K-Kt2 gives Black the opposition and an easy draw.

2 . . .   K-R3

What else is there? if *2* . . . RPxP *3* PxP, P-Kt6 *4* P-Kt6ch, K-R3 *5* P-Kt7, P-Kt7 *6* P-Kt8(Q) wins, or if *2* . . . KtPxP *3* P-Kt5, P-R6 *4* P-Kt6ch, K-R3 *5* P-Kt7, P-R7 *6* P-Kt8(Q), P-R8(Q) *7* Q-Kt6 mate.

3 K-B6!   RPxP

Or *3* . . . KtPxP *4* P-Kt5ch, K-R2 *5* K-B7 and White wins.

4 PxPch	K-R4
5 P-Kt6	P-Kt6
6 P-Kt7	K-Kt5
7 P-Kt8(Q)ch	K-B6
8 K-Kt5	P-Kt7
9 K-R4	K-B7
10 Q-Kt3ch	K-B8
11 Q-B3ch	K-Kt8
12 K-R3	K-R8
13 QxP mate	

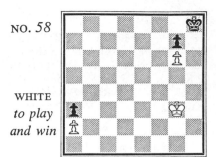

NO. *58*

WHITE

to play
and win

MORAVEC 1941

1 K-B4!

UNEXPECTED, but the obvious idea of immediately going after the Rook Pawn leads only to a draw: *1* K-B3, K-Kt1 *2* K-K3, K-B1 *3* K-Q3, K-K2 *4* K-B3, K-B3 *5* K-Kt3, KxP *6* KxP, K-B4 *7* K-Kt4, P-Kt4 *8* P-R4, and both sides will Queen at the same time.

1 . . .	K-Kt1
2 K-K5	K-B1
3 K-Q6!	K-K1
4 K-K6	K-B1

On *4* . . . K-Q1 *5* K-B7 is fatal.

5 K-Q7	K-Kt1
6 K-K7	K-R1

Now we see the reason for the tour White's King made. It will take only four moves now to capture Black's Rook Pawn instead of the six it would have taken from the original position. Black's King meanwhile has been unable to make any progress, having been forced back to the corner.

7 K-Q6	K-Kt1
8 K-B5	K-B1
9 K-Kt4	K-K2
10 KxP	

Black is in trouble. If he tries to get a passed Pawn, this is what happens: *10* . . . K-B3 *11* K-Kt4, KxP *12* P-R4, K-B4 *13* P-R5, P-Kt4 *14* P-R6, P-Kt5 *15* P-R7, P-Kt6 *16* P-R8(Q), K-B5 *17* Q-Kt2 and White wins.

10 . . .	K-Q3

So he tries another defense.

11 K-Kt4	K-B3
12 P-R4	K-Kt3
13 K-B4	K-B3
14 P-R5	K-B2
15 K-Q5	

White wins, since Black cannot stop the Rook Pawn and defend his own Pawn at the same time.

NO. *59*

WHITE
to play
and win

GRIGORIEV 1925

1 K-B2   K-R6

IF *1* . . . P-Kt6ch *2* K-Kt1 (not
2 K-Kt2 stalemate) leads to the actual play, while *1* . . . PxP loses by
2 KxP, K-R6 *3* P-B5, P-R5 *4* P-B6,
K-R7 *5* P-B7, P-R6 *6* P-B8(Q), K-
Kt8 *7* Q-KR8, P-R7 *8* Q-R1 mate.

2 K-Kt1

Certainly not *2* P-B5, K-R7, and
Black will be first to get a Queen.

2 . . .   K-R4

He must stop *3* P-B5, which wins
against other moves.

3 K-Kt2   P-Kt6
4 K-Kt1!

A fearful error would have been
4 K-R1, when White Queens his
Pawn but gets mated! The continuation would be *4* . . . K-R6 *5* P-B5,
P-Kt7ch *6* K-Kt1, K-Kt6 *7* P-B6, P-
R5 *8* P-B7, P-R6 *9* P-B8(Q), P-R7
mate!

4 . . .   P-Kt7
5 K-R2!

Naturally, *5* KxP stalemating Black
is unthinkable.

5 . . .   P-Kt8(Q)ch
6 KxQ   K-Kt6
7 P-B5

White wins, as the Pawn cannot be
headed off.

NO. *60*

WHITE
to play
and win

SELESNIEV 1927

1 K-B4!   KxP

NECESSARY, as *1* . . . P-R5 *2* P-Q5, P-R6 *3* K-Kt3 is hopeless for Black.

| *2* P-Q5 | K-K4 |
| *3* K-B5 | P-B5 |

Queening the Rook Pawn instead would result in this: *3* . . . P-R5 *4* P-Q6, P-R6 *5* P-Q7, P-R7 *6* P-Q8(Q), P-R8(Q) *7* Q-R8ch, and White wins the Queen on the diagonal.

| *4* P-Q6 | P-B6 |

Or *4* . . . K-K3 *5* K-B6, P-B6 *6* P-Q7, P-B7 *7* P-Q8(Q), P-B8(Q) *8* Q-K8ch, K-B3 *9* Q-B8ch, and White wins the Queen.

5 P-Q7	P-B7
6 P-Q8(Q)	P-B8(Q)
7 Q-K8ch	K-B4
8 Q-KB8ch	

White wins the Queen on the file.

71 ♟

NO. *61*

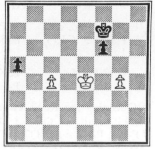

WHITE
*to play
and win*

REY 1938

A CLEVER sacrifice transforms a drawish-looking position into a pretty win.

1 K-Q4!

Not at once *1* P-B5, as after *1* . . . K-K3 *2* K-Q4, P-R5 *3* K-B4, P-R6 *4* K-Kt3, K-Q4, and White loses instead of winning.

1 . . .   K-K3

On *1* . . . P-R5 instead, *2* K-B3, K-K3 *3* K-Kt4 wins for White.

| *2* K-B5 | K-K4 |
| *3* K-Kt5 | K-Q5 |

Expecting the continuation *4* P-B5, P-R5 *5* P-B6, P-R6 with a comfortable draw. Instead of this, Black gets a rude shock.

| *4* P-Kt5! | PxP |
| *5* P-B5 | P-R5 |

Black can Queen the other Pawn, with this result: *5* . . . P-Kt5 *6* P-B6, P-Kt6 *7* P-B7, P-Kt7 *8* P-B8(Q), P-Kt8(Q) *9* Q-B5ch, and White wins the Queen.

6 P-B6	P-R6
7 P-B7	P-R7
8 P-B8(Q)	P-R8(Q)
9 Q-R8ch	

White wins the Queen and the game.

NO. *62*

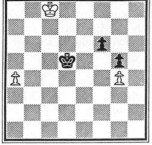

WHITE
to play
and win

GRIGORIEV 1930

AN APPARENTLY simple position, but how does White proceed? If *1* K-Q8 (to attack the Pawns) K-B3 *2* K-K7, P-B4! *3* PxP, P-Kt5, and both sides will Queen their Pawns with a drawn result.

1 P-R5!	K-B3
2 K-Kt8!	

Threatens to advance the Pawn and Queen with check.

2 . . .	K-Kt4
3 K-Kt7	KxP

Or *3* . . . P-B4 *4* P-R6, PxP *5* P-R7, P-Kt6 *6* P-R8(Q), P-B7 *7* Q-R1 and White wins.

4 K-B6	P-B4

The best chance. If instead *4* . . . K-R3 *5* K-Q5, P-B4 *6* PxP, P-Kt5 *7* K-K4 and Black's Pawn is lost. Or if *4* . . . K-Kt5 *5* K-Q5, P-B4 *6* PxP, P-Kt5 *7* P-B6, and the Pawn reaches B8 with check winning for White.

5 PxP	P-Kt5
6 P-B6	P-Kt6
7 P-B7	P-Kt7
8 P-B8(Q)	P-Kt8(Q)
9 Q-R3 mate!	

NO. *63*

WHITE
to play
and win

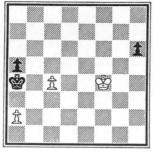

GRIGORIEV 1925

BLACK'S own King Rook Pawn loses the game for him. If White could only be induced to capture it, the position would be a draw!

1 P-R3!

The attractive *1* K-K5 instead leads to *1* . . . P-R4 *2* P-B5, K-Kt4! (but not *2* . . . P-R5 *3* P-B6, P-R6 *4* P-B7, P-R7 *5* P-B8(Q), P-R8(Q) *6* Q-B4ch, K-R6 *7* Q-Kt3 mate) *3* K-Q6, P-R5 *4* P-B6, P-R6 *5* P-B7, P-R7 *6* P-B8(Q), P-R8(Q) *7* Q-QB5ch, K-R3! and a draw.

1 . . .	P-R4
2 K-Kt3	P-R5ch
3 K-R3!	

It is important not to remove the Pawn.

3 . . .	KxP
4 P-B5	P-R5
5 P-B6	K-Kt7
6 P-B7	P-R6
7 P-B8(Q)	P-R7
8 Q-Kt7ch	K-B7
9 Q-B6ch	K-Kt7
10 Q-Kt5ch	K-B7
11 Q-R4ch	K-Kt7
12 Q-Kt4ch	K-B7
13 Q-R3	K-Kt8
14 Q-Kt3ch	K-R8

The threat of stalemate would allow Black to draw—if he didn't have an extra Pawn!

15 K-Kt4!	P-R6
16 Q-B2	P-R7
17 Q-B1 mate	

NO. *64*

WHITE
to play
and win

GRIGORIEV 1929

IN A position where the moves seem to be forced, it is easy to play mechanically—and let a sure win slip.

1 P-Kt6	P-Kt6
2 P-Kt7	P-Kt7
3 P-Kt8(R)!	

The unthinking promotion to a Queen instead allows *3* . . . P-Kt8(Q) *4* QxQ and stalemate.

3 . . .	K-R7
4 K-R4	P-Kt8(Q)
5 RxQ	KxR
6 K-Kt3	

White wins. He will capture Black's Pawn and proceed to Queen his own, while his opponent watches helplessly.

NO. 65

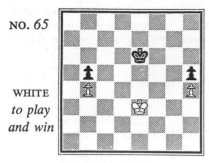

WHITE
*to play
and win*

CAPABLANCA 1921

1 K-K4

SEIZES the opposition and forces Black to give way. He has two plausible defenses:

A] 1 . . .   K-Q3
   2 K-Q4

The attractive alternative 2 K-B5 is premature. Starting with that move it takes White seven more moves to capture Black's Rook Pawn and then Queen his own. In the meantime, Black captures on the Queen side, Queens his Pawn, and draws.

2 . . .   K-K3

On 2 . . . K-B3 White plays 3 K-K5 and after the reply 3 . . . K-Kt3 can move 4 K-Q5, force the capture of the Knight Pawn and win, or he can switch to the King side by 4 K-B5, capture the Rook Pawn and win.

3 K-B5	K-B4
4 KxP	K-Kt5
5 K-B4	KxP
6 P-Kt5	K-Kt6
7 P-Kt6	P-R5
8 P-Kt7	P-R6
9 P-Kt8(Q)ch	K-Kt7
10 Q-Kt8ch	K-B7
11 Q-Q5	

Threatens to continue with *12 Q-R1*.

11 . . .	K-Kt8
12 Q-Kt5ch	K-B7
13 Q-R4ch	K-Kt7
14 Q-Kt4ch	K-R7
15 K-Q4	K-R8
16 QxPch and wins	

B] 1 . . .   K-B3
   2 K-B4!

White does not attack by 2 K-Q5. It would take eight moves to capture the Knight Pawn and Queen his own. In the same number of moves Black would capture the Rook Pawn, Queen his passed Pawn, and draw.

2 . . .   K-Kt3
3 K-K5!

White wins. He has the pleasant choice of winning on either side of the board, since he can force the capture of either of Black's Pawns.

NO. 66

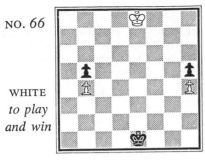

WHITE
to play
and win

GRIGORIEV 1929

A BEAUTIFUL example of distant opposition. The Kings are separated by the length of the board, but White's, believe-it-or-not, exerts irresistible pressure on Black's!

1 K-K7!

White seizes the opposition, and for the rest of the play leaves Black with only one reasonable move in reply.

    1 . . .   K-K7

If Black leaves the King file, White wins by attacking on the same file. For instance, if *1 . . .* K-Q7 *2* K-Q6, followed by *3* K-B5. Or if *1 . . .* K-B7 *2* K-B6, followed by 3 K-Kt5.

    2 K-K6!   K-K6

If *2 . . .* K-Q6 *3* K-Q5 and *4* K-B5 wins, or if *2 . . .* K-B6 *3* K-B5 and *4* K-Kt5 wins.

    3 K-K5!   K-K7
    4 K-K4!   K-K8

Here too *4 . . .* K-Q7 is met by *5* K-Q4 and *6* K-B5, while *4 . . .* K-B7 succumbs to *5* K-B4 followed by *6* K-Kt5.

    5 K-K3!   K-B8

Unfortunately, Black must leave the file. There is no square left on it for retreat.

6 K-B4	K-K7
7 K-Kt5	K-Q6
8 KxP	K-B5
9 K-Kt4	KxP
10 P-R5	K-R6
11 P-R6	P-Kt5
12 P-R7	P-Kt6
13 P-R8(Q)	P-Kt7
14 Q-B3ch	K-R7
15 Q-B2	K-R8
16 Q-R4ch	K-Kt8

The idea in this sort of position is to force Black to block his Pawn. Each time he does so, White gains time to bring his King closer.

17 K-B3	K-B8
18 Q-B4ch	K-Q7
19 Q-Kt3	K-B8
20 Q-B3ch	K-Kt8
21 K-K3	K-R7
22 Q-B2	K-R8
23 Q-R4ch	K-Kt8
24 K-Q3	K-B8
25 Q-B2 mate	

NO. 67

WHITE
*to play
and win*

KUPCZEWSKI 1931

1 P-R4   K-Q3

BLACK had no time to start his passed Pawn as White's Rook Pawn threatened to move up the board and Queen with check.

2 K-Kt6

Otherwise Black heads off the passed Pawn with 2 . . . K-B2.

2 . . .   K-Q2

If he can get to B1, White's Rook Pawn will be harmless.

3 K-Kt7	P-R4
4 P-R5	P-R5
5 P-R6	P-R6
6 P-R7	P-R7
7 P-R8(Q)	P-R8(Q)

This might be a draw, except that in Queening first White has the advantage of giving a few checks.

8 Q-B8ch	K-Q3
9 Q-B6ch	K-K4
10 P-B4ch	

White wins the Queen by discovered attack.

NO. 68

WHITE
to play
and win

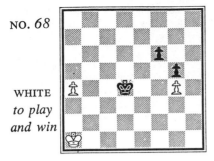

CHEKHOVER 1947

1 P-R5	K-B4
2 K-Kt2!	P-B4

IF BLACK attacks the Rook Pawn, the play goes like this: 2 . . . K-Kt4 3 K-B3, KxP 4 K-Q4, K-Kt4 5 K-K4, K-B3 6 K-B5, K-Q2 7 KxP, K-K1 8 KxP, K-B2 9 K-R6, K-B3 (or 9 . . . K-Kt1 10 K-Kt6) 10 P-Kt5ch, K-B2 11 K-R7 and White wins.

3 PxP   P-Kt5

Hoping to promote at the same time as White, and draw.

4 P-B6!

Threatens to reach B8 and Queen with check.

4 . . .   K-Q3

To stop the Pawn if it takes another step.

5 P-R6   P-Kt6

Black has no time to play 5 . . . K-K3 as 6 P-R7, P-Kt6 7 P-R8(Q) wins.

6 P-B7

Renewing the threat of Queening with check.

6 . . .	K-K2
7 P-R7	P-Kt7

Will both sides Queen their Pawns simultaneously?

8 P-B8(Q)ch	KxQ
9 P-R8(Q)ch	K-K2
10 QxP	

White wins. It is just a coincidence that the composer of this ending is named Chekhover.

NO. *69*

WHITE
*to play
and win*

GRIGORIEV 1930

1 P-B4

TO THIS Black cannot reply *1 . . .* P-Q4 as after *2* P-B5, P-Q5 *3* P-B6, P-Q6 *4* P-B7, P-Q7 White's Pawn promotes to a Queen *with check,* and wins.

| *1 . . .* | K-Kt5 |
| *2* P-R4 | |

Now if Black moves *2 . . .* K-B4 *3* P-R5, and the Rook Pawn cannot be caught.

2 . . .   P-Q4

The best defense: if White continues by *3* P-R5, then *3 . . .* P-Q5 and Black will Queen with check.

3 P-B5!

To meet *3 . . .* P-Q5 with *4* P-B6, threatening to Queen with check.

| *3 . . .* | K-B4 |
| *4* P-R5 | |

Stops the King from coming closer, the reply to *4 . . .* K-Q3 being *5* P-R6 followed by *6* P-R7 and *7* P-R8(Q).

4 . . .   P-Q5

♟ 80

Black in turn is ready to refute *5* P-R6 with *5 . . .* P-Q6.

5 P-B6

Renews the threat of Queening with check.

5 . . .   K-Q3

Stops the Bishop Pawn but now comes. . . .

6 P-R6

Preventing *6 . . .* K-K3 as then *7* P-R7 wins.

6 . . .   P-Q6

Now White cannot play *7* P-R7, so he threatens again to Queen with check.

7 P-B7!	K-K2
8 P-R7	P-Q7
9 P-B8(Q)ch	KxQ
10 P-R8(Q)ch	K-K2
11 Q-Q4	

White wins. A beautiful composition, with Black's alternation of King and Pawn moves the only possible defense to White's seesawing Pawns.

WHITE
*to play
and win*

THE outside passed Pawn keeps Black busy on one side of the board to the neglect of the other. White's King takes the opportunity to come down on the unprotected Pawns like a wolf upon the fold.

1 P-QR5   K-Kt4

Sooner or later the Pawn must be removed. If instead *1* . . . P-Kt4 *2* PxP, BPxP *3* K-K5, and Black must still play to capture the passed Pawn.

2 K-Q5	KxP
3 K-K6	P-B4
4 PxP	PxP
5 KxP	K-Kt3
6 K-Kt6	K-B2
7 KxP	K-Q2
8 P-R5	K-K2
9 K-Kt7	

White wins

NO. 71

WHITE

to play
and win

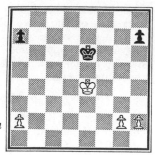

WHITE, a Pawn ahead, plays to exchange Pawns on the King side. This would leave a passed Pawn which Black would have to keep under surveillance. White meanwhile could switch his attack to the other side of the board and win the game there.

1 P-Kt4	P-QR4
2 P-QR4	K-B3
3 P-R4	K-K3

On 3 . . . K-Kt3 4 K-Q5, K-B3 5 K-B5, K-K4 6 K-Kt5, K-B5 7 KxP, KxP 8 K-Kt6, and White will Queen his Pawn.

4 P-Kt5	K-B2
5 K-B5	K-Kt2
6 P-R5	K-B2

If 6 . . . P-R3 7 P-Kt6, K-B1 8 K-K6, and the King goes over to the Queen side, since his King side Pawns are safe from capture.

7 K-K5	K-K2
8 P-Kt6	PxP
9 PxP	K-K1

On 9 . . . K-B1, White can win it on the King side if he wishes, by 10 K-B6, since the Pawn advances to the seventh rank without checking.

10 K-Q5	K-B1

Black's King, unfortunately for him, cannot be in two places at the same time.

11 K-B5

White wins

NO. 72

WHITE
*to play
and win*

WHITE has three Pawns to two. An exchange of Pawns, leaving him with two Pawns to one, would greatly increase his advantage. By means of a temporary sacrifice, White brings about an exchange.

> *1* P-Kt4ch!   PxPch

There is no hope in *1* . . . K-Kt3 *2* P-Kt5, and White has a passed Pawn on the King side.

> *2* K-Kt3   K-Kt3

If *2* . . . K-K5 *3* KxP, K-Q5 *4* P-R5, K-B5 *5* P-R6, and the Pawn Queens long before Black can promote his Pawn.

> *3* KxP   K-R3
> *4* K-B5

White can go gaily about his business, since Black must lose time disposing of the passed Pawn.

> | *4* . . . | K-R4 |
> |--------------|-------|
> | *5* K-K5 | KxP |
> | *6* K-Q5 | K-Kt4 |
> | *7* K-B5 | K-B3 |
> | *8* KxP | K-K2 |
> | *9* K-B6 | K-Q1 |
> | *10* K-Kt7 | K-Q2 |
> | *11* P-Kt5 | |

White wins

NO. 73

WHITE
to play
and win

FONTANA 1943

A CLEVER break-through by White's Pawns!

1 P-B6!   K-Kt3

If *1* . . . PxP instead, then *2* P-Q6 forces *2* . . . PxP, after which White plays *3* P-B5 and the Pawn marches merrily up the board.

2 P-Q6!   PxQP

Other moves lose instantly:
A] *2* . . . KxP   *3* PxP
B] *2* . . . PxBP   *3* PxP
C] *2* . . . P-K3   *3* PxP

3 P-B5   K-B2

He must try to stop the passed Pawn.

4 P-B6   K-Q1
5 P-QB7ch   KxP

The unhappy King cannot be in two places at once.

6 P-B7

White wins

NO. 74

WHITE
to play
and win

LOLLI 1763

1 P-Kt6!

THE only way to break through!
White threatens *2* PxP, winning on
the spot.

1 . . .   P-R3

The alternative *1* . . . PxP leads
to this: *2* RPxP, K-B1 *3* K-Q6 (diagonal opposition) K-K1 *4* K-K6, K-B1
(if *4* . . . K-Q1 *5* K-B7 ends the
struggle) *5* K-Q7, K-Kt1 *6* K-K7, K-
R1 *7* P-B6, PxP *8* K-B7, P-B4 *9* P-
Kt7ch and White mates in two.

2 K-Q5

Not at once *2* P-B6, PxPch *3* K-
B5, K-B1 *4* KxP, K-Kt1 *5* P-Kt7, K-
R2, and Black has a draw.

2 . . .   K-B3

On *2* . . . K-Q2 *3* P-B6 is decisive.

3 K-K4	K-Kt4
4 K-K5	KxRP
5 K-K6	K-Kt4
6 P-B6!	

Now!

6 . . .   PxP

Or *6* . . . KxP *7* P-B7 followed
by *8* P-B8(Q).

7 P-Kt7

White wins

85

NO. 75

WHITE
to play
and win

GRIGORIEV

1 K-Kt4	K-Q5
2 P-R4	K-Q4
3 P-R5	PxPch

IF *3* . . . K-Q3 instead, *4* PxP wins at once.

4 K-R4!

Unexpected, but the only way to win. After *4* KxP, Black forces a draw by *4* . . . K-B4 *5* K-R4, K-Kt3.

| 4 . . . | K-B4 |
| 5 KxP | |

Now we have the position in the previous note (after *4* . . . K-B4) but with *Black* to move.

| 5 . . . | K-Q3 |
| 6 P-Kt6 | PxPch |

No better is *6* . . . K-B3 when 7 PxP is conclusive.

7 KxP

White wins

NO. 76

WHITE
*to play
and win*

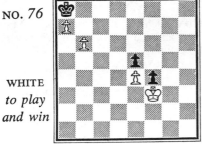

HORWITZ 1851

BOTH sides have Pawns which are immune from capture. White's are further advanced, so he can venture on a combination.

1 K-K2	K-Kt2
2 K-Q3	K-R1
3 K-B4	K-Kt2

Black must not push on by *3* . . . P-B6 as the reply *4* K-Q3 winning the Pawn is the penalty.

4 K-B5	P-B6
5 K-Q6	P-B7
6 P-R8(Q)ch	KxQ
7 K-B7	P-B8(Q)
8 P-Kt7ch	K-R2
9 P-Kt8(Q)ch	K-R3
10 Q-Kt6 mate	

NO. 77

WHITE
to play
and win

HORWITZ AND KLING 1851

1 K-K4 K-Kt5

OBVIOUSLY if *1* . . . KxP *2* P-Kt4, and the passed Pawn can never be caught.

2 P-R4

And now the Knight Pawn may not be captured.

2 . . .	K-R4
3 K-B4	K-R3
4 P-Kt4	K-Kt3
5 P-R5ch	K-R3
6 K-K4	K-Kt4
7 K-B3	K-R3
8 K-B4	K-R2
9 P-Kt5	K-Kt2
10 P-Kt6	K-R3
11 K-Kt4	K-Kt2

Naturally, if *11* . . . P-Q6 *12* K-B3 will win the Pawn.

12 K-Kt5!	P-Q6
13 P-R6ch	K-Kt1
14 K-B6	P-Q7
15 P-R7ch	K-R1
16 K-B7	P-Q8(Q)
17 P-Kt7ch	KxP
18 P-Kt8(Q)ch	K-R3
19 Q-Kt6 mate	

88

WHITE
to play
and win

GRIGORIEV 1930

1 P-R3!   P-B4

BLACK goes straight for a Queen. If he attacks the Rook Pawns instead, the play would go as follows: *1* . . . K-R4 *2* K-Kt7, KxP (or *2* . . . P-B4, changing plans in mid-stream, *3* PxP, P-Kt5 *4* P-B6, P-Kt6 *5* P-B7, P-Kt7 *6* P-B8(Q), P-Kt8(Q) *7* Q-Kt4 mate) *3* K-B6, KxP *4* K-Q5, K-Kt5 *5* K-K5, K-B4 *6* K-B6, K-Q3 *7* KxBP, K-K4 *8* K-Kt6, K-B5 *9* K-R5, K-K4 *10* KxP, K-K3 *11* K-Kt6, K-K2 *12* P-Kt5, K-B1 *13* K-R7 and White wins.

2 PxP	P-Kt5
3 P-B6	P-Kt6
4 P-B7	P-Kt7
5 P-B8(Q)	P-Kt8(Q)
6 Q-B8ch	K-R4

If *6* . . . K-Kt3 *7* Q-Kt7ch, K-B4 (on *7* . . . K-R4 *8* Q-Kt5 is mate) *8* Q-R7ch and White wins the Queen.

       7 Q-B3ch   K-Kt3

If *7* . . . K-R3 *8* Q-B4ch, K-Kt3 *9* P-R5ch, KxP   *10* Q-Kt4ch, K-R3 *11* Q-R4ch, K-Kt3 *12* Q-R7ch, and White wins the Queen.

8 P-R5ch	K-Kt4
9 Q-Kt4ch	K-R3

On *9* . . . K-B3 *10* Q-Kt7ch, K-Q3 *11* Q-Kt6ch is a brutal but convincing exchange of Queens.

10 Q-Kt7ch	KxP
11 Q-Kt4ch	K-R3
12 Q-R4ch	K-Kt3
13 Q-R7ch	

White wins the Queen and the game.

89

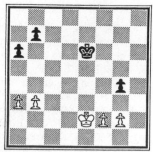

WHITE
*to play
and win*

1 P-B3

FORCING an exchange will leave White with a passed Pawn.

    1 . . .   PxPch

If Black avoids the exchange by *1* . . . P-Kt6, then *2* P-B4 followed by *3* K-B3 wins the luckless Pawn.

2 KxP	K-B4
3 P-Kt4ch	K-Kt4
4 P-Kt4	

In order to block the position on the Queen side. Black's Pawns will be easier to pick off if they are immovable.

4 . . .	P-Kt3
5 P-R4	K-Kt3
6 K-B4	K-B3
7 P-Kt5ch	K-Kt3
8 P-Kt5	P-R4
9 K-Kt4	K-Kt2
10 K-B5	K-B2
11 K-K5	

Poses a difficult problem. How does Black protect his Pawns while contending with the dangerous passed Pawn?

11 . . .	K-K2
12 P-Kt6	K-K1
13 K-Q6	K-B1
14 K-B6	

White wins

NO. *80*

WHITE
to play
and win

UNASSISTED by the King, White's Pawns break through by sheer force.

    1 P-B5   K-Kt5

Any Pawn move instead loses immediately: *1* . . . PxP *2* PxP followed by *3* P-Q6 wins, or if *1* . . . P-Kt3 *2* RPxP gives White a passed Pawn.

       2 P-Kt5!

Threatens to continue with *3* P-B6, PxBP *4* PxRP and White wins.

    2 . . .   PxBP

If *2* . . . PxKtP *3* P-B6 is decisive.

    3 P-Kt6   PxP
    4 P-Q6

White wins, his Queen Pawn having a clear road to the last square.

NO. *81*

WHITE
*to play
and win*

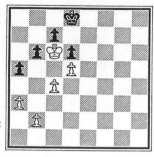

DAVIDSON

1 P-B5!

THE right moment for the break-through. Black must not be given time for *1 . . .* K-B1, consolidating his position.

1 . . .   KtPxP

If *1 . . .* QPxP   *2* P-Q6, PxP *3* KxQP followed by *4* K-B6, and all Black's Pawns will fall.

2 K-Kt5   K-Q2
3 P-R4

Not at once *3* KxP, as after *3 . . .* P-B3 Black has counter-play.

3 . . .   K-B1

Whereas if now *3 . . .* P-B3ch (instead of *3 . . .* K-B1) *4* PxPch, K-B2 *5* P-Kt3, and Black is helpless.

4 KxP   K-Kt2
5 K-Kt5   K-R2
6 K-B6   K-Kt1
7 P-R5   K-B1
8 P-R6   K-Kt1
9 P-R7ch   KxP

The rest is no strain on White.

10 KxP   K-R3
11 KxP   K-Kt4
12 P-Kt3   K-Kt5
13 K-B6

White wins

♟ 92

NO. *82*

WHITE
to play
and win

SACKMANN 1913

A FLOCK of Pawns can make life miserable for a Queen, however nimble she may be.

1 P-R6	P-B8(Q)
2 P-R7	

Threatens to advance, become a Queen and checkmate.

2 . . .	Q-QR8

If the King tries to flee by 2 . . . K-Kt1, then 3 P-R8(Q)ch, K-B2 4 Q-Kt7ch, KxP (on 4 . . . K-B1 5 Q-K7ch, K-Kt1 6 Q-K8 is mate) 5 Q-Kt7ch, K-B4 6 Q-B7ch, and Black's Queen falls.

3 P-B7	Q-R6

Prevents the Pawns on the seventh taking another step.

4 P-Q6

Poses a problem, since the Queen Pawn (which may not be taken) screens the Bishop Pawn, which threatens to Queen.

4 . . .	Q-KB6

Solves the problem—temporarily.

5 P-Q5!

How now?

5 . . .	QxBP
6 P-R8(Q)ch	Q-Kt1
7 Q-R1ch	Q-Kt2ch
8 QxQ mate	

White wins

93

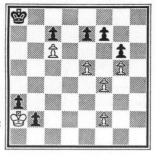

WHITE
*to play
and win*

HORWITZ AND KLING 1851

BLACK is a Pawn ahead, and has two connected passed Pawns. His advantage in Force, Space and Time is enough, according to Znosko-Borovsky, to guarantee a win. Despite his superiority in these elements Black is lost! White wins this by an intangible element—Strength of Position!

The fact that victory is brought about by the doubled Pawns, generally a weakness, is an amusing feature.

1 P-B5

Threatens to continue with *2* P-K6, breaking through for a Queen.

1 . . .   P-K3

If *1* . . . PxP instead, *2* P-K6, PxP *3* P-Kt6 does the trick.

2 PxKP	PxP
3 P-B4	K-Kt1
4 P-B5!	KPxP

Or *4* . . . KtPxP *5* P-Kt6, and White wins.

5 P-K6	K-B1
6 P-K7	

White wins

NO. *84*

WHITE
to play
and win

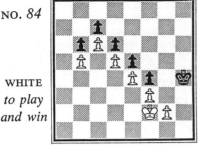

HORWITZ 1851

WHITE breaks through what seems an impregnable barrier.

1 P-Kt3ch   PxPch

Against a refusal to capture, White proceeds as follows: *1* . . . K-Kt4 *2* P-Kt4, K-R5 *3* K-Kt2, K-Kt4 *4* K-R3, K-R3 *5* K-R4, K-Kt3 *6* P-Kt5, K-Kt2 *7* K-R5, K-R2 *8* P-Kt6ch, K-Kt2 *9* K-Kt5, K-Kt1 *10* K-B6, K-B1 *11* K-K6, K-Kt2 *12* K-Q7, and White wins.

2 K-Kt2	K-R4
3 KxP	K-Kt4
4 P-B4ch	PxPch
5 K-B3	K-Kt3
6 KxP	K-B3
7 P-K5ch	PxPch
8 K-K4	K-B2
9 KxP	K-K2
10 P-Q6ch	PxPch
11 K-Q5	K-K1
12 KxP	K-Q1
13 P-B7ch	K-B1
14 K-K6	

Unforgivable would be the precipitate *14* K-B6, allowing a draw by stalemate.

14 . . .	KxP
15 K-K7	K-B1
16 K-Q6	K-Kt2
17 K-Q7	K-Kt1
18 K-B6	K-R2
19 K-B7	K-R1
20 KxP	K-Kt1
21 K-R6	K-R1

On *21* . . . K-B2 *22* K-R7 escorts the Pawn to the eighth square.

22 P-Kt6	K-Kt1
23 P-Kt7	K-B2
24 K-R7	

White wins

95 ♟

WHITE
to play
and win

TROITZKY 1913

IT IS clear that White's hopes of winning depend on Queening the Rook Pawn, but how does he start? If *1* P-R4 (the natural move) K-Kt6! *2* P-R5, P-R4 *3* P-R6, P-R5 *4* P-R7, P-R6 *5* P-R8(Q), P-R7 mate! Or if *1* KxP, K-Kt4 *2* P-R4, PxPe.p. *3* PxP, K-B3 *4* P-R4, K-K2 *5* P-R5, K-Q1 *6* P-R6, K-B1 *7* P-R7, K-Kt2, and Black wins the Pawn and the ending.

1 P-KB6!

Throws a Pawn in the path, so that Black's King cannot reach Q1 directly.

1 . . .	PxP
2 KxP	K-Kt4
3 P-R4	PxPe.p.
4 PxP	K-B4
5 P-R4	K-K4

Now if *6* P-R5, simply *6* . . . KxP, while *6* P-B6 is met by *6* . . . P-Q3 followed by *7* . . . KxP, winning for Black. Therefore:

6 P-Q6!   PxP

Clearly, if *6* . . . P-B3 *7* P-R5, K-Q4 *8* P-R6 wins.

7 P-B6!

White strews the Pawns about, and Black stops to pick them up, as Atalanta did the golden apples that Milanion threw in her path in their legendary race.

7 . . .	PxP
8 P-R5	

The Pawn, safely out of reach, is sure to reach the Queening square. White wins

NO. 86

WHITE
*to play
and win*

CHÉRON 1952

1 P-R6   Kt-Q3
2 P-R7   Kt-B2ch
3 K-K7   Kt-R1

IF *3* . . . Kt-K4 instead (playing for *4* P-R8(Q), Kt-Kt3ch winning the Queen) *4* K-B6, Kt-Q2ch *5* K-Kt7 keeps the Knight at a distance, and wins.

If White is careless now in chasing the Knight, this may happen: *4* K-B8, K-K4 *5* K-Kt7, K-K3 *6* KxKt, K-B2, and White has been stalemated.

4 K-B6!

Maintains the opposition. White will continue with *5* K-Kt7, capture the Knight and win.

NO. *87*

WHITE
to play
and win

MARWITZ 1937

1 P-K6!   Kt-K7ch

WHITE must move out of check, and has choice of seven squares. One, and only one, is the right square, that assures White of a win. Moving to any of the others leads to a draw, as follows:

A] *2* K-B3, Kt-Q5ch, winning the Pawn

B] *2* K-R3, Kt-B5ch, winning the Pawn

c] *2* K-Kt4, Kt-B6 *3* P-K7, Kt-Q4 *4* P-K8(Q), Kt-B3ch, winning the Queen

D] *2* K-R4, Kt-B5   *3* P-K7, Kt-Kt3ch, winning the Pawn

E] *2* K-B2, Kt-B6   *3* P-K7, Kt-K5ch *4* K-K3, Kt-Q3, stopping the Pawn (and capturing it later with the King).

F] *2* K-Kt2, Kt-B5ch, winning the Pawn

How that Knight hops around!

2 K-R2!!

This is the right move, to which there is no reply.

White wins

NO. 88

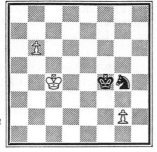

WHITE
to play
and win

RINCK 1937

1 K-Q5

IF AT once *1* P-Kt7, Kt-K4ch *2* K-Q5, Kt-Q2 *3* K-Q6, Kt-Kt1 *4* K-B7, Kt-R3ch *5* K-Kt6, Kt-Kt1 *6* K-R7, Kt-Q2, and Black draws.

1 . . .   Kt-K4

The best chance. There is no hope in *1* . . . Kt-K6ch *2* K-B5, nor in *1* . . . Kt-B3ch *2* K-B6. Now comes an amusing continuation:

2 P-Kt3ch	K-B4
3 P-Kt4ch	K-B3
4 P-Kt5ch	K-B4
5 P-Kt6	K-B3

The King is torn between obligation to his Knight, and the necessity (let alone desire) to capture the impudent Pawn.

6 P-Kt7

White wins, having set Black a task too much even for a King to cope with.

NO. *89*

WHITE
to play
and win

LAPIN

CLEVER defense disposes of one White Pawn, but the one that remains renders Black's Knight *hors de combat.*

1 P-Kt6	Kt-Q3
2 P-Kt7	Kt-K1
3 P-Kt8(Q)	Kt-B3ch
4 K-Kt5!	KtxQ
5 P-Q6!	

Prevents the Knight from emerging, and threatens to move on and Queen with check.

5 . . .	P-Kt6

All that is left, neither King nor Knight being able to head off the Queen Pawn.

6 P-Q7	P-Kt7
7 P-Q8(Q)ch	

White wins

♟ 100

NO. 90

WHITE
to play
and win

NEUMANN 1926

1 K-Kt6	Kt-K4ch
2 K-B6	Kt(K4)-Kt5ch
3 K-K6	KtxP
4 P-Kt6	Kt-B2

BLACK is willing to sacrifice one Knight so that the other can overtake the dangerous advanced Pawn.

| 5 KxKt | Kt-B5 |

Attacks both Pawns.

| 6 P-Kt7 | Kt-Q3ch |

Did White overlook this?

| 7 K-K7 | KtxP |
| 8 P-Kt4 | |

Paralyzes the Knight.

8 . . .	K-Kt4
9 K-Q7	K-B3
10 K-B7	

White captures the Knight and wins

WHITE
to play
and win

OTTEN

1 P-R5   B-B1

IN ORDER to stop the Pawn, Black tries to get his Bishop to the diagonal running from his QR2 to KKt8.

2 K-Q5

White of course plays to keep the Bishop off the line.

2 . . .   B-R3

Aiming at the square K6.

3 P-Kt5ch!   BxP

If *3 . . .* KxP *4* P-R6 followed by *5* P-R7 and the coronation at R8.

4 K-K4!   B-R5
5 K-B3!

White wins. His Pawn will march on, fearing neither the King who is too far off, nor the Bishop who can no longer interfere with its progress.

NO. 92

WHITE
to play
and win

RINCK 1937

1 K-Q5!

WHITE does not play *1* P-Kt7 immediately, as after *1* . . . B-K4 in reply followed by *2* . . . B-Kt1, the position is a draw.

1 . . .	B-K4
2 P-Kt3ch	K-B4
3 P-Kt4ch	K-B3

The alternative is *3* . . . K-B5 leading to *4* P-Kt5, K-B4 *5* P-Kt6, K-B3 *6* P-KKt7, and White wins.

| *4* P-Kt5ch | K-B4 |
| *5* P-Kt6 | K-B3 |

If *5* . . . B-B6 instead, then *6* P-QKt7, B-K4 *7* P-Kt8(Q), BxQ *8* P-Kt7 wins.

6 P-KKt7

White wins

NO. 93

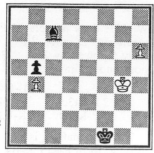

WHITE
*to play
and win*

DE FEIJTER 1932

1 K-B5

BEFORE advancing the passed Pawn, White fights to keep the Bishop from occupying the long diagonal.

| 1 . . . | B-Kt3 |
| 2 K-K4 | |

But not 2 K-K5, as after 2 . . . K-K7 *3* P-R7, K-Q6, and the Bishop reaches Q5.

| 2 . . . | B-Q1 |
| 3 K-K5! | B-Kt4 |

If Black tries *3* . . . B-K2, then *4* P-R7, BxP *5* K-Q4, B-R6 *6* K-B3, and control of the long diagonal wins for White.

4 P-R7	B-B8
5 K-Q5	B-Kt7
6 K-B5	K-B7
7 KxP	K-B6

Since the Bishop will not be able to cope with both passed Pawns, Black rushes his King over to dispose of the Rook Pawn.

8 K-B6	K-B5
9 P-Kt5	K-B4
10 P-Kt6	K-Kt3

Is Black in time?

11 P-Kt7	B-K4
12 P-Kt8(Q)	BxQ
13 P-R8(Q)	

White wins

WHITE
to play
and win

ISENEGGER 1946

| 1 K-Kt7 | B-Kt6 |
| 2 P-R5 | K-Q2 |

APPARENTLY Black will attend to the Rook Pawn with his Bishop, while his King blockades the King Pawn—but White has a few surprises!

| 3 P-R6 | B-B7 |
| 4 K-B7! | |

Threatens to win by 5 P-K6ch followed by 6 P-K7. The natural move 4 K-B6 (instead of 4 K-B7) allows Black to reply 4 . . . K-K1 and draw the position.

| 4 . . . | B-Kt6ch |
| 5 P-K6ch! | |

Astonishing! Not only does White give away a Pawn, but he lets it be captured with check!

5 . . .	BxPch
6 K-B6	B-Kt1
7 K-Kt7	

White wins

WHITE
*to play
and win*

HORWITZ AND KLING 1851

PASSED Pawns on both sides of the board can make life difficult for a lone Bishop.

1 P-B5	K-Kt4
2 P-B6	B-Q1
3 K-K5	K-R3

To meet *4* K-K6 with *4* . . . K-Kt2 *5* P-B6ch, K-B1, and Black has a draw.

4 P-B6!	K-R2
5 K-K6	K-Kt1
6 K-Q7	B-R4
7 K-K8	

White wins

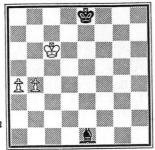

WHITE
*to play
and win*

1 P-R5!

THE plausible *1* P-Kt5 would be refuted by *1* . . . K-Q1 *2* K-Kt7, K-Q2 *3* P-Kt6, B-R4! *4* K-R7, BxPch *5* KxB, K-B1 *6* K-R7 (or *6* P-R5, K-Kt1) K-B2 *7* P-R5, K-B1 *8* P-R6, K-B2, and Black draws.

1 . . .   K-Q1

If *1* . . . BxP *2* P-R6, and the Pawn cannot be stopped.

2 P-R6	B-B7
3 K-Kt7	K-Q2
4 P-Kt5	K-Q1
5 P-R7	BxP
6 KxB	

White wins

WHITE
to play
and win

MORAVEC 1925

1 P-B7   B-B3ch
2 P-Kt7!

UNEXPECTED, but the move that wins. If instead 2 K-Kt8, B-Kt2 3 P-Kt5ch, KxP(Kt3), 4 P-B8(Q), BxQ 5 KxB, KxP, and Black draws. Or if 2 K-Kt8, B-Kt2   3 P-B8(Q), BxQ 4 K-B7, K-Kt4 (but not 4 . . . B-Kt2   5 P-Kt5ch, KxP   6 KxB,   and Black has been swindled) 5 KxB, KxP(Kt3) and the position is a draw.

    2 . . .   BxPch
    3 K-Kt8   K-Kt3
    4 P-Kt5!

White wins, as Black must either abandon his Bishop, or move it and allow the Pawn to Queen.

NO. *98*

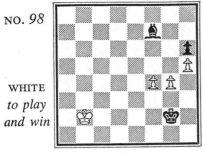

WHITE
to play
and win

HORWITZ 1884

EVEN without the help of the King, a couple of passed Pawns can be remarkably effective against a Bishop.

1 P-B5	K-Kt6
2 P-Kt5!	PxP

If 2 . . . BxP *3* PxP wins at once, or if 2 . . . K-Kt5 *3* P-Kt6, B-Q4 *4* P-B6, KxP *5* P-B7, and White wins.

3 P-R6	B-Kt1
4 P-B6	K-B5
5 P-R7	BxP
6 P-B7	

White wins

NO. 99

WHITE
to play
and win

HORWITZ AND KLING

1 K-Kt5

THE winning idea is to bring the King around to Q8.

1 . . .	K-B2
2 K-B5	B-Q2ch
3 K-K5	B-R5
4 K-Q6	B-Kt4
5 K-B7	B-R5
6 K-Q8	B-Kt4
7 P-Kt8(Q)ch	KxQ
8 P-K8(Q)ch	BxQ
9 KxB	

White wins

♟ 110

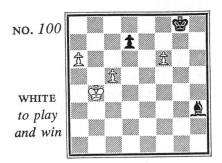

NO. *100*

WHITE
to play
and win

HOLM 1913

1 P-B6

THE impulsive *1* P-R7 is met by
1 . . . B-Kt7, wrecking White's
chances of a win.

1 . . .	PxP
2 K-B5	

Here too if *2* P-R7, P-B4ch *3* KxP,
B-Kt7, and Black draws.

2 . . .	B-B1
3 P-R7	B-Kt2
4 K-Q6	

Threatens to win by *5* K-K7 followed by *6* P-B7ch.

4 . . .	K-B2
5 K-B7	B-R1
6 K-Kt8	

White wins. He captures the imprisoned Bishop and then Queens his
Rook Pawn.

NO. *101*

WHITE
to play
and win

SAAVEDRA 1895

| 1 P-B7 | R-Q3ch |
| 2 K-Kt5 | |

EVERY move of White's must be timed right. For instance, if *2* K-Kt7, R-Q2 followed by capturing the pinned Pawn draws, or if *2* K-B5, R-Q8 followed by *3* . . . R-B8ch does likewise.

2 . . .	R-Q4ch
3 K-Kt4	R-Q5ch
4 K-Kt3	R-Q6ch
5 K-B2	R-Q5

With this idea: *6* P-B8(Q), R-B5ch! *7* QxR, and Black draws by stalemate.

6 P-B8(R)!

Under-promotes to a Rook, and foils the stalemate try. Pieces are now even, but White threatens to mate by *7* R-R8ch.

| 6 . . . | R-R5 |
| 7 K-Kt3 | |

Attacks the Rook and threatens *8* R-B1 mate. White wins a Rook and the game.

NO. *102*

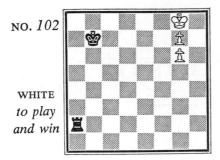

WHITE
*to play
and win*

HORWITZ AND KLING

1 K-B7   R-B7ch

OBVIOUSLY if *1* . . . R-R1 *2* P-Kt8(Q), RxQ *3* KxR, and the remaining Pawn becomes a Queen.

2 K-K6   R-K7ch

The idea is to annoy the King enough to make him come down the board, whereupon the Rook can get to the first rank and hold back the Pawns.

3 K-B5   R-B7ch

If at once *3* . . . R-K1, then *4* K-B6, K-B2 *5* K-B7, K-Q2 *6* P-Kt8(Q) wins for White.

4 K-K4   R-K7ch
5 K-B4!

The natural *5* K-B3 fails after *5* . . . R-K1 *6* K-B4, R-KKt1 *7* K-B5, RxP, and the Rook giving up his life for the second Pawn, draws for Black.

5 . . .	R-K1
6 K-Kt5	K-B2
7 K-R6	K-Q2
8 K-R7	K-K2
9 P-Kt8(Q)	

White wins

The Knight

THAT graceful creature, the Knight, showman of the chessboard, has always been popular with the beginner, the average player, the amateur, the neighborhood expert, the real expert, the master, the Grandmaster, and the World Champion. The Knight needs no further introduction.

For positions where the Knight executes the mate by itself see Carvajal No. 103, Berger No. 105, and Troitzky No. 108.

Amusing concepts are those by Chéron No. 114, Eisenstadt No. 121 and Prokes No. 124.

Interesting duels between Knight and Bishop (and in this section the Knight is always victorious) are Dimentberg No. 109, Kosek No. 110 and Kosek No. 111.

Worthy of special mention in the encounters between White Knight and Black are Pongracz No. 115, Kling No. 117, No. 118, Belenky No. 126, and Tapiolinna No. 127.

In No. 107 by Kubbel, the Knight makes a playful tour—to allow itself to be captured!

Delightful concepts are those by Rinck No. 120, Renner No. 122, Prokes No. 125, Réti No. 128, and Kotov No. 131.

Thoroughly absorbing are the Halberstadt No. 113, Réti No. 116, Halberstadt No. 119, Kaminer No. 132 and the deceptive Selesniev No. 133.

NO. *103*

WHITE
to play
and win

CARVAJAL 1889

A LONE Knight can mate! Without a Pawn on the board, Black would be quite safe. As it stands, the Pawn is compelled to move down and hem in its own King.

1 K-B1	P-R6
2 Kt-B2ch	K-R7
3 Kt-Q4	K-R8
4 K-B2	K-R7

Or *4* . . . P-R7 *5* Kt-Kt3 mate.

5 Kt-K2	K-R8
6 Kt-B1	P-R7
7 Kt-Kt3 mate	

115 🐎

WHITE
to play
and win

| 1 Kt-B5 | K-Q7 |
| 2 Kt-R4! | |

IF WHITE had played 2 Kt-K4ch instead, the reply 2 . . . K-Q6 would threaten to capture the Knight and then the Pawn. After White's actual move, Black must lose time chasing after the Knight.

2 . . .	K-Q6
3 K-Kt2	K-B5
4 K-B3	K-Kt6
5 K-K4	KxKt
6 K-Q5	

White has gained time to bring his King to a dominating position. The rest is elementary.

6 . . .	K-Kt4
7 P-B4ch	K-Kt3
8 K-Q6	K-Kt2
9 P-B5	K-B1
10 K-B6!	

White wins

NO. *105*

WHITE

*to play
and win*

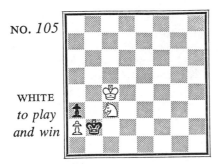

BERGER

1 K-Q3

WHITE does not go after the Pawn, as *1* K-Kt4, K-R8 *2* KxP is a draw by stalemate.

| *1* . . . | K-R8 |
| *2* Kt-R4! | |

Instead, he gives up his own valuable Pawn!

2 . . .	K-Kt8
3 K-Q2	K-R8
4 K-B1	

Forces Black to take it.

4 . . .	KxP
5 K-B2	K-R8
6 Kt-B5	K-R7
7 Kt-Q3	K-R8
8 Kt-B1	P-R7
9 Kt-Kt3 mate	

WHITE
to play
and win

GRIGORIEV 1933

1 Kt-R2!

IMMOBILIZES the Pawn, and avoids such dangers as this: *1* K-B5, K-Kt1 *2* K-Kt6, K-R1 *3* P-R7, P-R7 *4* KtxP, stalemate.

1 . . .	K-B1
2 K-B6!	K-Kt1
3 K-Kt6	K-R1
4 Kt-Kt4	K-Kt1
5 P-R7ch	K-R1
6 Kt-B6	P-R7
7 Kt-Q8	P-R8(Q)
8 Kt-B7 mate	

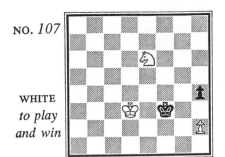

NO. *107*

WHITE
to play
and win

KUBBEL 1914

1 P-R3

ON *1* Kt-Kt5ch, K-Kt5 draws easily.

1 . . .	K-Kt6
2 Kt-Kt5	K-B5
3 Kt-K4	K-B6
4 K-Q4	K-B5

There is no fight in *4* . . . K-Kt7 *5* Kt-Kt5, K-Kt6 *6* K-K3, K-Kt7 *7* K-B4, K-B7 *8* K-Kt4, and White wins.

5 K-Q5	K-B4

Still keeping White's King at bay.

6 Kt-B3!

Very subtle! The natural *6* Kt-B2 leads to *6* . . . K-B5 *7* K-K6, K-B6 *8* K-B5, KxKt *9* K-Kt4, K-K6 *10* KxP, K-B5 *11* K-R5, K-B4 *12* K-R6, K-B3 *13* K-R7, K-B2 *14* P-R4, K-B1 *15* P-R5, K-B2 *16* P-R6, K-B1, and White must either play *17* K-Kt6 allowing Black to reach Kt1 and a draw, or imprison his own King in a humiliating stalemate position.

6 . . .	K-B5
7 Kt-K2ch	K-B6
8 Kt-Kt1ch	K-Kt7
9 K-K4	KxKt
10 K-B3	K-R7
11 K-Kt4	K-Kt7
12 KxP	K-B6
13 K-Kt5	K-K5
14 P-R4	K-K4
15 P-R5	K-K3
16 K-Kt6	

White wins, as the Pawn is free and Black can never reach Kt1, the drawing square.

NO. *108*

WHITE
to play
and win

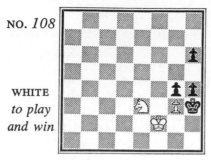

TROITZKY 1906

IT WOULD appear that Black has at least a draw, since White cannot hold on to his solitary Pawn—but White has hidden resources!

1 Kt-Kt2!   PxPch

The alternative is *1* . . . K-R7 2 KtxP, K-R6   3 Kt-B5, P-R4   4 K-Kt1, P-R5 (unfortunately forced) 5 PxP, and the Rook Pawn marches up the board to Queen.

   2 K-Kt1   P-R4
   3 K-R1   P-R5
   4 Kt-B4 mate

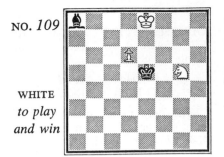

NO. *109*

WHITE
to play
and win

DIMENTBERG 1949

1 K-Q7!

BLOCKING the Pawn—a strange winning move! White does not advance the Pawn immediately, as after *1* P-Q7, B-B3 followed by *2 . . .* BxP draws the position.

1 . . .	K-Q4
2 K-B7	

Now threatening *3* P-Q7.

2 . . .	B-B3
3 Kt-K4!	

Black is in Zugzwang. He loses because he is compelled to move. He has these choices:

A] *3 . . .* KxKt *4* KxB, and the Pawn Queens.

B] *3 . . .* B-K1 *4* Kt-B6ch winning the Bishop.

C] *3 . . .* B-Kt4 *4* Kt-B3ch, K-B4 *5* KtxB, KxKt *6* P-Q7, winning.

D] *3 . . .* B-R5 *4* Kt-B3ch and *5* KtxB.

White wins

NO. *110*

WHITE
*to play
and win*

KOSEK 1923

1 Kt-B5	B-R1

OBVIOUSLY, if *1* . . . B-B1 *2* Kt-K7ch followed by *3* KtxB wins for White.

2 Kt-Q4ch	K-B4
3 Kt-K6ch	K-B3

The only move, since the King must stay near the Pawn, and *3* . . . K-Kt4 loses by *4* Kt-B7ch.

4 Kt-B7	B-Kt2
5 Kt-Q5!	

Leaves Black without resource. On *5* . . . KxKt (or any other move by the King) the reply *6* KxB wins for White. Should Black try *5* . . . B-B1, then *6* Kt-K7ch, K-Q2 *7* KtxB, KxKt *8* P-Kt7ch compels resignation. White wins

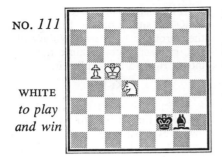

NO. 111

WHITE
*to play
and win*

KOSEK 1910

1 Kt-B6

SHUTS off the Bishop's action on the long diagonal so that the Pawn may march through. The Pawn now threatens to reach Kt7 safely.

1 . . .	B-B8
2 P-Kt6	B-R3
3 K-Q6	B-Kt2

If the King tries to help by *3* . . . K-K6, then *4* K-B7, K-K5 *5* Kt-Kt4 evicts the Bishop, enabling the Pawn to advance next move.

| *4* K-B7 | B-R1 |
| *5* Kt-Q8 | K-K6 |

On *5* . . . B-B6 *6* Kt-B6 shuts the Bishop out permanently, assuring the Pawn of Queening in two more moves.

6 Kt-Kt7

Brutal but necessary. The Bishop is imprisoned.

| *6* . . . | K-Q5 |
| *7* K-Kt8 | K-Q4 |

Unfortunately for Black, his King may not move to B4 attacking the Pawn.

| *8* KxB | K-B3 |
| *9* K-R7 | |

White wins

123

NO. *112*

WHITE
*to play
and win*

WHITE plans to maneuver his Knight to Kt7, shutting off the Bishop, and then promote his Pawn. White's object is clear, but he must time his moves right to accomplish it.

1 Kt-R5

The plausible try *1* K-Kt8, K-Q1 *2* Kt-R5 (threatening *3* Kt-Kt7ch followed by advancing the Pawn) fails after *2* . . . B-R1! *3* KxB, K-B2 *4* Kt-B4, K-B1 *5* Kt-Q6ch, K-B2 *6* Kt-Kt5ch, K-B1 due to the fact that the Knight cannot gain a move.

1 . . .   B-R1

White was threatening to shut off the Bishop by *2* Kt-Kt7 or *2* Kt-B6ch.

2 K-B8!

Gaining a move for the final maneuver—something the Knight cannot do. If at once *2* K-Kt8, K-Q1 *3* Kt-Kt7ch, K-Q2   *4* KxB, K-B1 *5* Kt-Q6ch, K-B2   *6* Kt-K8ch, K-B1, and the stubborn King cannot be ousted.

2 . . .	K-Q3
3 K-Kt8	K-Q2
4 Kt-Kt7	

Black's King needs a waiting move (so that *5* KxB can be met with *5* . . . K-B1) but he has none!

4 . . .	K-B3
5 KxB	K-B2
6 Kt-Q6!	

Prevents Black from moving to B1, and enables his own King to emerge.

| *6* . . . | KxKt |
| *7* K-Kt7 | |

White wins

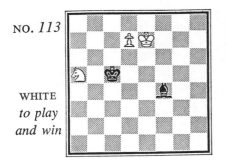

NO. *113*

WHITE
to play
and win

HALBERSTADT 1939

AN INTERESTING duel between Knight and Bishop.

1 Kt-Kt7ch   K-Kt5

The other defenses lead to the following play:

A] *1* . . . K-B3   *2* Kt-Q8ch, K-Kt4 (on *2* . . . K-Kt3, or Q4 *3* Kt-K6 followed by Queening with check wins, while *2* . . . K-B4 *3* Kt-K6ch costs the Bishop) *3* Kt-K6, B-Kt6 *4* K-B6, B-R5ch   *5* Kt-Kt5 wins.

B] *1* . . . K-B5 *2* Kt-Q6ch, K-Q4 *3* K-B6!, B-Kt6 *4* K-Kt5 wins. A beautiful variation.

C] *1* . . . K-Kt3, Q4 or Q5 *2* P-B8(Q)ch wins.

2 Kt-Q6   B-K6

On *2* . . . B-Kt4ch *3* K-K8, and White will then play *4* Kt-B5 followed by *5* Kt-K7, blocking the Bishop's action on the diagonal.

Black's actual move leaves the possibility of checking at Kt4 open, as well as the opportunity of shifting to another diagonal via QKt3.

3 Kt-B8   B-B5

Kept out of QKt3, the Bishop heads for B2.

4 Kt-Kt6!

Refutes *4* . . . B-B2 by *5* Kt-Q5ch winning the Bishop, and *4* . . . B-Kt4ch by *5* K-K8, K-B4 *6* Kt-B8 followed by *7* Kt-K7 shutting out the Bishop.

4 . . .   K-B4

After all the fencing, the position is almost identical with the opening scene.

5 Kt-Q5!

White wins. If *5* . . . KxKt *6* P-Q8(Q), the Pawn Queening with check, while on *5* . . . B-Kt4ch *6* Kt-B6 is decisive.

WHITE
to play
and win

CHÉRON 1952

A PRETTY tactical device in Pawn endings is the forcible displacement of a piece that prevents your Pawn from moving up the board.

A simple and pleasing example:

1 Kt-Kt7ch!   KtxKt

On *1* . . . K-B2 instead, *2* KtxKt, K-B3 *3* P-R6 wins for White. The Pawn and Knight stay where they are until the King comes up and helps.

2 P-R6   K-B2
3 P-R7

Certainly not the greedy *3* PxKt, when *3* . . . KxP drawing is fit retribution.

White wins

NO. *115*

WHITE
to play
and win

PONGRACZ

BEFORE the Pawn can advance, Black's Knight must be driven off and kept out of active play.

1 Kt-Q2	K-Kt2
2 Kt-B4	

Forces Black's Knight away from the center of action.

2 . . .	Kt-Kt8

On *2* . . . Kt-B7 *3* P-Kt5, Kt-K8 *4* P-Kt6, Kt-Q6ch *5* K-Kt5, Kt-B5 *6* P-Kt7 leaves Black helpless.

3 K-Q4!

Not at once *3* P-Kt5 as *3* . . . Kt-B6 attacks the Pawn, and after *4* P-Kt6, Kt-R5ch *5* K-B6, KtxP captures it and draws.

3 . . .	K-B2

For the moment Black's Knight is out of business.

4 P-Kt5	K-K2
5 P-Kt6	K-Q2
6 K-B5	Kt-B6
7 Kt-K5ch	K-B1

Black has no time to attack the Knight as after *7* . . . K-K3 *8* P-Kt7, Kt-R5ch *9* K-Kt4 wins.

8 K-B6	Kt-K7
9 P-Kt7ch	K-Kt1
10 K-Kt6	

White mates next move

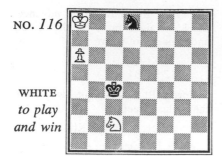

NO. *116*

WHITE
*to play
and win*

RÉTI 1929

1 K-R7!

A SUBTLE winning move. The natural *1* K-Kt8 leads to *1* . . . K-Kt4 *2* Kt-Kt4 (*2* P-R7, Kt-B3ch wins the Pawn) Kt-B3ch *3* K-Kt7 (*3* K-B7, KtxKt *4* P-R7, Kt-Q4ch followed by *5* . . . Kt-Kt3 draws) Kt-R4ch *4* K-R7, KxKt *5* K-Kt6, Kt-B5ch *6* K-B7, K-R4 *7* P-R7, Kt-Kt3 and Black draws.

| *1* . . . | K-Kt4 |

If *1* . . . Kt-B3ch *2* K-Kt6, K-Q4 (or *2* . . . Kt-K2 *3* K-Kt7) *3* Kt-Kt4ch, KtxKt *4* P-R7 wins, or if *1* . . . K-B4 *2* Kt-Q4 (a pretty sacrifice to prevent the King coming closer) KxKt *3* K-Kt6, and White wins.

| *2* Kt-Kt4! | K-R4 |

If *2* . . . KxKt *3* K-Kt6 wins, or if *2* . . . K-B4 *3* K-Kt8, KxKt *4* K-B7 (certainly not *4* P-R7, Kt-B3ch followed by *5* . . . KtxP) Kt-K3ch *5* K-Kt6, and the Pawn cannot be stopped.

3 K-Kt8	Kt-B3ch
4 K-Kt7	Kt-Q1ch
5 K-B7	Kt-K3ch
6 K-Kt8	Kt-B4

On *6* . . . K-Kt3 *7* P-R7, Kt-B2 *8* Kt-Q5ch wins.

7 P-R7	Kt-Q2ch
8 K-B7	Kt-Kt3
9 K-Kt7	K-Kt4
10 Kt-Q5	

White wins. Black's Knight must not move and dares not stay. A full-bodied instructive Réti composition.

NO. *117*

WHITE

to play

and win

KLING 1867

WHITE must draw Black's Knight away from its post, so that his Pawn may advance and Queen.

1 Kt-K6

Intending to attack the Knight by 2 Kt-B8.

1 . . .   K-Q4

Vacates B3 for later occupation by his Knight.

2 Kt-B8   Kt-K4
3 K-R8

Clearly   not   *3* P-Kt8(Q), Kt-B3ch, and the newly-crowned Queen comes off the board.

3 . . .   Kt-B3
4 Kt-Q7   K-K3

If *4* . . . K-Q3 *5* Kt-Kt6, K-B2 (on *5* . . . K-B4 *6* Kt-B8 followed by 7 Kt-R7 wins) 6 Kt-Q5ch, K-Q3 7 Kt-Kt4 wins for White.

5 Kt-Kt6   K-Q3
6 Kt-B8ch   K-B2
7 Kt-R7   Kt-Kt1
8 Kt-Kt5ch   K-Kt3
9 KxKt

White wins

WHITE
*to play
and win*

1 Kt-B6

TO PREVENT a perpetual check by
1 . . . Kt-Q2ch   *2* K-R8, Kt-Kt3ch
3 K-Kt8, Kt-Q2ch *4* K-B8, Kt-Kt3ch
etc.

1 . . .   Kt-R1!

A clever defense. If Black had
played *1* . . . K-B4, then *2* K-Kt7,
K-Kt4 *3* Kt-Q5 evicts the Knight and
wins.

2 Kt-Q5!

A fine reply. White avoids *2* KxKt,
K-B2 *3* Kt-Q5ch, K-B1 *4* Kt-K7ch,
K-B2, and Black draws, the Knight
being unable to gain a move to dislodge Black's King.

2 . . .   K-Q2

Ready to meet *3* KxKt with *3* . . .
K-B1, and Black draws.

3 K-Kt7

Restricts Black to one move by his
King, since his Knight may not come
out.

3 . . .   K-Q1

The only move to keep in touch
with the square B1. On *3* . . . K-Q3
instead, White replies *4* KxKt followed by *5* K-Kt8, winning.

4 Kt-Kt6   Kt-B2
5 K-B6

White wins
Black must either move his King,
losing the Knight, or move the Knight
and allow White's Pawn to Queen.

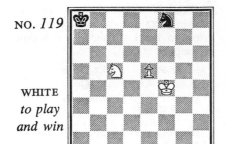

NO. *119*

WHITE
to play
and win

HALBERSTADT 1949

A REWARDING ending where the variations are as brilliant as the main play.

1 K-Kt5!

Moving in on the Knight. Straightforward attack by *1* K-B5 leads to this: *1* . . . K-R2! *2* K-B6 (or *2* Kt-Q7, KtxKt *3* P-K6, Kt-Kt3 *4* P-K7, Kt-B1 *5* P-K8(Q), Kt-Q3ch and Black wins the Queen) K-Kt3 *3* K-Kt7, KxKt *4* KxKt, K-Q4, and Black captures the Pawn and draws. Or *1* K-B5, K-R2 *2* K-Kt5, K-Kt3 *3* Kt-Q7ch, KtxKt *4* P-K6, Kt-B4 *5* P-K7, Kt-K3ch *6* K-B6, Kt-B2, and the Pawn can never move on to Queen.

$$1 . . . \qquad K\text{-}R2$$
2 K-B5!

The natural attack *2* K-R6 is met by *2* . . . K-Kt3 *3* Kt-Q7ch (if *3* K-Kt7, KxKt draws) KtxKt *4* P-K6, Kt-B3 *5* K-Kt6 (*5* P-K7, Kt-Kt1ch) Kt-Q4 and Black draws.

$$2 . . . \qquad K\text{-}Kt3$$

If Black returns instead by *2* . . . K-Kt1, then *3* K-B6, K-B1 (or *3* . . . Kt-R2ch *4* K-Kt6, Kt-B1ch *5* K-Kt7, and the Knight is trapped) *4* K-Kt7, Kt-Q2 *5* KtxKt, KxKt *6* K-B7, and the Pawn will Queen.

3 Kt-Q7ch!	KtxKt
4 P-K6	Kt-B4

If *4* . . . K-B2 *5* P-K7 followed by *6* P-K8(Q) wins.

$$5 \text{ P-K7} \qquad Kt\text{-}Kt2$$

A last flicker of hope. If White precipitately Queens his Pawn then *6* . . . Kt-Q3ch removes the Queen.

$$6 \text{ K-K5}$$

White wins

131

NO. *120*

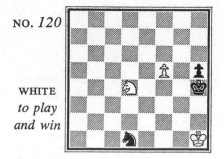

WHITE
to play
and win

RINCK 1915

THERE is classic economy in this pleasing example of persuasion exerted on Black's Knight to abandon his important post.

1 P-B6	Kt-B7ch
2 K-Kt2	Kt-Q6
3 P-B7	Kt-B5ch
4 K-R2	

In order later to restrict the moves of Black's King.

4 . . .	Kt-Kt3

The Pawn is stopped, but White has a counter-combination.

5 Kt-B3ch	K-Kt5
6 Kt-K5ch!	KtxKt
7 P-B8(Q)	

White wins

NO. *121*

WHITE
to play
and win

EISENSTADT 1948

GALLOPING furiously after the passed Pawn, Black's Knight heads it off just in time—or does he?

1 P-B5	Kt-K6
2 P-B6	Kt-B4
3 P-B7	Kt-K2ch
4 K-Kt7	Kt-Kt3

The Pawn is stopped, but now comes. . . .

5 KtxP

Ready to reply to *5* . . . KtxKt with *6* P-B8(Q) and White wins, or if Black plays *5* . . . P-R6, then the continuation is *6* KtxKt, P-R7 *7* P-B8(Q), P-R8(Q), *8* Q-R8ch will remove Black's Queen.

5 . . .	Kt-B1
6 Kt-B6 mate!	

133

NO. *122*

WHITE
*to play
and win*

RENNER 1941

WHITE'S first move is obvious, but how will his King hide from all the the checks?

1 PxP	R-Kt6ch
2 K-B7	R-B6ch
3 K-Q7	

The King must not leave the seventh rank. If for example 3 K-Q3, R-B1 solves Black's problems, or if 3 K-Q8, RxKt, and White does not dare Queen his Pawn.

3 . . .	R-Q6ch
4 K-K7	R-K6ch
5 K-B7	R-B6ch
6 K-Kt7	R-Kt6ch
7 Kt-Kt5!	

Chess players are generous!

| 7 . . . | RxKtch |

Now the Rook is closer, which is the purpose of White's sacrifice.

8 K-B7	R-B4ch
9 K-K7	R-K4ch
10 K-Q7	R-Q4ch
11 K-B7	R-B4ch
12 K-Kt7	R-Kt4ch
13 K-B6!	

White wins. The Rook has no more checks, and cannot return to the first rank.

NO. *123*

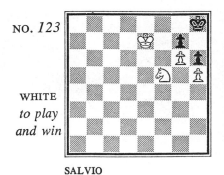

WHITE
to play
and win

SALVIO

WHITE is a whole piece ahead, but how does he win? Moving closer with his King stalemates Black, and meaningless Knight moves do not force the win.

Clearly, giving up the Knight will break through, but the sacrifice must be timed right. If for example *1* KtxP(R6), PxKt   *2* K-B6, K-Kt1 *3* P-Kt7, K-R2 *4* P-Kt8(Q)ch (*4* K-B7 stalemates Black) KxQ *5* K-Kt6, and White can win the remaining Pawn but not the ending.

1 Kt-Q6	K-Kt1
2 Kt-K8	K-R1
3 Kt-B6!	

Leaves no choice.

3 . . .	PxKt
4 K-B7	P-B4
5 P-Kt7ch	K-R2
6 P-Kt8(Q) mate	

135 🐴

NO. *124*

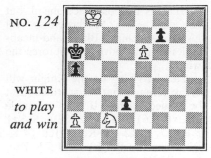

WHITE
*to play
and win*

PROKES 1947

HOW does White win? He can Queen his advanced Pawn, but so can Black.

1 Kt-Kt4ch!	PxKt
2 P-K7	P-Q7
3 P-K8(Q)	P-Q8(Q)
4 Q-B6ch	K-R4
5 K-Kt7!	

Threatens mate on the move.

   5 . . .   Q-Q6

The alternative *5* . . . P-Kt6 is answered by *6* P-R3, and Black is faced with an additional threat of mate in two by *7* Q-B5ch, K-R5 *8* Q-Kt4 mate.

6 Q-Kt6ch	K-R5
7 Q-R7ch	K-Kt4
8 Q-R6ch	

White wins the Queen and the game.

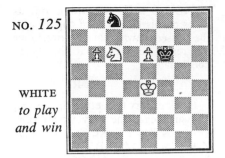

NO. *125*

WHITE
to play
and win

PROKES 1938

1 P-Kt7   Kt-Q3ch
2 K-Q4!

NOT at once *2* K-Q5, as after *2 . . .* KtxP *3* P-K7, K-B2, Black has a draw.

2 . . .   KtxP
3 K-Q5

The difference is that Black is now confined to two plausible defenses.

3 . . .   K-Kt2

Moving away from the Pawn, but if he makes the only move open to his Knight then this happens: *3 . . .* Kt-B4 *4* P-K7, Kt-R3 *5* K-Q6 (of course not *5* P-K8(Q), Kt-B2ch winning the Queen) K-B2 *6* Kt-Q8ch, K-K1 *7* Kt-K6, K-B2 *8* Kt-Kt7, Kt-B2 *9* K-Q7, K-B3 *10* Kt-K8ch, KtxKt *11* KxKt and White wins.

4 Kt-Q8!   KtxKt
5 P-K7

White wins

NO. *126*

WHITE
*to play
and win*

BELENKY 1955

BLACK is so busy warding off attacks on his Knight, and coping with the passed Pawns, that he overlooks a greater danger—that of being checkmated!

1 K-K7   Kt-R2

Black can try to capture the Pawns, in which case the play would run: *1* . . . K-Kt4 *2* KxKt, KxP *3* K-Kt7, K-Kt5 *4* Kt-K4, K-B6 *5* K-Kt6, K-Kt5 *6* K-B6, K-B6 *7* K-B5 and White wins.

2 K-B7   K-Kt4

The alternative is *2* . . . Kt-B3 when *3* P-R6, K-Kt4 (on *3* . . . K-K4 *4* Kt-Q7ch wins) *4* Kt-K4ch, KtxKt *5* P-R7 wins for White.

3 Kt-K4ch	KxP
4 K-Kt7	Kt-Kt4
5 Kt-B6 mate	

138

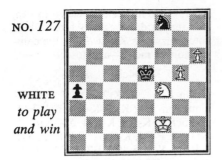

NO. *127*

WHITE
to play
and win

TAPIOLINNA 1929

1 P-Kt6	K-B3
2 P-Kt7	K-B2
3 Kt-Q5	

THREATENS to win by *4* Kt-B6 followed by *5* P-Kt8(Q)ch.

| 3 . . . | Kt-K3 |

Other defenses are:

A] *3* . . . Kt-Q2 (or R2) *4* Kt-K7, Kt-B3 *5* P-Kt8(Q)ch, KtxQ *6* P-R7 and wins.

B] *3* . . . Kt-Kt3 *4* Kt-B6, Kt-K2 *5* P-Kt8(Q)ch, KtxQ *6* P-R7 and wins.

| 4 Kt-K7 | KtxP |
| 5 P-R7! | |

White wins

NO. *128*

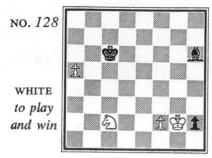

WHITE
to play
and win

RÉTI 1922

ONLY two moves are needed to win, but they are enough to force Black into zugzwang. Zugzwang is the compulsion to move—and lose.

1 Kt-Q4ch   K-B4

On *1* . . . K-Kt2 instead, the continuation is *2* KxP, K-R3 *3* Kt-Kt3, B-B5ch *4* K-R3, K-Kt4 *5* K-Kt4, B-Kt1 *6* P-B4, K-Kt5 *7* P-B5, KxKt *8* P-B6, K-Kt5 *9* P-B7, B-Q3 *10* P-R6, and White wins, the Bishop being outdistanced by the Pawns.

2 K-R1!

White wins! There are no threats, and if Black could pass nothing could happen to him. But zugzwang—the compulsion to move when it's one's turn to move—has him in its grasp, and he is lost. The proof: If

A] *2* . . . B-B1 *3* Kt-K6ch wins the Bishop.

B] *2* . . . B-Kt2 *3* Kt-K6ch wins the Bishop.

C] *2* . . . B-Kt4 *3* Kt-K6ch wins the Bishop.

D] *2* . . . B-B5 *3* Kt-K6ch wins the Bishop.

E] *2* . . . B-Q7 *3* Kt-Kt3ch wins the Bishop.

F] *2* . . . B-B8 *3* Kt-Kt3ch wins the Bishop.

G] *2* . . . K-Q3 *3* Kt-B5ch wins the Bishop.

H] *2* . . . K-Q4 *3* P-R6, and the passed Pawn becomes a Queen.

WHITE
to play
and win

MATTISON 1914

1 P-B6

BEFORE starting his Rook Pawn, White blocks the long diagonal.

1 . . .	PxP
2 P-R6	B-B6

If 2 . . . P-B4 3 Kt-K5 prevents the Bishop from getting on the diagonal.

3 Kt-Kt5	B-Q4
4 Kt-K6	P-B4

Black may not bring his King closer, as after 4 . . . K-Q2 5 Kt-B5ch, K-B2 6 P-R7 leaves him helpless.

5 Kt-B7ch	K-Q2
6 KtxB	K-B1

On 6 . . . K-B3 7 K-Kt2, P-B5 8 K-B2, P-B6 9 K-K3, and White overtakes the Pawn.

7 Kt-Kt6ch	K-Kt1

Forced, as 7 . . . K-B2 allows 8 P-R7 followed by Queening.

8 Kt-Q7ch	K-R2
9 KtxP	

White wins. His King simply comes up the board and escorts the Pawn to the Queening square.

NO. *130*

WHITE
*to play
and win*

BERGER 1889

1 P-B5

THREATENING to win by *2* P-B6, PxP *3* P-Kt7.

| *1* ... | B-Kt8 |
| *2* Kt-K6! | |

Ready to circumvent *2* . . . B-K5 by *3* Kt-Kt5ch, K-B5 *4* KtxB, KxKt *5* P-B6, etc.

2 ...	PxKt
3 P-B6	B-K5
4 P-B7	

White wins

NO. *131*

WHITE
to play
and win

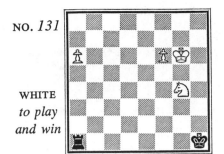

KOTOV 1945

1 P-B7	RxPch
2 Kt-B6	R-R1
3 Kt-K8	R-R3ch
4 K-Kt5	

THE King must find a way to evade the Rook's checks. He may not move to the seventh rank, as after *4* K-Kt7 for example, *4* . . . R-R2 followed by sacrificing the Rook for the Pawn, draws. Nor may he move to the Bishop file, as after *4* K-B5, R-R8 followed by *5* . . . R-KB8 (with or without check) draws for Black.

4 . . .	R-R4ch
5 K-Kt4	R-R5ch
6 K-Kt3	R-R6ch
7 K-B2	R-R7ch
8 K-K3	R-R6ch

Now we go up the board.

9 K-K4	R-R5ch
10 K-K5	R-R4ch
11 K-K6	R-R3ch
12 K-Q7	R-R2ch
13 Kt-B7	

White wins, as the Rook has no more checks and cannot stop the Pawn.

NO. 132

WHITE
*to play
and win*

KAMINER 1925

| 1 P-Kt7 | R-B1 |
| 2 Kt-Kt4ch | K-K5 |

BLACK plays to capture or render impotent the King Knight Pawn. Moving to the Queen side instead would lead to this: 2 . . . K-B5 3 Kt-B6, K-B4 4 P-Kt8(Q), RxQ 5 KtxR, K-Q4 6 P-Kt4, K-K4 7 P-Kt5, K-B4 8 Kt-Q7, K-B5 9 Kt-B6 and White wins.

| 3 Kt-B6 | K-B5 |

Hoping for this: 4 P-Kt8(Q), RxQ 5 KtxR, K-Kt6, and Black captures the Pawn next move and draws.

| 4 P-Kt4! | KxP |

What else is there? Black must prevent 5 P-Kt5 followed by 6 P-Kt8(Q)ch, and if he tries 4 . . . R-B3ch (instead of 4 . . . KxP) then 5 K-Kt7 (not 5 KxP which is refuted by 5 . . . R-B2ch, and White loses the ambitious Queen Knight Pawn) R-Kt3ch 6 KxP and White wins.

| 5 K-Kt7 | R-K1 |

The only square open along the rank.

| 6 K-B7 | R-KR1 |

Once again the only square left.

| 7 K-K7! |

Threatens 8 Kt-Q8, cutting off the Rook, after which the Pawn could advance.

| 7 . . . | R-KKt1 |
| 8 Kt-Q8 | R-Kt2ch |

If White should now get out of check by moving his King, the reply 9 . . . RxP would draw easily, the Knight alone being unable to force mate.

| 9 Kt-B7 | R-Kt1 |

But now the Rook returns to the first rank. Does Black get a draw after all?

| 10 Kt-R6ch |

Certainly not! The Knight fork wins the Rook and the game.

 144

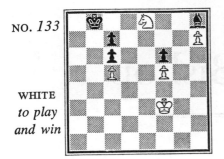

NO. *133*

WHITE
to play
and win

SELESNIEV 1920

WHITE cannot save his stranded Knight, but he can close in and capture the badly-placed Bishop in return. At the critical moment though, he must find the pretty surprise move that turns an apparent draw into a win.

1 K-Kt4	K-B1
2 K-R5	K-Q1
3 Kt-Kt7!	BxKt
4 P-R8(Q)ch!	

Unexpected, and the only way to win. If instead *4* K-Kt6, B-R1 *5* K-B7, K-Q2 *6* K-Kt8, K-K2 *7* KxB, K-B2, and White is stalemated.

4 . . .	BxQ
5 K-Kt6	K-K2
6 K-R7	K-B2
7 KxB	K-B1
8 K-R7	K-B2
9 K-R6	K-B1
10 K-Kt6	K-K2
11 K-Kt7	K-K1
12 KxP	K-B1
13 K-K6	K-K1
14 P-B6	K-B1
15 P-B7	K-Kt2
16 K-K7	

White wins

The Bishop

THE Bishop may not be so glamourous as the Knight, since its whole life must be spent on diagonals of one color. Despite this, endings in which the Bishop is the star actor can be quite entertaining.

For example, there are these sprightly inspirations: Sachodakin No. 134 (mate by a lone Bishop) Fritz No. 137 (in which the Bishop makes only one move) Efron No. 138, Selesniev No. 172 and Fritz No. 175.

Winning with "the wrong Bishop" is nicely demonstrated in Troitzky No. 136, Duras No. 139 (the Bishop makes a couple of ingenious moves in this one) Horwitz and Kling No. 140, and Horwitz No. 144.

Sometimes the Bishop's role is to be sacrificed for the good of the cause, as in Selesniev No. 141, Kayev No. 142, Neustadt No. 143, Del Rio No. 145, Bledow No. 148, Neustadt No. 177 (the Bishop offers itself on three squares!) Troitzky No. 176 and Karstedt No. 179.

In combat with the Knight, the Horwitz and Kling No. 147 shows the Bishop winning by triangulation, while the Selesniev No. 155 has the King casually invading the enemy territory.

The basic battle of Bishop against Bishop is instructively demonstrated by Centurini in his No. 149, No. 150, No. 152, No. 153 and No. 154.

Noteworthy Bishop endings are the deceptive Weenink No. 156, the delightful Heuacker No. 157, the classic Horwitz No. 158, and the pleasantries by Platov Nos. 159 and 160.

Domination over a Rook is beautifully illustrated in Fritz No. 161, while other entertaining instances of the Rook being outwitted by a Bishop can be seen in Mattison No. 162, Halberstadt No. 163, Kubbel No. 164 and Vancura No. 178.

Engaging subtleties in Bishop endings are those in Fritz No. 165 (a little beauty!) Isenegger No. 166 and Selesniev No. 173.

Last there is the Queckenstedt No. 180, which has this composer's own characteristic touch. The interplay of Pawns and Bishops is amusing.

NO. *134*

WHITE
to play
and win

SACHODAKIN 1932

A LONE Bishop *can* mate—if the King is imprisoned by his own friends!

1 K-B7	P-R6
2 B-R4	P-R7
3 K-B6	P-R8(Q)

The Pawn must push on and become a Queen (or some other piece) though the enemy is closing in on his King.

4 B-Kt5 mate

WHITE
to play
and win

BISHOP and Rook Pawn win easily against the lone King if the Bishop controls R8, the Queening square. If the Bishop is the wrong color, as in the diagrammed position, the win can only be attained if the adverse King is kept out of the corner square. Once he reaches that square, a win is impossible.

1 P-R6	K-B2	
2 B-R7!		

To prevent *2* . . . K-Kt1 followed by *3* . . . K-R1, which would assure Black of a draw.

2 . . .	K-B3
3 K-B4	K-B2
4 K-B5	K-B1
5 K-B6	K-K1
6 B-B5	K-B1
7 P-R7	K-K1
8 P-R8(Q) mate	

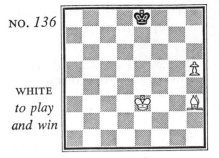

NO. *136*

WHITE
to play
and win

TROITZKY 1896

AGAINST a Rook Pawn and a bad Bishop (one that does not control the Pawn's Queening square) Black can draw if his King can reach the corner square.

White's play to win is easily understood once we realize that his purpose is to keep Black's King from reaching Kt1 or Kt2, from whence he can move to R1 and the safety of a draw.

1 B-K6!	K-K2
2 P-R6	K-B3
3 B-B5!	

To prevent *3* . . . K-Kt3 attacking the Pawn.

3 . . .	K-B2

Now threatening to move to Kt1, and a sure draw.

4 B-R7!	K-B3
5 K-B4	K-B2
6 K-B5	K-B1
7 K-B6	K-K1
8 B-B5	K-B1

White mates in two moves

WHITE
to play
and win

FRITZ 1939

CAN White overtake the Rook Pawn?

  1 K-B7   P-R4
  2 K-K6

But not *2* B-B6 as *2* . . . K-Kt6 *3* K-Kt6, P-R5 *4* BxP, KxP and Black has a draw.

  2 . . .   P-R5

This time if Black had played *2* . . . K-Kt6, *3* K-B5 would close in on the Pawn.

    3 K-Q5

Ready to meet *3* . . . K-Kt6 with *4* K-K4 and the Rook Pawn is doomed.

    3 . . . P-R6

But this certainly looks good!

  4 K-B4!   P-R7
  5 B-Kt4   P-R8(Q)
  6 P-Kt3 mate!

And not a moment too soon.

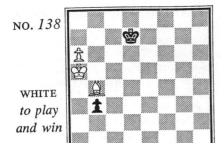

NO. *138*

WHITE
*to play
and win*

EFRON

1 P-R7

WHITE can try to prevent Black from Queening his Pawn, but after *1* B-B3, K-B1 *2* B-K5 (to stop *2* . . . K-Kt1 when Black has a certain draw) P-Kt7 *3* BxP, K-Kt1, and White cannot possibly force a win.

1 . . .	P-Kt7
2 P-R8(Q)	P-Kt8(Q)

With Black's King and Queen so far apart from each other, it seems incredible that the Queen will either be lost or the King driven into a *cul-de-sac* in a half-dozen moves.

3 Q-Kt7ch   K-K3

If *3* . . . K-K1 *4* Q-K7 mate, or if *3* . . . K-Q1 *4* B-K7ch, discovering an attack on the Queen.

4 Q-K7ch   K-Q4

The alternative is *4* . . . K-B4 *5* Q-R7ch winning the Queen.

5 Q-Q6ch   K-B5

Here if *5* . . . K-K5 *6* Q-Kt6ch wins the Queen.

6 Q-B5ch	K-Kt6
7 Q-B3ch	K-R7
8 Q-R3 mate	

WHITE
to play
and win

DURAS 1908

IT IS clear that Black can draw if his King reaches QR1, since White has a Rook Pawn and his Bishop does not control the Pawn's Queening square. How does White keep the King out? If he plays the natural *1* B-B5, the continuation would be *1* . . . K-B2 *2* P-R4, K-K3 (but not *2* . . . K-K1 *3* P-R5, K-Q1 *4* B-Q6, K-B1 *5* P-R6, K-Q1 *6* P-R7 and White wins) *3* P-R5, K-Q4 *4* P-R6, K-B3 *5* K-Kt2, K-B2 (aiming for the square Kt1 and a sure draw) *6* B-R7, K-B3 (threatens to win the Pawn) *7* B-Kt8, K-Kt3 *8* P-R7, K-Kt2, and White must concede the draw.

1 B-Kt4!

A subtle move, whose purpose will shortly be manifest.

1 . . .	K-B2
2 P-R4	K-K3
3 P-R5	K-Q4
4 P-R6	K-B3
5 B-R5!	

Prevents *5* . . . K-B2, and closes all the roads leading to Black's QR1.

5 . . .	P-Q4
6 K-Kt2	P-Q5
7 K-B3	P-Q6
8 K-K3	K-Q2

The King has nothing left but retreat.

9 P-R7

White wins

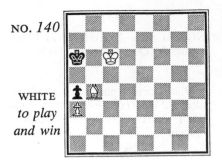

NO. *140*

WHITE
*to play
and win*

HORWITZ AND KLING 1851

BEFORE Black can be subdued, his King must be prevented from reaching the corner square, and his remaining Pawn captured.

1 B-B5	K-R4
2 K-Kt7	K-Kt4
3 B-Kt6!	

Forces Black to move down the board.

3 . . .	K-B5
4 K-B6	K-Kt6

Black can try a roundabout route to R1, with this result: *4* . . . K-Q6 *5* K-Kt5, K-K5 *6* KxP, K-Q4 *7* K-Kt5, K-Q3 *8* K-R6, K-B3 *9* P-R4, K-Q2 *10* K-Kt7, and Black is kept out.

5 B-B5	K-B5
6 B-Q6	K-Q5
7 K-Kt5	K-Q4
8 B-R2	K-K3
9 KxP	K-Q2
10 K-Kt5	K-B1
11 K-B6	

White wins

WHITE
to play
and win

SELESNIEV 1916

1 B-Q4!

NOT at once *1* P-B8(Q), as Black replies by Queening with check.

1 . . .   P-Kt8(Q)

Black cannot play *1* . . . KxB as after *2* P-B8(Q), P-Kt8(Q) *3* Q-B5ch forfeits his newly-crowned Queen.

2 BxQ   P-R7

Now this Pawn looks dangerous!

3 B-Q4!

Obviously, if White had played *3* P-B8(Q) instead, then *3* . . . P-R8(Q) would have drawn for Black.

3 . . .   KxB
4 P-B8(Q)   P-R8(Q)
5 Q-R8ch

White wins the Queen and the game.

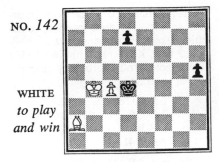

WHITE
*to play
and win*

KAYEV 1940

WHITE must do something about the menacing Rook Pawn, but after the plausible *1* B-Kt1, P-R5 *2* B-B5, P-Q3 *3* B-R3, K-Q6 *4* B-B1ch, K-Q5 *5* K-Kt5, K-B6 *6* K-B6, P-R6 *7* K-Q5 (or *7* KxP, P-R7 *8* B-Kt2, KxP and a draw) P-R7 *8* B-Kt2, K-Q6, he can capture the Queen Pawn only at the expense of his own Pawn. Therefore:

1 P-B5!		P-R5
2 B-K6!		

A bit of generosity saves miles of analysis.

2 . . .	PxB
3 P-B6	P-R6
4 P-B7	P-R7
5 P-B8(Q)	P-R8(Q)
6 Q-B3ch	K-Q4
7 Q-B5ch	K-K5
8 Q-B6ch	

White wins the Queen and the game.

NO. *143*

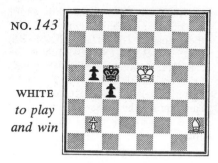

WHITE
to play
and win

NEUSTADT 1930

WHITE must retain his Pawn in order to win. He must prevent something like this happening: *1* . . . P-B6 *2* PxP, K-B5, and his invaluable Pawn comes off the board, enabling Black to draw.

1 B-Kt1ch	K-Kt5
2 B-Q4	K-Kt6
3 B-B3	P-Kt5
4 K-Q4!	

But not *4* B-Q4, P-B6, and Black forces the draw.

4 . . .	PxB
5 PxP	K-R5
6 KxP	

White wins

NO. *144*

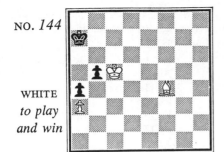

WHITE
*to play
and win*

HORWITZ 1885

ORDINARILY, Black could move his King to the corner and draw easily against a Rook Pawn and a Bishop of the wrong color. White wins the position though, by effecting a change of identity in his impotent Rook Pawn!

1 K-B6   K-R1

If Black plays *1* . . . K-R3 instead, there comes *2* B-K3, K-R4 *3* B-B5, K-R3 *4* B-Kt6, P-Kt5 *5* PxP, P-R6 *6* P-Kt5 mate.

2 K-Kt6!

White does not blunder into *2* KxP, after which there is no possible way to win.

2 . . .   P-Kt5
3 PxP

But now the Rook Pawn has been transformed into a Knight Pawn!

3 . . .   P-R6
4 P-Kt5   P-R7
5 B-K5   P-R8(Q)
6 BxQ   K-Kt1
7 B-K5ch   K-R1
8 K-B7   K-R2
9 P-Kt6ch

White wins

NO. *145*

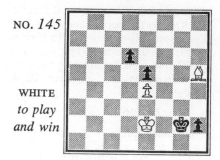

WHITE
to play
and win

DEL RIO 1750

BLACK has a wicked-looking Rook Pawn, but an alert sacrifice renders it harmless.

1 B-B3ch	K-Kt8
2 B-R1!	KxB
3 K-B1	P-Q4
4 PxP	P-K5
5 P-Q6	P-K6
6 P-Q7	P-K7ch
7 KxP	K-Kt8
8 P-Q8(Q)	P-R8(Q)

Black gets his Queen after all, but will never have a chance to move it.

9 Q-Q4ch

Care must be taken in checking. Such a move as *9* Q-Kt5ch for example allows Black to interpose his Queen with check, forcing a draw.

9 . . .	K-R7
10 Q-R4ch	K-Kt7

On *10* . . . K-Kt8 *11* Q-B2 is mate.

11 Q-Kt4ch	K-R7
12 K-B2	

White wins

NO. *146*

WHITE
*to play
and win*

GORGIEV 1938

BLACK is a piece behind, but his passed Pawns on both sides of the board can be a worry to a Bishop.

1 B-Kt1!

Stops the dangerous-looking Rook Pawn from moving on.

1 . . .	P-B5

Or the following: *1* . . . K-Kt6 *2* K-B6, K-Kt7   *3* P-Q7, KxB   *4* P-Q8(Q), P-R7   *5* Q-Kt6ch, K-R8   *6* QxP, K-Kt7   *7* Q-Kt4ch, K-B7   *8* Q-R3, K-Kt8   *9* Q-Kt3ch, K-R8   *10* Q-B2, P-B5   *11* Q-B1 mate.

2 K-B6	P-B6
3 K-B5!	

Threatens mate on the move.

3 . . .	K-Kt6
4 P-Q7	P-B7
5 P-Q8(Q)	P-B8(Q)
6 Q-Q5ch	K-B6

Or *6* . . . K-Kt7 *7* Q-R2ch, K-B6 *8* Q-B2 mate.

7 Q-Q4ch	K-Kt6
8 Q-R4ch!	KxQ

If he refuses the Queen by *8* . . . K-Kt7, then *9* Q-B2ch, K-R8 *10* Q-R2 is mate.

9 B-B2 mate

NO. *147*

WHITE
to play
and win

HORWITZ AND KLING

IN THIS battle of Bishop against Knight, White plays to force his opponent into zugzwang.

| *1* B-B7 | K-Kt4 |

The King stays near the Pawn, preventing White from capturing the Knight.

| *2* B-K8ch | K-R4 |
| *3* B-Q7 | |

Not *3* B-R5 when Black draws by *3* . . . Kt-K3ch *4* K-B6, Kt-Q1ch *5* K-B5, Kt-K3ch *6* K-B6, Kt-Q1ch, and Black has a perpetual check.

| *3* . . . | K-R3 |
| *4* B-R3 | K-R4 |

Black may not move the Knight as after *4* . . . Kt-Kt2, White can win the beast either by *5* B-B8 or *5* B-B1ch.

| *5* B-Kt4 |

Still keeping an eye out for the Knight check.

| *5* . . . | K-Kt4 |
| *6* B-K2ch | K-R4 |

If *6* . . . K-B4 instead, the reply *7* B-B4 leaves Black helpless.

| *7* B-B4 |

Now we have the diagrammed position, with *Black* to move. But Black is in zugzwang—he has no moves!
White wins

NO. *148*

WHITE
to play
and win

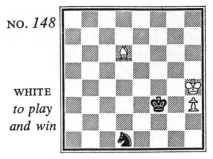

BLEDOW 1843

1 K-Kt5	Kt-B7
2 P-R4!	Kt-K5ch
3 K-Kt6	KtxB

IF BLACK refuses the Bishop, then after *3* . . . Kt-B7 *4* P-R5, Kt-Kt5 *5* K-Kt5, the Knight must retreat, since the King can no longer move and still protect it.

4 P-R5	Kt-B5
5 P-R6	Kt-K4ch
6 K-Kt7	

White wins

NO. *149*

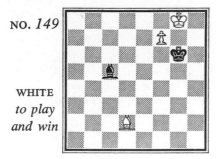

WHITE
to play
and win

CENTURINI 1856

TO WIN this, Black's Bishop must be driven off either of the two diagonals leading to White's QB8, the Queening square of the Pawn.

The first step:

1 B-B3	B-R6
2 B-Kt7	B-Kt5
3 B-B8	

Moving *in front of the Pawn,* even though it blocks the Pawn for the time being, to force Black's Bishop to leave the diagonal.

3 . . .	B-Q7

The second step:

4 B-B5	B-R3

Ousted from one diagonal, the Bishop seizes another, also leading to QB8.

5 B-Q4

Prevents Black from playing *5* . . . B-Kt2.

5 . . .	K-B4

Black moves his King, since his Bishop must stay where it is.

6 B-Kt7

Now the Bishop moves *beside the Pawn,* assuring its advance next move.

White wins

NO. *150*

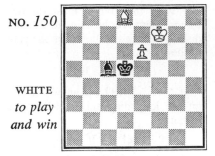

WHITE
to play
and win

CENTURINI 1856

IN ORDER that his Pawn advance to K7 (after which it is assured of Queening) White must drive the opposing Bishop off either of the two diagonals leading to that square.

1 B-K7

As in the previous example, White's first step is to move his Bishop *in front of the Pawn*. This will evict Black's Bishop from one diagonal.

| *1* . . . | B-K6 |
| 2 B-B8 | B-Kt4 |

Black of course seizes the other diagonal leading to K7.

| *3* B-Kt7 | K-Q3 |
| *4* B-B6 | |

The second step: the Bishop moves *beside the Pawn* to dislodge Black from his occupancy of the critical diagonal.

| *4* . . . | B-Q7 |

The alternative, exchanging Bishops, is obviously hopeless.

5 P-K7

White wins

WHITE
to play
and win

TO WIN this, White must do two things: maneuver his King to B7, and dislodge Black's Bishop from the path of the Pawn.

<blockquote>

1 B-Kt5   B-B1

</blockquote>

If *1* . . . B-Kt7 (or anywhere else on the long diagonal) *2* B-B6 wins instantly.

<blockquote>

2 K-B6!   B-K2ch

</blockquote>

Or *2* . . . K-Kt5 *3* B-Q2, B-B4 (*3* . . . K-R4 *4* K-B7, and Black is out of moves) *4* B-B3, B-B1 *5* K-B7, K-B4 *6* B-Q2 and White wins.

<blockquote>

3 K-B7   B-B1
4 B-K3

</blockquote>

Black is in zugzwang—he must move, and he has no moves!
White wins

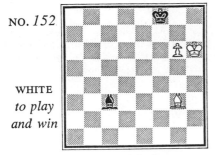

NO. *152*

WHITE
to play
and win

CENTURINI 1856

1 K-R7!

TO PREVENT *1* . . . K-Kt1, after which Black's King could not be evicted.

1 . . .   B-Kt7

Or anywhere else on the long diagonal.

2 B-B4	B-Q5
3 B-R6ch	K-K1
4 B-Kt7	

Moving in front of the Pawn, the Bishop drives the adverse Bishop off the long diagonal.

4 . . .   B-B4

The only move, since *4* . . . B-K6 is refuted by *5* B-Kt2 followed by *6* P-Kt7, winning.

5 B-K5   B-B1

In accordance with principle, White can now deploy his Bishop to B4, and then R6 alongside the Pawn, but there is a faster win available.

6 B-Q6!

White wins. After *6* . . . BxB *7* P-Kt7 is decisive.

NO. *153*

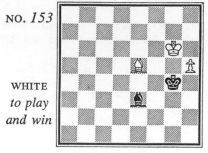

WHITE
to play
and win

CENTURINI 1847

1 B-Kt7   B-Kt4

IF BLACK tries *1* . . . B-Q7, then
2 B-R6, B-B6 *3* B-Kt5, B-Kt2 (to
prevent *4* P-R6) *4* B-K7!, B-B6 *5* P-
R6, B-Q5 *6* B-B6, and White wins.

2 B-R6

Moving in front of the Pawn to dislodge Black's Bishop.

2 . . .   B-B3

If *2* . . . B-K2 *3* B-K3, B-B1 *4* B-
Q4, K-R5 (on *4* . . . K-B5 *5* B-Kt7
is conclusive) *5* B-K5, K-Kt5 *6* B-
B6, K-B5 *7* B-Kt7, and the Pawn has
a clear road ahead.

3 B-K3

Threatening to advance the Pawn.

3 . . .	B-Kt2
4 B-Kt5	B-B1
5 B-B6	K-B5
6 B-Kt7	

White wins

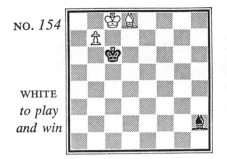

NO. *154*

WHITE
*to play
and win*

CENTURINI 1856

1 B-R4   K-Kt3

ON A Bishop move instead, say
1 . . . B-K4, White continues with
2 B-B6, B-R7   *3* B-Q4, B-Kt6   *4* B-R7, B-B5   *5* B-Kt8, B-K6   *6* B-R2, B-R2   *7* B-Kt1, and wins.

2 B-B2ch   K-R3

To prevent White from moving his
Bishop to R7 and Kt8, after which it
is easy to dislodge the enemy Bishop.
For example, if *2* . . . K-B3 *3* B-R7,
B-Kt6   *4* B-Kt8, B-B7   *5* B-R2, B-R2
6 B-Kt1, and it is done.

3 B-B5!

Forces the opposing Bishop out of
the corner, since his King must stay
where it is.

3 . . .   B-Kt6
4 B-K7   K-Kt3

Otherwise, the maneuver *5* B-Q8
and *6* B-B7 is decisive.

5 B-Q8ch   K-B3

Stops *6* B-B7, but the exposed position of Black's Bishop enables
White to gain a tempo.

6 B-R4!

Had Black at his third move
played the Bishop to Bishop five,
then White's sixth move would have
been B-Kt5, or if *3* . . . B-K4, then
White's sixth would have been B-B6.

6 . . .	B-R7
7 B-B2	K-Kt4
8 B-R7	K-R3
9 B-Kt8	B-Kt8
10 B-B4	B-R2
11 B-K3	

White wins

WHITE
*to play
and win*

SELESNIEV 1915

1 B-B6!

IT IS important to blockade the Pawn. If instead *1* K-K5, P-B3 *2* BxP, K-B2 *3* B-Kt2, Kt-R1! *4* BxKt (other moves do not affect Black's reply) K-Kt3 *5* B-Kt2, KxP and Black has drawn.

1 . . .	K-Q1
2 K-B5!	

The natural move *2* K-B7 (to force *2* . . . K-B1 *3* K-K8, and an easy win) is beautifully demolished by the subtle *2* . . . Kt-B1 (attacking the Pawn) *3* P-R8(Q), stalemate!

Another pitfall is *2* K-K5, when *2* . . . K-K2 gives Black the opposition and a draw.

2 . . .	K-K2
3 K-K5!	

White seizes the opposition, the objective being to work his King around to QKt7.

3 . . .	K-B2
4 K-Q4	K-K3
5 K-B5	K-K2

It is clear that throughout all this, the Knight must stay rooted to the spot.

6 B-B3	K-Q2
7 B-Kt4ch	K-K2
8 K-B6	K-Q1
9 K-Kt7	

Black's position now comes apart. He must not move the Knight, dares not move the Pawn, and should not move his King.

White wins

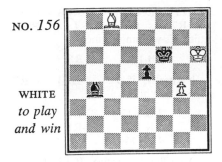

NO. *156*

WHITE
to play
and win

WEENINK 1919

THE win seems simple and straight-forward—but it is easy to fall head-long into a hidden trap prepared by Black.

1 P-Kt5ch	K-K2
2 P-Kt6	K-K1

At this point 99 out of 100 players would move *3* P-Kt7, confidently and unhesitatingly, only to be set back on their heels by *3* . . . B-B1 (pinning the Pawn) followed by *4* . . . BxP (sacrificing the Bishop for the precious pawn), the resulting position being a draw.

3 B-Q7ch!	KxB

White meets other replies with *4* P-Kt7.

4 P-Kt7

White wins

NO. *157*

WHITE
to play
and win

HEUACKER 1930

WHITE must not be hasty and move *1* P-R7, as the reply *1* . . . P-K5 ruins his winning chances.

1 B-R7!	B-R8

Naturally, if *1* . . . BxB *2* P-R7 wins for White.

2 K-Kt1	B-B6
3 K-B2	B-R8
4 B-Q4!	

A brilliant sacrifice. If Black captures by *4* . . . PxB, then *5* K-Q3 blocks the Bishop's path and assures the Rook Pawn of Queening.

4 . . .	BxB
5 K-Q3	B-R8

On *5* . . . K-Kt4 *5* P-R7, P-K5ch *6* KxB, and the Pawn cannot be overtaken.

After the actual move, White must not play *6* P-R7, as after *6* . . . P-K5ch the liberated Bishop will prevent White's Pawn from Queening.

6 K-K4

White wins, as his Pawn cannot be headed off.

WHITE
*to play
and win*

HORWITZ 1884

THE King is urged to the top of the board, into a crowded position that can only end in mate.

1 B-B2ch	K-R4
2 P-Kt4ch	K-R3
3 K-B6	K-R2

Evidently not relishing *3* . . . B-R2 *4* B-K3 mate.

4 P-Kt5	K-R1
5 B-Q4	K-R2

Or *5* . . . B-R2 *6* KxP mate.

6 B-R1	K-R1
7 P-Kt6!	PxP

If *7* . . . B-R2 *8* KxP mate.

8 KxP mate

WHITE
*to play
and win*

PLATOV 1907

ONLY one piece can stop White's passed Pawn—Black's Bishop. So the Bishop must be persuaded to leave the critical diagonals!

1 P-K5	B-Kt2
2 P-K6	B-B1
3 P-K7	B-Q2
4 B-R3!	

Without a moment's delay! If *4* K-B8 instead, *4* . . . P-B4 wins for Black!

4 . . .	B-K1
5 K-B8	B-R4
6 B-Kt4	

But not *6* B-K6 (intending 7 B-B7) as Black's reply is *6* . . . P-B6 giving him a draw.

6 . . .	B-Kt3

Still keeping an eye on the Pawn.

7 B-B5ch	BxB
8 P-K8(Q)	

White wins

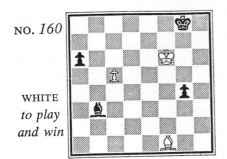

NO. *160*

WHITE
to play
and win

PLATOV 1907

VARIOUS offers are made to decoy Black's rampant Bishop, and one of them must be accepted.

    1 P-B6   B-R5

If *1* . . . B-Q4 *2* B-B4 (pins the Bishop) BxB (or *2* . . . P-Kt6 *3* BxBch and the Knight Pawn is harmless) *3* P-B7 and White wins.

2 P-B7	B-Q2
3 K-K7	B-B1
4 K-Q8	B-B4

On *4* . . . B-Kt2 *5* B-Kt2, BxB *6* P-B8(Q) wins.

5 B-Q3	B-K3
6 B-B4	K-B2
7 P-B8(Q)	

White wins

NO. *161*

WHITE
to play
and win

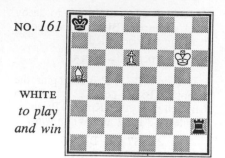

FRITZ 1931

A BEAUTIFUL ending with minimal means.

1 P-Q7   R-R1

If instead *1* . . . R-Kt7ch 2 K-B7 (White's moves are intended to keep the Rook from reaching the first rank) R-B7ch *3* K-K7, R-K7ch *4* K-Q6, and the Rook is out of checks.

2 K-Kt7   R-QKt1

The only square available on the first rank.

3 B-B7 (Domination)

White wins

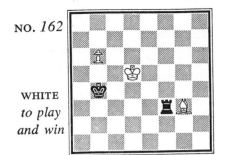

NO. *162*

WHITE
to play
and win

MATTISON 1924

1 P-Kt7	R-Q6ch

THE only way the Rook can get back to the first rank. If Black tries *1* . . . R-B4ch, then *2* B-K5, R-B1 *3* B-Q6ch wins the Rook.

2 K-K6!	R-Q1
3 B-B7	R-KR1
4 B-K5	R-Q1

If Black moves *4* . . . R-K1ch instead, then *5* K-B7, R-Q1 *6* B-B7, R-KR1 *7* B-Q6ch leads by a transposition of moves into the actual play.

5 K-K7	R-KKt1
6 K-B7	R-Q1
7 B-B7	R-KR1
8 B-Q6ch	K-R4
9 B-B8	

Cuts off the Rook from the Pawn, but does Black have another resource?

9 . . .	R-R2ch
10 B-Kt7	

White wins, as the Pawn will Queen.

NO. *163*

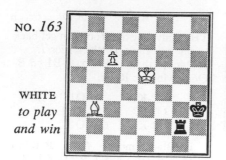

WHITE
*to play
and win*

HALBERSTADT 1938

1 P-B7	R-K7ch

THE Rook tries to return to the first rank, to prevent the Pawn's Queening. Should the Rook attempt to get behind the Pawn, then this would occur: *1* . . . R-Kt4ch *2* K-Q4, R-Kt5ch *3* K-B3, R-Kt6ch *4* K-Kt2, R-Kt7ch *5* K-R3, and White wins.

2 K-B6	R-K1
3 B-R4!	R-KKt1
4 K-B7	R-KR1
5 K-Kt7	R-R1

The only square left, as *5* . . . R-QB1 allows *6* B-Q7ch winning the Rook.

6 B-B6	R-R2

The Rook could not remain on the first rank. This looks good though, as the Pawn is pinned and cannot advance.

7 B-Q7ch!

Cleverly interposing the Bishop, so that the Pawn is freed.

7 . . .	K-R5
8 P-B8(Q)	

White wins

NO. *164*

WHITE
*to play
and win*

KUBBEL 1909

AN INTERESTING battle between Bishop and Rook.

> *1* P-R7   R-B4ch

The Rook must get back to the first rank, to stop the Pawn. It cannot do so by *1* . . . R-R1 as *2* B-B6ch wins the Rook.

> *2* K-K2   R-K4ch

If *2* . . . R-B1 *3* B-B6ch, K-B4 *4* B-K7ch wins the Rook.

> *3* K-Q2   R-K1
> *4* B-B2ch

Now it's the Bishop's turn to check.

> *4* . . .   K-K4
> *5* B-Kt3ch   K-B4
> *6* B-Kt8

Shuts off the Rook and wins for White.

NO. *165*

WHITE
to play
and win

FRITZ 1933

THERE is a great deal of brilliant play in this innocent-looking miniature.

1 P-Kt7	R-R4ch
2 K-Q6!	

On *2* KxB for example, Black draws by *2* . . . R-R3ch (but not by *2* . . . R-Kt4 *3* B-B6ch, K-Q1 *4* BxR, K-B2 *5* B-R6, and White wins) *3* K-Q5, R-Kt3 followed by *4* . . . RxP.

2 . . .   R-Kt4!

A subtle defense involving the sacrifice of the Rook and an offer of the Bishop!

There was no hope in *2* . . . R-R3ch *4* B-B6ch, and the Pawn will advance, since Black must drop all business to get out of check.

3 B-B6ch	K-Q1
4 BxR	B-B1!

The idea being that *5* P-Kt8(Q) or *5* P-Kt8(R) stalemates Black.

5 P-Kt8(B)!

A clever under-promotion. Two Bishops do not generally win against one Bishop, but Black is cramped and in a mating net.

5 . . .   B-Kt5

If the Bishop moves to the other diagonal by *5* . . . B-Kt2, then *6* B-B7ch, K-B1 *7* B-Q7 is mate.

6 B-B7ch	K-B1
7 B-R6 mate	

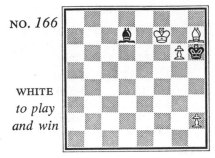

NO. *166*

WHITE
to play
and win

ISENEGGER 1951

BEFORE we see how White wins, let us look at some interesting tries:

A] *1* P-Kt7, B-K6ch *2* KxB, KxP, and Black draws against the Rook Pawn and a Bishop that does not control the Pawn's Queening square.

B] *1* K-B6, B-K1 *2* P-R4, BxP, *3* BxB, and Black draws by stalemate.

C] *1* B-Kt8, B-K3ch *2* KxB, KxP, and again Black gets to the corner and draws.

The solution is:

> *1* K-Kt8!   B-K3ch

A pretty alternative is *1* . . . B-B4 *2* P-Kt7!, BxBch *3* K-R8, K-Kt3 (the Bishop must obviously stay where it is) *4* P-R4, K-R3 *5* P-R5, and Black is in zugzwang. He must move, though every move loses.

> *2* K-R8   B-B4

Against *2* . . . B-Q4, White proceeds with *3* P-Kt7, B-K3 *4* B-Kt8, B-B4 *5* B-Q5, B-R2 *6* B-K4, BxB *7* P-Kt8(Q) and wins.

> *3* P-Kt7!   BxB
> *4* P-R3!

The key move! If *4* P-R4 instead, *4* . . . K-Kt3 *5* P-R5ch, K-R3, and it is White who is in zugzwang, and must give up both Pawns.

> *4* . . .   K-Kt3
> *5* P-R4   K-R3
> *6* P-R5

White wins: Black is out of moves.

WHITE
*to play
and win*

BERGER

1 P-Kt6

THE first step in the process of promoting one of the Pawns is to bring them both to the sixth rank.

1 . . .	B-B7
2 P-B5	B-Kt6
3 K-Kt5	B-B7
4 P-B6	B-Kt6
5 B-Kt4ch	K-Kt1

On *5* . . . K-K1, White comes around by *6* K-R6, and *7* K-Kt7 followed by *8* P-B7ch and *9* P-B8(Q), Black being unable meanwhile to do anything but watch.

6 K-B4

To swing the King around to K7 where it will help the Bishop Pawn's advance.

6 . . . B-B5

On *6* . . . B-B7 *7* P-B7ch wins at once.

7 K-K5	B-Kt6
8 K-Q6	K-B1

Here too, if *8* . . . B-B7 *9* P-B7ch, K-Kt2 *10* K-K7 is decisive.

9 K-Q7ch	K-Kt1
10 K-K7	B-B5
11 P-B7ch	

White wins

NO. *168*

WHITE
*to play
and win*

TARRASCH 1921

| 1 B-B4ch | K-K2 |
| 2 K-K4! | |

PREMATURE would be *2* P-B5, B-Kt2 *3* K-B4, B-R1 and Black has an easy draw. White would have no winning chances after the anti-positional *4* P-K6, while *4* P-B6ch allows the Bishop to sacrifice itself for the two Pawns.

2 . . .	B-Kt2
3 K-B5	B-R3
4 K-Kt4!	B-B1

Choice is fearfully limited. If *4* . . . B-Kt2 *5* K-Kt5 leads to the actual play, while *4* . . . K-K1 *5* P-B5, K-K2 *6* P-B6ch, K-K1 *7* P-K6 wins easily.

| 5 K-Kt5 | B-Kt2 |
| 6 K-Kt6 | |

White moves his King to a dominating position before advancing his Pawns.

| 6 . . . | B-B1 |

On *6* . . . K-B1 *7* K-R7 wins the Bishop, while *6* . . . B-R1 allows *7* K-R7, cornering the Bishop literally and figuratively.

| 7 P-B5 | K-K1 |
| 8 P-B6 | |

Note that White keeps his Pawns as much as possible *on squares opposite in color to those controlled by his Bishop.*

8 . . .	B-B4
9 K-Kt7	B-B1ch
10 K-Kt8	B-B4
11 P-K6	B-Kt5
12 B-Kt5ch	K-Q1
13 K-B7	B-B4
14 P-K7ch	

White wins

181

NO. *169*

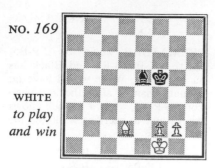

WHITE
*to play
and win*

AVERBACH 1954

IN CONVOYING the Pawns up the board, care must be taken that the enemy Bishop does not sacrifice itself for both Pawns, thereby forcing a draw.

1 K-K2	K-Kt5
2 B-K1	

Not at once *2* P-B3ch, K-Kt6, and time will be lost evicting the King.

2 . . .	B-Q3
3 P-B3ch	K-B5
4 P-Kt3ch	K-B4
5 P-Kt4ch	

The Pawns, you will notice, occupy whenever possible squares *opposite in color to those controlled by the Bishop.* In this way, the Pawns and the Bishop dominate as many squares as possible. Here, for example, the Pawns attack the white squares, while the Bishop attacks the black.

5 . . .	K-K3

If *5* . . . K-B5 *6* B-Q2ch, K-Kt6 *7* P-Kt5, B-K4 *8* P-Kt6, B-Kt2 (otherwise *9* B-R6 followed by *10* P-Kt7 wins) *9* K-K3, K-R5 (clearly if *9* . . . B-R3ch *10* K-K4, B-Kt2

11 B-B4ch, K-Kt7 *12* B-K5 is decisive) *10* K-K4, K-R4 *11* K-B5, B-Q5 *12* B-Kt5, B-Kt2 *13* B-B6, B-B1 *14* P-Kt7 wins.

6 K-Q3	K-Q4
7 B-Q2	B-B2
8 P-B4	B-Kt3

To prevent White's intended maneuver *9* K-K3, *10* K-B3, *11* P-Kt5 and *12* K-Kt4.

9 B-B3	B-B4
10 P-Kt5	

The Pawns now occupy black squares (the color of those controlled by the Bishop). They do so when they can move without hindrance to the white squares.

10 . . .	B-Kt3
11 P-Kt6	K-K3
12 K-K4	B-Q1
13 P-B5ch	K-K2
14 K-Q5	K-B1

If *14* . . . B-B2 *15* P-B6ch, K-B1 *16* B-Kt4ch, K-Kt1 *17* P-B7ch, and White wins.

15 K-K6	B-Kt4
16 P-B6	B-K6
17 B-Kt4ch	

White wins

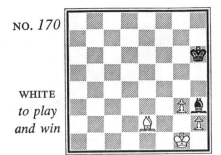

NO. *170*

WHITE
to play
and win

BERGER 1890

1 B-B1	B-Kt5
2 P-R4	B-B4
3 K-B2	B-Kt5
4 K-K3	B-K3
5 K-B4	B-Q2
6 B-Q3	

CAREFULLY avoiding *6* P-Kt4 (to continue with *7* B-K2 and *8* P-Kt5ch) as Black would sacrifice his Bishop for the Knight Pawn, and then have a draw against a Rook Pawn and a Bishop of the wrong color (one that does not control the Pawn's Queening square).

6 . . .	B-R6
7 B-B5	B-B8
8 P-Kt4	B-K7

Threatening to force a draw by *9* . . . BxP.

9 P-Kt5ch	K-R4

If *9* . . . K-Kt2, White continues with *10* B-Kt4 followed by *11* P-R5.

10 K-Kt3!

Avoiding the pitfall *10* P-Kt6, K-R3 *11* K-K5, B-R4 *12* K-B6, BxP *13* BxB, stalemate.

10 . . .	B-Q8
11 B-K4	B-Kt6

Otherwise *12* B-B3ch forces an exchange of Bishops.

12 B-B3ch	K-Kt3
13 K-B4	B-B2
14 P-R5ch	K-Kt2
15 K-K5	B-Kt6
16 B-K4	

Note how possession is taken of the white squares before playing P-R6ch.

16 . . .	B-B2
17 P-R6ch	

The Pawns of course occupy whenever possible squares opposite in color to those controlled by the Bishop.

17 . . .	K-R1
18 K-B6	B-R4
19 B-Q5	

Not *19* P-Kt6 allowing *19* . . . BxP, and a draw, nor *19* B-Kt6 (to drive off Black's Bishop) since it blocks the Knight Pawn.

19 . . .	K-R2
20 B-B7	B-K7
21 P-Kt6ch	

White wins

NO. *171*

WHITE
to play
and win

1 P-B4ch	K-Q3
2 P-B5	K-K4
3 P-Q4ch	K-B3
4 K-B4	B-Kt6
5 B-B6	B-B7
6 B-Q7	

PROTECTS the BP and threatens to advance the QP.

6 . . .	B-Kt6
7 K-K4	B-B5

If Black plays *7* . . . B-B7ch, then *8* K-Q5, BxP *9* BxB, KxB *10* K-B6 wins for White.

8 P-Q5	B-Kt6
9 B-K6	B-B5
10 K-Q4	B-K7

If *10* . . . B-R7 *11* K-B5, B-Kt6 *12* P-Q6 wins.

11 P-Q6	B-Kt4
12 P-Q7	K-K2
13 P-B6ch	K-Q1
14 P-B7	K-K2
15 P-B8(Q)ch	KxQ
16 P-Q8(Q)ch	

White wins

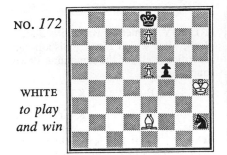

NO. *172*

WHITE
to play
and win

SELESNIEV 1920

A WIN for White seems optimistic, his Pawns look so shaky.

> *1* K-Kt5   Kt-Kt5

On *1* . . . KxP, White replies *2* KxP, and Black's Knight is stranded. The continuation could then be: *2* . . . K-B2 *3* P-K6ch, K-K2 *4* K-K5, K-K1 *5* K-B6, K-B1 *6* P-K7ch, K-K1 *7* B-Kt5 mate.

> *2* KxP

But not *2* BxKt, PxB *3* KxP, KxP, as after *4* K-B5, K-B2 *5* P-K6ch, K-K2! (in King and Pawn against King positions the defender blockades the Pawn whenever possible) *6* K-K5, K-K1! (so that the Pawn, when it reaches the seventh rank, can do so only with check) *7* K-B6, K-B1 *8* P-K7ch (delaying the Pawn's advance does not help, as White cannot force a win) K-K1 *9* K-K6 and Black draws by stalemate.

> *2* . . .   KtxP
> *3* K-K6!   Kt moves

4 Bishop mates accordingly

NO. *173*

WHITE
*to play
and win*

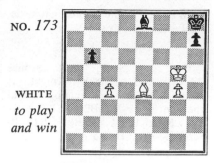

SELESNIEV 1919

1 K-R6   B-B2

READY to meet *2* BxP with *2* . . . BxP, after which Black's Bishop can sacrifice itself for the remaining Pawn and draw.

2 B-Q3   B-K3

Obviously if *2* . . . K-Kt1, White takes the Rook Pawn with check, while *2* . . . B-Kt1 is refuted by *3* P-Kt5, B-B2 *4* BxP, BxP *5* P-Kt6 followed by *6* P-Kt7 mate.

     3 P-Kt5   B-Kt1
     4 BxP!

This can bowl a fellow over!

     4 . . .   BxB

There is no relief in *4* . . . BxP *5* P-Kt6 and mate next move.

     5 P-Kt6   BxP

All that is left. If *5* . . . B-Kt1 *6* P-Kt7 mate, or if *5* . . . K-Kt1 *6* PxBch, K-R1 *7* K-Kt6, P-Kt4 *8* P-B5, P-Kt5 *9* P-B6, P-Kt6 *10* P-B7, P-Kt7 *11* P-B8(Q) mate.

6 KxB	K-Kt1
7 K-B6	K-B1
8 K-K6	K-K1
9 K-Q6	K-Q1
10 K-B6	K-B1
11 KxP	K-Kt1
12 P-B5	K-B1
13 K-B6!	

White wins

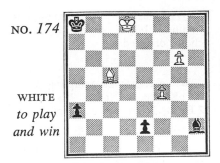

NO. *174*

WHITE
*to play
and win*

TROITZKY 1916

E] *5* . . . Q-R5ch *6* B-K7ch winning the Queen.

F] *5* . . . Q-Kt6 *6* B-B2ch winning the Queen.

G] *5* . . . Q-B6 *6* B-Kt4ch winning the Queen.

H] *5* . . . Q-Q7 *6* Q-Q7ch winning the Queen.

I] *5* . . . Q-KR8 *6* Q-Kt7ch winning the Queen.

J] *5* . . . Q-Q8 *6* Q-Q7ch winning the Queen.

K] *5* . . . Q-QB8 *6* B-K3ch winning the Queen.

L] *5* . . . Q-QR8   *6* B-Q4ch, KxB *7* Q-K5ch winning the Queen.

White wins

| *1* P-Kt7 | P-K8(Q) |
| *2* P-Kt8(Q) | K-Kt2 |

THE King must flee. If Black tries aggressive action, then after *2* . . . Q-R4ch *3* K-Q7ch, K-Kt2 *4* Q-B8 is mate, or if *2* . . . Q-R5ch *3* K-B7ch and mate follows next move.

| *3* Q-Kt3ch | K-B3 |

Or *3* . . . K-R1 *4* Q-R4ch, K-Kt2 *5* Q-Kt5ch, K-R1   *6* Q-R6ch, K-Kt1 *7* B-Q6 mate.

| *4* Q-Kt6ch | K-Q4 |
| *5* Q-Kt5! | |

A quiet move, leading to a remarkable position. The threat is *6* B-B2, discovering check and attacking the Queen.

It is Black's turn to move, but despite all the moves at his command, he is helpless. The proof:

A] *5* . . . K-K3 *6* Q-K8ch winning the Queen.

B] *5* . . . K-K5 *6* Q-K8ch winning the Queen.

C] *5* . . . Q-K3 *6* Q-Kt3ch winning the Queen.

D] *5* . . . Q-K5 *6* Q-Kt7ch winning the Queen.

NO. *175*

WHITE
to play
and win

FRITZ 1951

WHITE has two pretty winning possibilities, based on his opponent's choice of defense.

1 P-R7

White resists the tempting pin of the Knight, as after *1* B-B3, KxP *2* BxKt, Black has been stalemated.

1 . . .   Kt-B3

If *1* . . . K-R3   *2* K-Kt8, Kt-B3ch *3* K-B7, KtxP *4* P-Kt4, Kt-B1 *5* KxKt, K-R2   *6* K-B7, K-R3 *7* K-B6, K-R2 *8* KxP(Kt5) and wins.

2 K-Kt7   KtxP
3 B-B3ch

The hasty *3* KxKt allows *3* . . . K-Kt5 followed by *4* . . . KxP, and Black draws.

3 . . .   P-Kt5
4 B-Q4

Threatens to capture the Knight.

4 . . .   Kt-Kt4

Saves the Knight, but at fearful cost.

5 BxP mate

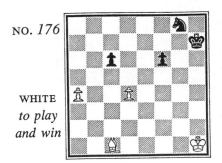

NO. *176*

WHITE
to play
and win

TROITZKY 1924

1 B-R3

IF WHITE pushes the Pawn instead, then after *1* P-R5, Kt-K2 *2* P-R6, Kt-Q4 *3* P-R7, Kt-Kt3, and the Pawn can go no further.

The actual move is intended to prevent the Knight from approaching the Pawn by way of K2.

1 . . .   P-KB4

Frees the square KB3 for the use of the Knight.

2 P-Q5!

White in turn takes away a square from the Knight! Black is now forced to occupy Q4 with a Pawn.

2 . . .	PxP
3 P-R5	Kt-B3
4 P-R6	Kt-K1

On *4* . . . Kt-Q2 (to meet 5 P-R7 with *5* . . . Kt-Kt3) *5* B-B5!, KtxB *6* P-R7 wins for White. With the actual move (*4* . . . Kt-K1) Black expects to reply to *5* P-R7 with *5* . . . Kt-B2.

5 B-Q6!

When instead, he is offered the Bishop—an unwelcome gift!

5 . . .	KtxB
6 P-R7	

White wins

NO. *177*

WHITE
*to play
and win*

NEUSTADT

A ROOK is almost always helpless against two connected passed Pawns on the sixth rank. Knowing this bit of endgame lore makes it easy to find the winning combination, including the repeated offers of the Bishop.

1 B-R5!   K-Kt6

If *1* . . . PxB instead, *2* P-R7, R-B1 *3* P-Kt6, and the Pawns cannot be stopped. One of them will become a Queen.

2 BxP!   K-B5

Here if Black had played *2* . . . RxB, the continuation *3* P-R7, R-R3ch *4* K-Kt4, R-R1 *5* P-Kt6 should be convincing.

3 P-R7   R-B1

Or *3* . . . R-B6ch *4* K-Kt4, R-KR6 *5* B-R5!, RxB *6* P-Kt6 and White wins.

4 B-K8!

The sacrifice of the Bishop gains a tempo for White's next move.

4 . . .   RxB
5 P-Kt6

White wins, his Pawns being too strong for the Rook to cope with.

NO. *178*

WHITE
*to play
and win*

VANCURA 1916

1 P-K8(Q)	RxQ
2 B-B8	R-K7ch
3 K-R3!	

IF *3* K-Kt3 (to answer *3* . . . R-K6ch with *4* K-B4) R-K3 *4* P-Kt8(Q), R-Kt3ch *5* QxR, PxQ lets Black get away with a draw.

3 . . .	R-K6ch
4 K-R4	R-K5ch
5 K-R5	R-K4ch
6 K-R6	R-K8

Now if White plays *7* P-Kt8(Q), R-R8ch *8* K-Kt7, R-Kt8ch wins the Queen.

| *7* B-B5! | R-K1 |

Naturally, *7* . . . R-R8ch *8* K-Kt5 (threatening to Queen with check) leaves Black no play.

Black's actual move restrains the Pawn for the time being.

8 KxP

Intending *9* B-B8 and *10* P-Kt8(Q).

| *8* . . . | R-Q1 |

Now if *9* B-B8, R-Q2 pins the Pawn and draws, the Rook sacrificing itself next move for the Pawn.

| *9* B-K7! | R-QB1 |
| *10* B-B8 | |

Threatens to Queen the Pawn next move.

| *10* . . . | R-B2 |

Pins the dangerous Pawn. Has Black squeezed out a draw?

11 B-Q6!

Pins the pinner and wins! White will capture the paralyzed Rook and then Queen the Pawn.

191

NO. *179*

WHITE
to play
and win

KARSTEDT 1916

1 P-R7   B-Q4

IF NOT for Black's Bishop, White's Pawn could Queen. White therefore entices the Bishop away, and then sets up an impenetrable barrier between Bishop and Pawn.

2 P-B4   B-Kt2

The Bishop stays on the diagonal, avoiding such palpable traps as *2* . . . BxP *3* P-R8(Q)ch.

3 B-B3   BxB
4 P-Q5

Shuts the Bishop out and wins.

NO. *180*

WHITE
to play
and win

QUECKENSTEDT

WHITE has a strong passed Pawn as compensation for his opponent's extra Pawn. It is the threat of Queening this Pawn that makes life difficult for Black.

| *1* P-Kt3ch! | KxP |

Black must take this Pawn, as after *1* . . . K-R4 *2* P-Kt4ch, K-R5 *3* P-QB4, B-K1 *4* P-Kt5 shuts his Bishop off the long diagonal and lets the passed Pawn advance unhindered to the Queening square. The alternative capture by *1* . . . BxP leads to *2* P-QB4, B-B7 *3* P-R7, B-K5ch *4* B-B3 and White wins.

| *2* P-QB4 | B-K1 |
| *3* B-B3 | P-K5 |

Chases White's Bishop off the long diagonal so that Black can occupy it with his own Bishop.

| *4* B-R5! | B-B3 |
| *5* B-B7 | |

Ready to meet *5* . . . K-Kt5 with *6* B-Q5, or *5* . . . K-R5 with *6* B-K8, in either case rendering Black's Bishop impotent.

| *5* . . . | B-R1 |
| *6* B-Q5 | P-B3 |

Black avoids the exchange of Bishops, which loses quickly, but the move he plays seems effective since White must leave the diagonal.

7 P-B5ch!

But he chooses not to!

| *7* . . . | PxB |
| *8* PxKtP | |

White wins, his next move being *9* P-Kt7.

The Rook

THE importance of Rook endings may be gauged from the fact that they appear more frequently in actual play than any other type of ending. It is therefore vital to the success of the practical player that he know how to conduct them, that he know how to win a winning position.

Despite the limitation imposed on the Rook of moving in straight lines only, endings which feature the Rook as protagonist lend themselves to the expression of remarkable subleties and a wealth of beautiful ideas.

Probably the most useful of all Rook endings is one illustrating "bridge-building" composed by Lucena in 1497 (almost 500 years ago!) No. 211 in this collection. It is probably responsible for more wins, even today, than any other single ending.

Shapiro No. 190 is an instructive treatment of Rook against two connected passed Pawns on the sixth rank, while Kivi No. 191, with Rook versus two Pawns on the Rook file has its points of interest.

Domination is the theme of the elegant Birnov No. 192.

Rooks are generously given away in Williams No. 193, Richter No. 194, Prokes No. 195, Rinck No. 197, Duras No. 216, Fritz No. 223 (the sacrifice is sudden here) and Troitzky No. 229, in which each side sacrifices his Rook.

Prokop's No. 196 shows the powerful Rook making things uncomfortable for Black's minor pieces, while sparkling wins by discovered check provide the *motif* for the Selesniev No. 198 and the famous Troitzky No. 201.

The skewer attack, a basic winning idea in Rook endings, is demonstrated neatly in Puder No. 203, Prokes No. 236 and Gabor No. 238.

Winning by zugzwang is nicely shown in No. 206, which first appeared in slightly different form in Chess Players Chronicle in 1878.

Bright and entertaining are the endings by Prokes No. 217, Selesniev No. 221, Fritz No. 222 and Pfeiffer No. 226.

Imaginative, ingenious play abounds in the compositions of Kok No. 218, Prokop No. 228, Kantorovich No. 230, Vlk No. 232, Eisenstadt No. 233, and Libiurkin No. 240.

Lasker's No. 225, with Black being forced down rank by rank, has found its way into all the treatises, while Botvinnik's No. 242 is a good specimen of the former World Champion's skill in the endgame.

Enchanting endings are those of Selesniev No. 234, Herbstmann No. 235, Moravec No. 237, Selesniev No. 239 (highly esteemed by Lasker) and Selesniev No. 241.

Masterpieces in the field of Rook and Pawn against Rook are Chéron's Nos. 204, 205, 207, 210, 214 and 215 (which I particularly recommend) and Grigoriev's Nos. 208, 209 and 213.

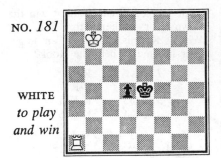

NO. *181*

WHITE
to play
and win

EUWE 1934

BLACK threatens to draw by bringing his King and Pawn to the seventh rank and forcing the Rook to sacrifice itself for the Pawn.

To win this, White must capture the Pawn outright.

1 K-B6

The King hastens towards the Pawn, as there is not a moment to lose.

1 . . .	P-Q6
2 K-B5	K-K6
3 K-B4	P-Q7
4 K-B3	K-K7
5 R-R2	

Pins the Pawn. White captures it next move and wins.

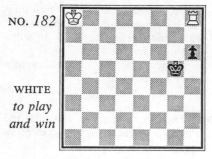

NO. *182*

WHITE
to play
and win

EUWE 1940

THE Rook by itself cannot win the Pawn (for nothing, that is). But White's King is far away. Can he get over in time to help the Rook?

1 K-Kt7	P-R4
2 K-B6	P-R5
3 K-Q5	K-Kt5
4 K-K4	K-Kt6

If *4* . . . P-R6 *5* R-Kt8ch, K-R5 *6* K-B4 (threatens *7* R-R8 mate) K-R4 *7* R-R8ch, winning the Pawn.

     5 K-K3   P-R6

There is no hope in *5* . . . K-R6 *6* K-B3, and Black must abandon the Pawn, nor in *5* . . . K-Kt5 *6* K-B2, P-R6 *7* R-R7, and again the Pawn falls.

     6 R-Kt8ch   K-R7

Or *6* . . . K-R5 *7* K-B3, K-R4 *8* K-Kt3, and White wins the Pawn.

     7 K-B2   K-R8
     8 R-QR8

White can win the Pawn by *8* K-Kt3, P-R7 *9* R-KR8, K-Kt8 *10* RxP, but the actual move is faster since it forces mate.

     8 . . .   K-R7

Or *8* . . . P-R7 *9* R-R1 mate.

     9 R-R8   K-R8
     10 RxP mate

NO. *183*

WHITE
to play
and win

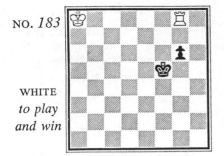

EUWE 1940

1 K-Kt7	P-Kt4
2 K-B6	P-Kt5
3 K-Q5	K-B5
4 K-Q4	K-B6

BLACK would lose quickly after *4* . . . P-Kt6 *5* R-B8ch, K-Kt5 *6* K-K3, K-R6 (*6* . . . P-Kt7 *7* K-B2 wins) *7* K-B3 (threatens mate) K-R7 *8* R-R8ch.

5 K-Q3	P-Kt6
6 R-B8ch	K-Kt7

If *6* . . . K-Kt5 *7* K-K2, K-R6 *8* K-B1, K-R7 *9* R-R8 mate.

7 K-K2	K-Kt8

If *7* . . . K-R7 *8* R-KKt8, K-Kt7 (or *8* . . . P-Kt7 *9* K-B2, and the Pawn is doomed) *9* R-Kt7, K-R7 *10* K-B3, and White wins the Pawn.

8 R-KKt8	P-Kt7
9 K-B3	K-R8

Last chance! If White pounces on the Pawn without thinking, he stalemates Black.

10 K-B2

White wins

NO. *184*

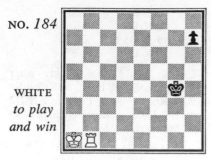

WHITE
to play
and win

BERGER 1890

1 R-Kt1ch

WHITE does not start with *1* R-R1 as *1* . . . P-R4 in reply saves the Pawn and advances its career.

1 . . .   K-B4

The only square, since moving to the Rook file would block his Pawn.

2 R-R1   K-Kt3

Thus the King has been driven back.

3	K-Kt2	P-R4
4	K-B3	K-Kt4
5	K-Q2	P-R5
6	K-K2	K-Kt5
7	K-B2	P-R6
8	R-R2	K-R5
9	K-B3	

White captures the Pawn next move and wins.

NO. *185*

WHITE
to play
and win

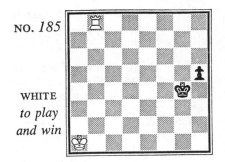

FINE 1941

1 R-Kt8ch   K-B6
2 R-KR8   K-Kt5

FORCED, as the Pawn must be protected. Black's pieces are now back to the position in the diagram, but White has gained time to place his Rook in the best possible position in Rook endings—*behind the passed Pawn.*

    3 K-Kt2   P-R5
    4 K-B2   P-R6
    5 K-Q2   K-Kt6
    6 K-K2!   K-Kt7

If *6* . . . P-R7 *7* K-B1, and Black must give up the Pawn.

    7 R-Kt8ch   K-R8

Playing for a stalemate possibility. There is no fight in *7* . . . K-R7 *8* K-B2, K-R8   *9* R-Kt1ch, K-R7 *10* R-Kt3, K-R8 *11* RxP mate.

    8 K-B3   P-R7
    9 K-Kt3!

A little device for lifting the stalemate.

    9 . . .   K-Kt8
    10 K-R3ch   K-R8
    11 R-Q8   K-Kt8
    12 R-Q1ch

White wins

NO. *186*

WHITE
to play
and win

ISENEGGER

WHILE the finishing touch here is similar to that in the previous example, there is a fine point in White's first move.

It is clear that White's King must hurry down to the Pawn, but the natural series of moves does not succeed in winning the Pawn: *1* K-K6, K-Kt6 *2* K-Q5, P-R6 *3* K-Q4 (or *3* R-Kt6ch, K-B7 *4* K-B4, P-R7 *5* R-QR6, K-Kt7, and White cannot win) P-R7 *4* K-Q3, K-Kt7 *5* R-Kt6ch, K-B8 *6* R-QR6, K-Kt7, and Black has a draw.

1 R-QKt6!

Shuts the King in! Unable to move past the Rook file, Black cannot prevent White's King from coming in to attack the Pawn. True, White must still guard against allowing a draw by stalemate.

1 . . .	K-R7
2 K-K6	P-R6
3 K-Q5	K-R8
4 K-B4	P-R7
5 K-Kt3!	K-Kt8
6 K-R3ch	K-R8
7 R-K6	K-Kt8
8 R-K1ch	

White wins

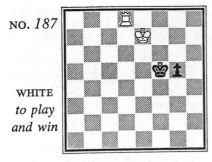

NO. *187*

WHITE
to play
and win

EUWE 1934

1 R-B8ch   K-Kt3

ON *1* . . . K-K5, White's King swings around to the far side of the Pawn to win: *2* K-B6, P-Kt5 (if *2* . . . K-B5 *3* K-Kt6ch, K-Kt5 *4* R-B5) *3* K-Kt5, P-Kt6 *4* K-R4, P-Kt7 *5* R-KKt8, K-B6 *6* K-R3, and the Pawn falls next move.

    2 R-B6ch   K-R4

Against *2* . . . K-Kt2, play proceeds: *3* K-K6, P-Kt5 *4* K-B5, P-Kt6 *5* R-Kt6ch followed by *6* RxP.

       3 K-K6   P-Kt5
       4 K-B5   P-Kt6

Or *4* . . . K-R5 *5* R-R6ch, K-Kt6 *6* R-KKt6 and White wins the Pawn.

       5 R-KKt6   K-R5

Holds on to the Pawn—at fearful expense.

       6 R-R6 mate

WHITE
*to play
and win*

HORWITZ AND KLING

WHITE'S threats of mate on one side of the board, facilitate his attack on the Pawns on the other side.

| *1* R-B7ch | K-Kt1 |

If *1* . . . K-R3 *2* R-B2, and Black must give up his Knight Pawn to prevent mate.

| *2* R-Kt7ch | K-R1 |

If *2* . . . K-B1 *3* R-Kt7, and the mate threat wins the Knight Pawn.

| *3* R-Kt7 | P-R6 |
| *4* K-Kt6 | |

White mates in two moves

NO. *189*

WHITE
to play
and win

SOZIN 1935

1 R-KKt6!

HOLDS both Pawns fast! In nearly all endings the Rook's best position is behind the passed Pawns—his own or the opponent's.

1 . . .	K-Q2
2 R-Kt4!	P-Kt7

On *2* . . . K-K3 instead, *3* RxBP, K-K4 *4* R-KKt4 wins.

3 RxKtP	K-K3
4 R-Kt5!	

Separates Black's King and Pawn. The King is confined to the first three ranks, while the Pawn must not take another step.

4 . . .	K-B3

Black dares not move his Pawn. If for example, *4* . . . P-Kt6 *5* R-KKt3 attacks and wins the Pawn.

5 R-QB5	K-K3
6 K-Kt7	K-B3

On *6* . . . K-Q3 *7* R-B5 wins, while *6* . . . P-B6 loses the Pawn by *7* R-B3, P-B7 *8* R-B3.

7 K-Kt6	K-K3
8 K-Kt5	K-B3
9 K-B4	K-K3
10 K-Q3	K-B3
11 K-K4	

White wins

NO. *190*

WHITE
to play
and win

SHAPIRO 1914

THE Pawns are so far advanced that it is useless to attack them directly. Black would simply allow one Pawn to be captured while the other moved on to become a Queen.

To win this, White keeps his opponent busy with mating threats, while his own King gradually moves over to the Pawns.

1 R-Q2ch   K-Kt8

Black avoids *1* . . . K-R8, the penalty being *2* K-Kt3 followed by *3* R-Q1 mate.

2 K-B3   K-B8

Pawn moves are answered as follows:

A] *2* . . . P-Kt7 *3* R-Q1ch, K-R7 *4* R-KKt1, P-R7 (*4* . . . K-R6 *5* R-R1 mate) *5* RxPch, K-R6 *6* RxP.

B] *2* . . . P-R7 *3* R-Q1ch, K-R7 *4* R-KR1, P-Kt7 (*4* . . . K-R6 *5* R-R1 mate) *5* RxP, and the remaining Pawn, being pinned, will fall next move.

3 R-QR2   K-Q8

If *3* . . . K-Kt8 instead, then *4* R-K2, P-Kt7 (a King move is of course unthinkable) *5* R-K1ch, K-R2 *6* R-KKt1, and White wins both Pawns.

4 K-Q3   K-B8

On *4* . . . K-K8 *5* K-K3 (threatens mate) K-Q8 (or *5* . . . K-B8 *6* K-B3 followed by capturing the Pawns) *6* K-B3, P-Kt7 (*6* . . . P-R7 *7* KxP) *7* K-B2 wins.

5 K-K3   P-R7

If *5* . . . P-Kt7 *6* K-B2 is decisive, while *5* . . . K-Kt1 loses by *6* R-K2, P-R7 *7* R-K1ch, K-Kt2 *8* K-B3.

6 R-R1ch   K-Kt2
7 R-R1   P-Kt7

If *7* . . . K-B6 *8* K-B3 wins the Pawns.

8 RxP

White wins

NO. *191*

WHITE
to play
and win

KIVI 1932

1 R-R2	P-R6
2 K-K5	P-R7
3 K-Q4	K-Kt8
4 K-B3	P-R8(Kt)

IF *4* . . . P-R8(Q)ch *5* K-Kt3, and Black must give up his Queen to avoid mate.

| 5 R-Kt2ch | K-B8 |
| 6 R-QR2 | K-Kt8 |

Forced, as the Knight is immediately captured if it emerges.

| 7 RxP | Kt-B7 |
| 8 R-K6! | Kt-R6 |

The alternatives are amusing:

A] *8* . . . Kt-R8 *9* R-K2, and to avoid mate, *Black must move the Knight, and lose it.*

B] *8* . . . K-B1 *9* R-K2, and to avoid mate, *Black must give up his Knight at once.*

| 9 R-K1ch | K-R7 |
| 10 R-K2ch | K-R8 |

If *10* . . . K-Kt8 *11* K-Kt3 threatens mate and wins the Knight.

| 11 K-Kt3 | Kt-Kt1 |

Other moves of the Knight allow its capture or instant mate.

12 R-R2 mate!

WHITE
*to play
and win*

BIRNOV 1946

A DELIGHTFUL ending, in which Black's Pawn turns out to be a liability.

    1 R-Kt5ch   K-B1

Clearly, if *1* . . . K-R2 *2* R-R5ch wins the Bishop.

    2 R-KR5   B-B2

The only move, the alternatives being:

A] *2* . . . B-Kt6 (or Kt8) *3* R-B5ch, K-K1 (on *3* . . . K-Kt2 *4* R-Kt5ch wins the Bishop) *4* R-KKt5, and Black must give up the Bishop to avoid mate.

B] *2* . . . B-B5 *3* R-B5ch winning the Bishop

C] *2* B-Kt1 *3* R-R8ch winning the Bishop

    3 K-Q7   B-Kt3

The only stopping-place, *3* . . . B-Kt6 being met by *4* R-B5ch followed by *5* R-Kt5ch.

    4 R-QKt5   B-R2
    5 R-QR5   B-Kt3
    6 R-R8ch   K-B2
    7 K-B6

White wins, the Bishop having no flight square.

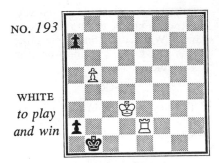

NO. *193*

WHITE
to play
and win

WILLIAMS 1894

HOW does White proceed? There is nothing but a draw after *1* RxP, while *1* K-B3, P-R8(Q)ch *2* K-Kt3, Q-R4! scuttles the mate threat and wins for Black.

1 R-K1ch	K-Kt7
2 R-QR1!	

Rather unexpected!

2 . . .	K-Kt6

Postpones the capture, but sooner or later Black will have to take the Rook.

3 K-Q2	K-Kt7
4 K-Q1	KxR

On *4* . . . K-Kt6 *5* K-B1, K-R6 *6* K-B2, K-Kt5 *7* RxP wins.

5 K-B2	P-R4
6 P-Kt6	P-R5

Black hopes to draw by stalemate if his King is hemmed in, while if the King is freed, his Pawn will threaten to Queen.

7 P-Kt7	P-R6
8 K-B3!	K-Kt8
9 P-Kt8(Q)ch	K-B8

If *9* . . . K-R8 *10* Q-Q6, K-Kt8 *11* Q-Q1 mate.

10 Q-B4ch	K-Q8(or Kt8)
11 Q-KB1 mate	

NO. *194*

WHITE
to play
and win

RICHTER 1939

WHITE'S own King being in the way, his Rook is unable to stop the passed Pawns. White must find some other means to win the position—or even to save the game!

1 K-Q6!

The key move. If instead *1* K-Q4, P-Q7, or if *1* K-B4, P-Q7 *2* R-Q6, P-K7 wins for Black.

1 . . .	P-Q7
2 K-B7	P-Q8(Q)

If *2* . . . P-Kt3 instead, *3* RxKtP followed by *4* R-R6 mate.

3 R-R6ch!	PxR
4 P-Kt6ch	K-R1
5 P-Kt7ch	K-R2
6 P-Kt8(Q) mate	

WHITE
*to play
and win*

PROKES 1924

1 R-Kt5   P-R6

IF *1* . . . P-Kt5ch *2* K-B4, P-R6 (on *2* . . . P-Kt6 *3* K-B5 forces mate) *3* R-Kt4 leads into the main line of play.

    2 R-Kt4ch   P-Kt5ch
    3 K-B4   P-R7

On *3* . . . P-Kt6 *4* K-B5 discovers check and mate.

    4 R-Kt3   P-Kt8(Q)

Here if *4* . . . P-Kt6 *5* RxQKtP, P-Kt8(Q) *6* R-R3 mate.

    5 R-R3ch!   PxR
    6 P-Kt3 mate

NO. *196*

WHITE
*to play
and win*

PROKOP 1924

1 R-B7   B-Kt8

THE only refuge. If *1* . . . B-Kt3 instead, *2* R-KKt7 wins a piece, or if *1* . . . B-K5 *2* R-B4 pins the Bishop.

2 P-Kt5

Stalemates the Knight, and threatens by *3* R-R7ch, K-Kt6 (*3* . . . K-Kt5 *4* R-Kt7ch wins the Bishop) *4* R-KKt7 to win it.

2 . . .   B-R7

The only chance, since King moves lose as follows:

A] *2* . . . K-Kt4 *3* R-Kt7ch
B] *2* . . . K-Kt5 *3* R-Kt7ch
C] *2* . . . K-Kt6 *3* R-KKt7
D] *2* . . . K-R4   *3* R-KKt7, B-R7 *4* R-R7ch
E] *2* . . . K-R6 *3* K-B3 (threatens mate) K-R5 *4* R-R7ch, K-Kt4 *5* R-Kt7ch

In all these variations White wins a piece.

3 R-R7ch   K-Kt6
4 K-B1

White wins. Black, completely helpless, must either give away his Knight or desert his Bishop.

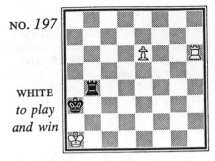

NO. *197*

WHITE
to play
and win

RINCK 1930

1 P-K7   R-K5

SHOULD Black play *1* . . . R-Kt1 instead, to stop the Pawn, then *2* R-R6ch, K-Kt5 *3* R-Kt6ch (diverting the Rook by force) RxR *4* P-K8(Q) wins for White.

After Black's actual move (*1* . . . R-K5), he threatens mate as well as capture of the Pawn.

    2 R-R3ch   K-Kt5
    3 R-R4!

A powerful pin by the unprotected Rook.

    3 . . .   RxR
    4 P-K8(Q)

White wins

WHITE
*to play
and win*

SELESNIEV 1923

1 P-R6   K-B3

IF BLACK tries *1* . . . R-B1, then
2 P-R7, R-KR1 (the King cannot
help, as after *2* . . . K-B3 *3* R-B1ch,
K-Kt2 *4* RxR wins) *3* K-Kt5, K-K3
4 K-Kt6, K-K2 *5* K-Kt7, and Black
will have to give up his Rook for the
Pawn.

2 P-R7   K-Kt2

Apparently Black has a draw, as
after   *3* K-Kt4, R-B1   *4* K-Kt5, R-
KR1, he captures the Pawn. But
White has an effective little combination that finishes Black.

3 P-R8(Q)ch!   KxQ
4 K-Kt4 dis.ch

White wins the Rook and the game

NO. *199*

WHITE
*to play
and win*

AN ATTEMPT to drive the Rook off
the Queen file could only succeed *if
White's Pawn stood on the fifth rank*.
Should White try it now, this would
be the result: *1* K-K4, R-K1ch *2* K-
B5, R-Q1 *3* K-K5, R-K1ch *4* K-Q6,
R-Q1ch *5* K-B5, R-B1ch, and White
makes no progress.

But a little artifice gets the Pawn
up a step, and enables White to carry
out his idea.

1 P-Q5!   K-R4

Black may not play *1* . . . RxPch
as the reply *2* K-B4, threatening mate
and attacking the Rook, is killing.

2 K-Q4   K-R3
3 K-K5

Now that the Pawn is on the fifth
rank, White can attack with his King,
drive the Rook away, and advance
the Pawn.

3 . . .   R-K1ch
4 K-B6   R-Q1

Or *4* . . . R-B1ch *5* K-K7, and
White proceeds as in the main line of
play.

5 K-K6   R-K1ch
6 K-Q7   R-KR1
7 P-Q6   R-R2ch
8 K-B6   K-R4

To avoid being mated.

9 P-Q7   R-R1
10 K-B7   R-R2
11 K-B8

White wins

NO. *200*

WHITE
to play
and win

PONZIANI 1782

1 K-Kt8	R-Kt7ch
2 K-B8	R-QR7
3 R-Kt6ch	

WHITE'S idea is to drive the King down, rank by rank.

3 . . .	K-B4

The alternatives are:

A] 3 . . . K-Kt4 4 K-Kt7 followed by Queening the Pawn.

B] 3 . . . K-Q4 4 K-Kt7, R-Kt7ch 5 R-Kt6, R-QR6 6 R-QR6, and again the Pawn will Queen.

4 K-Kt7	R-Kt7ch
5 K-B7	R-QR7
6 R-Kt5ch	

Taking care to avoid *6* R-B6ch, K-Q4 *7* K-Kt7 (intending to play *8* R-QR6 next move) as *7* . . . RxPch brusquely forces a draw.

6 . . .	K-B5
7 K-Kt7	R-Kt7ch
8 K-B6	R-QR7
9 R-Kt4ch	K-B6
10 K-Kt6	R-Kt7ch

Otherwise, White will continue with *11* R-Kt8, followed by *12* P-R8(Q).

11 K-B5	R-QR7
12 R-Kt3ch	K-B7
13 R-Kt2ch	K-Kt6
14 RxR	KxR
15 P-R8(Q)ch	

White wins

NO. *201*

WHITE
to play
and win

TROITZKY 1896

1 K-B4

THREATENS *2* R-Kt8ch followed
by *3* P-R8(Q).

1 . . .   K-B7

Hides behind White's King to
evade the check.

2 K-K4   K-K7

Black must keep on hiding, as
should he try *2* . . . R-R5ch for example, the continuation would be
3 K-Q3, R-R6ch   *4* K-B2, R-R7ch
5 K-Kt3, R-R8 *6* R-B8ch, and White
wins.

3 K-Q4   K-Q7
4 K-B5   K-B6

Black stays in the shadow of
White's King. If he plays *4* . . . R-
B8ch instead, then *5* K-Kt4, R-Kt8ch
6 K-R3, R-R8ch *7* K-Kt2, R-R3 *8* R-
Q8ch wins for White.

5 R-QB8!   RxP

Otherwise the Pawn advances.

6 K-Kt6 dis.ch

White wins the Rook and the game.

NO. *202*

WHITE
*to play
and win*

KARSTEDT 1909

1 R-B8   K-Q3

IF *1* . . . K-Q2 *2* R-QKt8, R-KR8 *3* K-Kt7, R-Kt8ch *4* K-R6, R-R8ch *5* K-Kt6, R-Kt8ch *6* K-B5 and White wins.

2 R-QKt8	R-KR8
3 K-Kt7	R-Kt8ch
4 K-B8	R-B8ch
5 K-Q8	R-KR8

Threatens mate. White does not reply to this by *6* K-K8 as *6* . . . R-R1ch *7* K-B7, R-R2ch wins the Pawn.

6 R-Kt6ch   K-B4

If *6* . . . K-K4 *7* K-B7, R-R2ch *8* K-Kt8, R-R1ch *9* K-Kt7, R-R2ch *10* K-R6, R-R1 *11* R-Kt8, and White wins.

7 R-B6ch!

The only way to win. If instead *7* R-K6, R-R8 *8* R-K7, K-Kt3 draws, or if *7* R-QR6, R-R1ch *8* K-K7, R-R2ch *9* K-B8 (moving to K6 or B6 costs a Rook) R-R1ch *10* K-Kt7, R-R1 *11* K-B7, K-Kt4 *12* R-R1, K-Kt3 and Black draws by taking the Pawn.

7 . . .   K-Kt4

If *7* . . . K-Q4 (certainly not *7* . . . KxR *8* P-R8[Q]ch) *8* R-QR6, R-R1ch *9* K-B7, R-R2ch *10* K-Kt6, R-R3ch *11* K-Kt5 wins.

8 R-B8	R-R1ch
9 K-B7	R-R2ch
10 K-Kt8	

White wins

NO. 203

WHITE
*to play
and win*

PUDER

ROOK endings are full of tactical tricks, and the one shown here occurs frequently.

1 P-R7	R-Kt8ch
2 K-R6	R-R8ch
3 K-Kt6	R-Kt8ch
4 K-B5	R-QR8

Or 4 . . . R-B8ch 5 K-Kt4, R-Kt8ch 6 K-B3, R-B8ch 7 K-Kt2, R-B2 8 R-R8 (threatens to Queen the Pawn) RxP 9 R-R7ch and White wins the Rook.

     5 R-R8   RxP

Otherwise the Pawn advances to the magic square.

     6 R-R7ch

White wins the Rook and the game.

NO. 204

WHITE
to play
and win

CHÉRON 1926

ALTHOUGH his King is cut off from the Queen side, Black puts up a tough battle and is not easily subdued.

1 K-Kt5	R-Kt1ch
2 K-B6	R-B1ch
3 K-Kt7	R-B8
4 P-R6	R-Kt8ch

On 4 . . . R-QR8 5 R-QKt3 shields the King from checks, after which the Pawn marches up without hindrance.

5 K-B6	R-B8ch
6 K-Kt5	R-Kt8ch
7 K-R4	R-Kt1

Black rejects 7 . . . R-R8ch as then 8 R-R3, R-R8 9 P-R7, R-R1 10 K-Kt5, R-R1 11 K-Kt6 wins easily.

| 8 K-R5 | R-QR1 |

Here, if 8 . . . R-Kt8 9 R-QR3 is decisive.

9 K-Kt6	R-Kt1ch
10 K-B7	R-Kt8
11 R-QR3	R-B8ch
12 K-Kt6	R-Kt8ch
13 K-R5	R-Kt1
14 P-R7	R-QR1
15 K-Kt6	

White wins

WHITE
*to play
and win*

CHÉRON 1926

1 K-Kt4　　R-K2
2 R-QR3

WHITE avoids the exchange of Rooks, as after *2* RxRch, KxR *3* K-Kt5, K-Q2 *4* K-Kt6, K-B1 *5* P-R5 (or *5* K-R7, K-B2 and White can make no progress) K-Kt1, and Black has an easy draw.

2 . . .	K-K1
3 P-R5	K-Q1
4 P-R6	R-QR2
5 K-Kt5	K-B1

Black's King had been cut off from the Queen side, but the offer to exchange Rooks enabled it to move over and help in the fight against the passed Pawn.

6 R-R3　　K-Kt1

Two alternatives are:

A] *6* . . . R-QB2 *7* R-R8ch, K-Q2 *8* P-R7, RxP *9* R-R7ch winning the Rook.

B] *6* . . . R-Q2 *7* R-R8ch, K-B2 *8* P-R7, and the Pawn will Queen.

7 R-R8ch

But not the tempting *7* K-Kt6, R-Kt2ch! *8* K-R5 (*8* PxR stalemates Black) R-Kt8, and White has been swindled out of a win.

7 . . .	K-B2
8 R-KKt8	K-Q3

Compulsory, since *8* . . . K-Q2 loses a Rook by *9* R-R7ch.

9 K-Kt6	R-KB2
10 P-R7	

White wins

NO. 206

WHITE
*to play
and win*

1 R-R7ch	K-Kt4
2 P-Kt7	

INTENDS *3* K-R8 followed by Queening the Pawn.

2 . . .	R-R1ch
3 K-B7	R-R2ch
4 K-K6	R-R3ch
5 K-Q5!	

The point! If at once *5* K-K5, R-KKt3, and White is in zugswang: if he moves the Rook, *6* . . . RxP draws, while a move by his King allows the reply *6* . . . K-B3 and the Pawn will fall.

5 . . .	R-KKt3

The Rook gets behind the Pawn, further checks being useless, and *5* . . . R-R1 (to head off the Pawn) ineffective after *6* R-R8.

6 K-K5!

The difference is now apparent. It is Black who is short of moves. His Rook must stay where it is, to prevent the Pawn from advancing, while his King has only one legal move.

6 . . .	K-Kt5
7 R-R1	K-Kt4

Or *7* . . . R-Kt4ch *8* K-K4, K-Kt6 (if *8* . . . RxP *9* R-Kt1ch wins the Rook) *9* R-Kt1ch, K-R5 *10* RxR, KxR *11* P-Kt8(Q)ch, and White wins.

8 R-Kt1ch	K-R3
9 RxRch	KxR
10 P-Kt8(Q)ch	

White wins

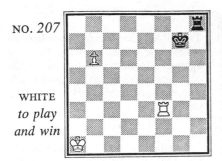

NO. *207*

WHITE
*to play
and win*

CHÉRON 1944

1 K-Kt2	R-QKt1
2 R-QKt3	K-B2
3 K-R3!	

PLAYING *3* P-Kt7 instead would be premature, as after *3* . . . K-K2 *4* K-R3, K-Q2 *5* K-R4, K-B2, the Pawn is lost.

3 . . .	K-K2
4 K-R4	K-Q2
5 K-Kt5	K-B1

On *5* . . . R-Kt2 instead, White has several ways of winning:

A] *6* R-QB3, K-Q1 (if *6* . . . R-Kt1 *7* R-Q3ch, K-B1 *8* K-B6, R-Kt2 *9* R-Q8ch, KxR *10* KxR, K-Q2 *11* K-R7) *7* K-R6, R-Kt1 *8* K-R7, R-B1 *9* RxRch.

B] *6* K-R6, K-B1 *7* R-B3ch, K-Kt1 *8* R-KR3, K-R1 (if *8* . . . K-B1 *9* R-R8ch wins the Rook) *9* R-R8ch, R-Kt1 *10* P-Kt7 mate.

| 6 R-B3ch | K-Kt2 |

If *6* . . . K-Q2 *7* R-Q3ch, K-B1 (*7* . . . K-K2 *8* K-B6 with an easy win) *8* K-B6, R-Kt2 *9* R-Q8ch, KxR *10* KxR, and the Pawn will Queen.

| 7 R-B7ch | K-R1 |
| 8 R-R7 mate! | |

NO. *208*

WHITE
to play
and win

GRIGORIEV 1937

1 R-Q4!

THE Rook does double duty here: it guards the Pawn, frees the King for aggressive action, and it shuts out the opposing King from the Queen side where he might take part in the struggle.

1 . . .   K-K3

If Black tries exchanging Rooks (so that his King can get to the Queen side) the play would go thus: *1* . . . R-Q1 *2* RxR, KxR *3* K-R4!, K-B1 *4* K-R5 (not *4* K-Kt5, K-Kt2, and Black, having the opposition, draws) K-B2 *5* K-R6, K-Kt1 *6* K-Kt6, and White wins.

2 K-B4!   R-B1ch

If *2* . . . K-K4 *3* R-Q5ch, K-K3 *4* P-Kt5, R-B1ch *5* R-B5, K-Q2 (on *5* . . . RxRch *6* KxR, K-Q2 *7* K-Kt6, K-B1 *8* K-R7 wins) *6* P-Kt6 (but not *6* RxR, KxR *7* K-B5, K-B2, and Black has a draw) RxRch *7* KxR, K-Q1 *8* K-Q6!, K-B1 *9* K-B6, and White wins.

3 K-Kt5

This and the following moves constitute a zigzag maneuver, customary in this type of position, and worth noting.

3 . . .	R-Kt1ch
4 K-B6	R-B1ch
5 K-Kt7	R-B1
6 P-Kt5	

White wins

NO. *209*

WHITE
to play
and win

GRIGORIEV 1937

THE fact that Black's King is cut off from the Queen side helps White in what might seem to be a difficult task, his Pawn being so far away from the Queening square.

1 K-B3	R-B1ch
2 K-Q4	R-QKt8
3 K-B4	R-B1ch
4 K-Q5	R-QKt1

If *4* . . . R-Q1ch *5* K-B6, R-B1ch *6* K-Kt7, R-B6 *7* R-QKt1, K-K3 *8* P-Kt4, K-Q3 *9* P-Kt5, and White wins.

5 R-QKt1	K-B3

If *5* . . . R-Kt4ch *6* K-B6, R-Kt5 *7* K-B5, R-Kt1 *8* P-Kt4, K-K3 *9* K-B6, R-B1ch *10* K-Kt7, and White has no troubles.

6 P-Kt4	K-K2
7 K-B6!	K-Q1
8 R-Q1ch	K-B1
9 R-KR1	K-Q1
10 R-R8ch	

White wins a Rook and the game.

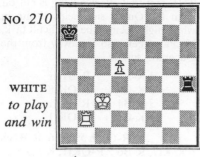

NO. 210

WHITE
*to play
and win*

CHÉRON 1944

Blockading the Pawn is suicide:
9 . . . K-Q1 *10* R-B8 mate.

10 R-KR2!

A brilliant surprise move, and the only way to win.

10 . . .   R-KKt1

Clearly, *10 . . .* RxR allows White to Queen his Pawn and win.

11 K-B7	R-QR1
12 K-K7	K-B2
13 P-Q8(Q)ch	RxQ
14 R-B2ch	K-Kt2
15 KxR	

White wins

1 K-Q3!

THE plausible *1* P-Q6 does not win, the continuation being *1 . . .* R-R3 *2* R-Q2 (if *2* P-Q7, R-B3ch *3* K-Kt4, R-Q3, and Black wins the Pawn) R-R1 *3* K-Q4 (here if *3* P-Q7, R-Q1 *4* K-B4, K-Kt3 and the Pawn will fall) K-Kt2 *4* R-QB2, R-R5ch, and White cannot escape perpetual check or loss of the Pawn.

1 . . .	R-KKt5
2 K-K3	R-KR5
3 P-Q6	R-R3
4 R-Q2!	

The advance *4* P-Q7 would be premature as *4 . . .* R-K3ch in reply followed by *5 . . .* R-Q3 will remove the Pawn.

4 . . .	R-R1
5 P-Q7	R-Q1
6 K-K4	K-Kt2
7 K-K5	K-B2
8 K-K6	R-KR1

Moving the King instead loses immediately, e.g. *8 . . .* K-B3 *9* R-B2ch, K-Kt2 *10* K-K7, and Black must give up his Rook for the Pawn.

9 R-B2ch	K-Kt2

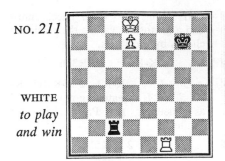

NO. *211*

WHITE
to play
and win

LUCENA 1497

White zigzags down the board until Black runs out of checks, then Queens his Pawn and wins.

The second method, beginning with the position in the diagram, is to Queen the Pawn by building a protecting bridge, as follows:

1 R-B4!	R-B8
2 K-K7	R-K8ch
3 K-Q6	R-Q8ch
4 K-K6	R-K8ch

On *4* . . . R-Q7 *5* R-B5 followed by *6* R-Q5, shutting off Black's Rook, insures the advance of the Pawn.

5 K-Q5	R-Q8ch
6 R-Q4	

White wins

THE Lucena position is almost 500 years old, but it is still one of the most important positions to know in the conduct of Rook endings.

White, as we can see, cannot win by simply moving his King out of the way, and Queening his Pawn. For example, if *1* K-K7, R-K7ch *2* K-Q6, R-Q7ch *3* K-B6, R-B7ch *4* K-Kt5 (moving towards the Rook to escape the checks) R-Kt7ch *5* K-B4, R-Q7, and Black wins the Pawn and draws.

Despite the apparent difficulties, White has two methods of winning:

1 R-QR1

Intending to evict Black's Rook from the Bishop file so that White's King may emerge without being annoyed by checks.

1 . . .	K-B2
2 R-R8	R-B8

If *2* . . . K-K3 *3* K-K8, R-KR7 *4* R-R6ch, K-B4 *5* P-Q8(Q) and White wins.

3 R-B8	R-Q8
4 K-B7	R-B8ch
5 K-Kt6	R-Kt8ch
6 K-B5	

NO. *212*

WHITE
to play
and win

TARRASCH 1906

THE King, who is in check, must find a means of evading the persistent checks by the Rook.

1 K-K6   R-R3ch

On *1* . . . R-R1   *2* R-Kt1ch, K-R2 *3* K-B7, threatening mate as well as Queening the Pawn, wins for White.

2 K-K5!

But not *2* K-B5, K-B2 *3* R-K1, R-R1 *4* R-K2, R-K1, and White cannot save his Pawn.

2 . . .	R-R4ch
3 K-B6	R-R3ch
4 K-Kt5	R-R4ch

Getting behind the Pawn by *4* . . . R-K3 yields to *5* R-B8ch, K-Kt2 *6* P-K8(Q), and White wins.

5 K-Kt6	R-R3ch
6 R-B6	R-R1
7 R-Q6	

White wins, his Rook's next stop being Q8—with or without check.

NO. *213*

WHITE
to play
and win

GRIGORIEV 1937

1 K-Q8   R-Kt1ch

BLACK can attack with his King instead, with this result: *1* . . . K-B3 *2* P-K7!, R-Kt1ch (if *2* . . . RxP *3* R-B1ch, K-K3   *4* R-K1ch costs Black his Rook) *3* K-B7, R-K1 *4* K-Q6, R-QKt1 *5* R-B1ch, K-Kt2 *6* K-B7, R-QR1 *7* R-QR1!, R-R1 *8* K-Q7, K-B2 *9* R-B1ch, K-Kt2 *10* P-K8(Q) and White wins.

2 K-B7	R-Kt7
3 R-K1	R-B7ch
4 K-Q7	R-Q7ch
5 K-K8	R-QR7
6 P-K7	R-R1ch
7 K-Q7	R-R2ch
8 K-B6	

White wins

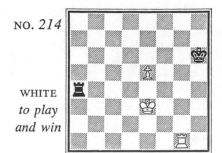

NO. *214*

WHITE
to play
and win

CHÉRON 1926

THE winning moves, in this fine ending of Chéron's, are as brilliant as they are forceful.

1 K-Q3!

In reply to this, Black is practically forced to move his Rook. Moving his King instead leads to one of these pretty possibilities:

A] *1* . . . K-R4 *2* P-K6!, R-R3 *3* K-K4! (in order to assist the Pawn by continuing with *4* K-K5 and *5* K-B6) RxPch *4* K-B5, and White's attack on the Rook combined with a threat of mate on the move forces Black to give up his Rook.

B] *1* . . . K-R4 *2* P-K6!, K-R3 *3* P-K7, R-R1 *4* K-K4, R-K1 *5* K-K5!, RxPch *6* K-B6, and again Black must lose his Rook or be instantly mated.

C] *1* . . K-R4 *2* P-K6!, K-R5 *3* R-Kt8, R-R2 (otherwise the Pawn simply moves on to K7 and K8) *4* K-K4, K-R4 *5* K-B5, K-R3 *6* K-B6, K-R2 *7* R-Q8, R-R3 *8* K-B7, and the rest plays itself.

1 . . .   R-QKt5

Black's best defense is a move by his Rook, and that along the fifth

rank. Had he played something like *1* . . . R-R3 instead (to prevent the Pawn from advancing) the win for White would be elementary. The continuation would be *2* K-K4 and *3* K-B5, and Black could offer no resistance, his King being confined to the Rook file.

2 P-K6!   R-Kt3
3 R-K1

Threatens to advance the Pawn, and forces . . .

3 . . .   R-Kt1
4 P-K7   R-K1
5 K-Q4   K-Kt2
6 K-Q5   K-B2
7 K-Q6

Threatens *8* R-B1ch, K-Kt2 *9* K-Q7, R-QR1 *10* P-K8(Q), and Black will have to give up his Rook.

7 . . .   R-QR1

Or *7* . . . R-KR1 *8* K-Q7, R-K1 *9* R-B1ch, and Black must abandon his Rook.

8 R-B1ch   K-Kt2

Naturally, if *8* . . . K-K1 instead, the penalty is *9* R-B8 mate.

If White is hasty now and plays *9* K-Q7 (threatening to promote the Pawn) Black replies with a series of checks from which the King cannot escape without loss of the Pawn. The play would be: *9* K-Q7, R-R2ch *10* K-Q6, R-R3ch *11* K-Q5, R-R4ch *12* K-B6, R-R3ch, and if White approaches the Rook by *13* K-Kt7 or K-Kt5, the response *13* . . . R-K3 wins the Pawn.

The winning move brilliantly eliminates the possibility of perpetual check as a defense.

228

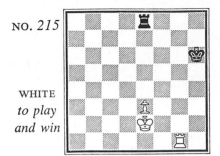

NO. 215

WHITE
to play
and win

CHÉRON 1927

THERE are delightful finesses in the position, innocuous though it looks.

1 K-Q3!   R-Q1ch

On a King move instead, White simply pushes his Pawn up a square.

2 K-B4	R-B1ch
3 K-Q5	R-Q1ch
4 K-K5	R-K1ch

Must White lose time now by retreating, in order to save his Pawn?

5 K-B6!

Not at all, since he threatens instant mate.

5 . . .   R-B1ch

On *5* . . . K-R4 instead, White replies *6* R-K1 followed by advancing the Pawn.

6 K-K7	R-B4
7 P-K4!	R-K4ch
8 K-B6	

Once again rescuing the Pawn by the threat of mate.

8 . . .	R-KR4
9 P-K5	R-R7
10 R-KB1	K-R2
11 K-B7	

White wins

---

9 R-QR1!   R-QKt1

Obviously if *9* . . . RxR instead, *10* P-K8(Q) wins for White.

10 K-B7	R-K1
11 K-Q7	K-B2

No better is *11* . . . R-QKt1 *12* P-K8(Q).

12 R-B1ch

White wins the Rook and the game.

WHITE
to play
and win

DURAS 1903

ORDINARY tactics do not suffice, so White gives it a touch of brilliancy.

1 R-Q2ch

The King must be dislodged if White's King is to emerge.

1 . . .   K-K2

White could now move 2 K-B7 but after *2 . . .* R-B6ch, the King would have to return.

2 R-Q6!   R-QB6

If *2 . . .* KxR instead, *3* K-B8, R-B6ch *4* K-Q8, R-KR6 (threatens mate) *5* P-Kt8, and the Pawn's promoting with check wins for White.

3 R-QB6!   RxR
4 K-R7

White wins

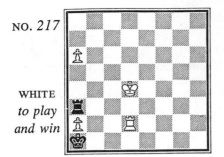

WHITE
to play
and win

PROKES 1941

THIS seems to be a dead draw, as White's Pawns are doomed, but White turns the dead draw into a neat win.

1 K-B4   RxP(R3)

Forced, as otherwise the King protects the Pawn and then escorts it up the board to be Queened.

2 P-R4!

Again threatening to proceed by *3* K-Kt5 and to march the Pawn up.

2 . . .   RxPch
3 K-Kt3!

Attacks the Rook on one hand, and threatens mate on the other.
White wins

231

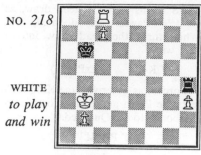

NO. *218*

WHITE
*to play
and win*

KOK 1936

WHITE is three Pawns ahead, but threatened with loss of two of them by *1* . . . RxPch *2* K-Kt4, K-Kt2 and *3* . . . KxP, after which Black could draw against the remaining Pawn.

The win requires care and finesse.

| *1* R-Q8 | RxPch |

Or *1* . . . KxP *2* R-Q3 and White has an easy win.

| *2* R-Q3! | RxRch |

Black must accept the offer, as the alternative *2* . . . R-R1 leaves no hope after *3* R-QB3.

| *3* K-B2! |

If *3* K-B4 instead, *3* . . . R-Q8, and the threat of *4* . . . R-QB8 (with or without check) draws.

| *3* . . . | R-Q3! |

Clever defense! If White plays *4* P-B8(Q), then *4* . . . R-B3ch *5* QxRch, KxQ *6* K-Kt3, K-Kt4, and Black, having the opposition, draws.

4 P-B8(Kt)ch!	K-B3
5 KtxR	KxKt
6 K-Kt3!	K-B3
7 K-R4	K-Kt3
8 K-Kt4	K-B3
9 K-R5	

White wins

NO. *219*

WHITE
*to play
and win*

RINCK 1906

SOME pretty ideas are concealed in a modest setting.

    1 R-R3ch   K-Kt2

If *1* . . . K-Kt4 *2* R-Kt3ch, K-B4 *3* RxR, KxR *4* P-R7 and White wins.

    2 R-Kt3!   RxR

If Black refuses to capture, White exchanges Rooks, and Queens the Pawn.

    3 P-R7   R-Kt8
    4 K-Kt2

Prevents the Rook from moving to QR8.

    4 . . .   R-Kt7ch
    5 KxP   R-Kt6ch
    6 K-Kt4

Moving to the Bishop file allows *6* . . . R-QR6, while *6* K-R4 lets Black draw by *6* . . . R-Kt8 followed by *7* . . . R-QR8, with or without check.

    6 . . .   R-Kt5ch
    7 K-Kt5   R-Kt4ch
    8 K-Kt6   R-Kt3ch
    9 K-Kt7

White wins

233 ♖

NO. *220*

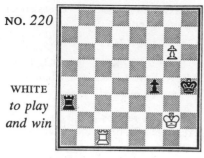

WHITE
*to play
and win*

HORWITZ

1 R-KKt1

IN ACCORDANCE with principle, the Rook supports the passed Pawn by moving behind it.

       1 . . .   R-R1

On *1* . . . R-Kt6ch *2* K-B2, K-R4 *3* P-Kt7, K-R3 *4* P-Kt8(Q) wins.

2 P-Kt7	K-R4
3 K-B3	R-KKt1
4 KxP	K-R3
5 K-B5	K-R2

If *5* . . . RxP instead, *6* R-R1 is mate.

6 K-B6	R-QR1
7 R-R1ch	K-Kt1
8 R-R8 mate	

234

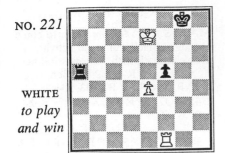

NO. *221*

WHITE
to play
and win

SELESNIEV 1923

WHITE can gain a Pawn by *1* RxP
or *1* PxP, but the reply *1* . . . R-
R2ch leads to a drawing position.

The point of the winning combination is not to gain a Pawn, but to give
one up!

1 R-Kt1ch	K-R2
2 P-K5!	RxPch

Otherwise the passed Pawn is irresistible. For example, if *2* . . . R-
R2ch *3* K-B6 followed by *4* P-K6
wins easily, Black's King being cut
off from the scene of action.

3 K-B7

Threatens mate on the move.

3 . . .	K-R3
4 K-B6	

Threatens mate again, whilst attacking the Rook.

White wins—first the Rook, then
the game.

WHITE
*to play
and win*

FRITZ 1953

1 K-Kt5!   K-R6

MAKES room for the Pawn to come through. Black can try to activate his Rook instead, with these possibilities:

A] *1* . . . R-R1 *2* R-R3ch, K-B7 *3* KxP, R-QB1 *4* R-QB3, K-K7 *5* K-B4, K-Q7 *6* R-B5, K-Q6 *7* K-K5, and White wins.

B] *1* . . . R-R8 *2* R-QB2, K-B6 *3* R-B3ch, K-K5 *4* P-B7, R-R1 *5* P-B8(Q), RxQ *6* RxR, P-Kt6 *7* K-R4, P-Kt7 *8* R-KKt8, K-B6 *9* K-R3, and White wins.

2 R-R2ch!	KxR
3 KxR	P-Kt6
4 P-B7	P-Kt7
5 P-B8(Q)	P-Kt8(Q)
6 Q-R3 mate!	

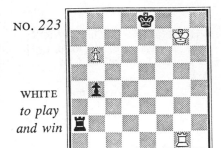

NO. *223*

WHITE
to play
and win

FRITZ 1953

THE move that breaks the pin is as brilliant as any I've seen in a long time.

1 P-Kt7	R-R2
2 R-K1ch	K-Q1
3 R-K7!	

Frees the Pawn and threatens to transform it into a Queen.

| 3 . . . | KxR |
| 4 P-Kt8(Q) | |

White wins. Black cannot hold on to his Pawn, since *4* . . . R-R5 loses the Rook after *5* Q-B7ch followed by *6* Q-B6ch.

NO. 224

WHITE
*to play
and win*

MORAVEC 1949

1 K-K7!

WHITE avoids the hasty *1* R-Kt8, since it allows Black to draw by *1* . . . R-Q2ch followed by *2* . . . RxP.

1 . . .   R-QR1

Not *1* . . . R-KR1, which loses immediately by *2* R-Kt8.

2 K-Q7!   R-KB1

Clearly, *2* . . . KxP is fatal after the reply *3* K-B7, while *2* . . . RxPch leads to the main line of play.

3 R-KB2!   R-QR1

On *3* . . . R-KKt1 (or *3* . . . R-KR1) *4* K-B7 (intending to continue by *5* R-R2ch and *6* P-R8) R-QR1 *5* R-R2ch, K-Kt4 *6* K-Kt7, and White wins.

4 K-B7   RxPch
5 K-B6

Threatens mate on the move.

5 . . .   K-R4
6 R-R2ch

White wins the Rook and the game.

238

NO. 225

WHITE
to play
and win

LASKER 1890

THE win is accomplished by a maneuver which forces Black's King to retreat rank by rank, until he is in position for the decisive blow.

1 K-Kt8

Threatens to Queen the Pawn.

1 . . .	R-Kt7ch
2 K-R8	R-B7

The Rook must return, to keep an eye on the Pawn.

3 R-B6ch	K-R4
4 K-Kt8	

Renews the procedure, Black's King meanwhile having had to move down a rank.

4 . . .	R-Kt7ch
5 K-R7	R-B7
6 R-B5ch	K-R5
7 K-Kt7	R-Kt7ch
8 K-R6	R-B7
9 R-B4ch	K-R6
10 K-Kt6	R-Kt7ch
11 K-R5	R-B7
12 R-B3ch	K-Kt7
13 RxP	RxR

Black, unfortunately, may not capture White's Pawn in return.

14 P-B8(Q)

White wins

239

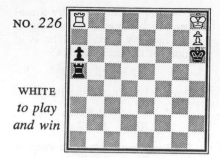

NO. 226

WHITE
to play
and win

PFEIFFER 1939

1 R-KB8

INTENDING to continue with *2* R-B6ch, K-R4 *3* K-Kt7, R-Kt4ch *4* K-B7, and the Pawn moves on to become a Queen and win.

1 . . .	R-KKt4
2 R-B6ch	K-R4
3 R-B5!	RxR
4 K-Kt7	R-Kt4ch
5 K-B7	

White avoids *5* K-B6, when *5* . . . R-Kt3ch *6* K-B7, R-R3 wins for Black.

5 . . .	R-B4ch
6 K-K7	R-K4ch
7 K-Q7	R-Q4ch
8 K-B7	R-B4ch
9 K-Kt7	R-Kt4ch

The last check, as the King hides behind the Pawn.

10 K-R7

White wins

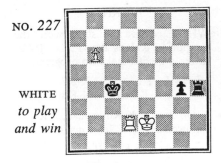

NO. 227

WHITE
*to play
and win*

RINCK 1911

1 P-Kt7

A FORCEFUL beginning. A prelim-
inary check instead leads to this:
1 R-B2ch, K-Q4   *2* P-Kt7, R-R7ch
3 K-Q1 (or *3* K-Q3, R-R6ch followed by *4* . . . R-QKt6) R-R8ch
4 K-Q2, R-QKt8, and Black draws
easily, his Rook now being behind
the Pawn.

| *1* . . . | R-R7ch |
| *2* K-K3 | R-R6ch |

Rushing back to the first rank in-
stead is useless: *2* . . . R-R1 *3* R-
B2ch, K-Q4 *4* R-B8, and White wins.
With the actual move, Black hopes
for *3* K-B4, R-QKt6 *4* R-B2ch, K-
Q4, and he has a drawn position.

| *3* K-K4! | R-QKt6 |
| *4* R-B2ch | K-Kt4 |

Such a move must be distressing,
Black having to obstruct the action of
his own Rook.

5 P-Kt8(Q)ch

White wins

NO. 228

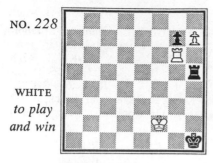

WHITE
*to play
and win*

PROKOP 1925

1 R-Kt1ch

WHITE does not start with the tempting *1* RxP as after *1* . . . R-R6 in reply he can make no progress.

| *1* . . . | K-R7 |
| 2 R-Kt2ch | K-R8 |

On *2* . . . K-R6 instead, *3* K-Kt1 followed by *4* R-R2ch wins for White.

3 K-Kt3!

Prevents *3* . . . RxP as *4* R-Q2 with a dire mate threat would be the penalty.

3 . . .   R-R3

What else is there:

A] *3* . . . R-Kt4ch *4* K-B3, RxR *5* P-R8(Q)ch, and White wins.

B] *3* . . . R-Kt4ch *4* K-B3, R-KR4 *5* RxP, K-R7 *6* K-Kt4, R-R3 *7* K-Kt5, R-R6 *8* K-Kt6, R-R5 *9* K-B7 followed by *10* K-Kt8, and White wins.

C] *3* . . . R-Kt4ch *4* K-B3, R-B4ch *5* K-Kt4 (threatens to Queen the Pawn) R-B1 *6* K-Kt3 (now the idea is *7* R-R2ch, followed by Queening) R-KR1 *7* R-K2, and it's all over.

| *4* P-R8(Q)! | RxQ |
| *5* R-QR2 | |

White wins

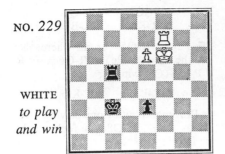

NO. 229

WHITE
*to play
and win*

TROITZKY 1908

A STRANGE duel of Rooks, where both sacrifice themselves to help their Kings!

1 P-K7   R-B1

An immediate offer of the Rook instead, leads to this: *1* . . . R-K4 *2* KxR, P-K7 *3* R-B3ch, K-Q7 (otherwise *4* R-K3, and the Rook gets behind the Pawn) *4* R-B2, K-Q8 *5* RxP, and White wins.

2 R-B8   R-B3ch

Black has no time for *2* . . . P-K7 as White captures the Rook with check, in response.

3 K-B5   R-K3!

Brilliant, and Black's best chance to save the game.

    4 KxR   P-K7
    5 R-B3ch   K-Q5

Here too, if *5* . . . K-Q7 *6* R-B2 pins the Pawn and wins.

    6 R-B4ch   K-Q6

To prevent *7* R-K4—or so he thinks!

        7 R-K4!

"A Roland for an Oliver," as the old novelists used to say.

    7 . . .   KxR
    8 P-K8(Q)   P-K8(Q)

The position on the board (almost symmetrical) is artistic.

       9 K-B6 dis.ch

White wins the Queen and the game.

NO. *230*

WHITE
*to play
and win*

KANTOROVICH 1952

| 1 P-Kt7 | R-Q1 |
| 2 R-K6ch | K-B5 |

IF *2 . . .* K-Q5 (or anywhere else on the Queen file) *3* R-Q6ch, RxR *4* P-Kt8(Q) wins.

| 3 R-B6ch | K-Kt6 |

Prevents White from playing *4* R-B8 as *4 . . .* R-Q8ch in reply would be fatal.

| 4 R-Kt6ch | K-R6 |

Ready to circumvent *5* P-Kt8(Q) with *5 . . .* RxQ *6* RxR, and Black is stalemated.

| 5 K-Kt1 | R-KKt1 |

Now Black's threat is *6 . . .* RxP *7* RxR, and he draws by stalemate.

| 6 K-B2 | K-R7 |
| 7 R-Kt4! | K-R6 |

The alternative is *7 . . .* P-R6 *8* R-Kt3, K-R8 (a Rook move allows the Pawn to Queen) *9* RxP mate.

8 K-B3	K-R7
9 RxPch	K-Kt8
10 R-R7	R-Q1

Or *10 . . .* K-B8 *11* R-R1 mate.

| 11 R-R8 |

White wins. A beautifully timed study.

NO. *231*

WHITE
to play
and win

TROITZKY 1924

A BLOCKADING action to make Black's Rook impotent, is the winning idea in this ending.

1 K-B3

Threatens mate on the move.

1 . . .   K-R5

Or *1* . . . K-R7 *2* P-Kt7, R-KKt7 *3* R-Kt2ch (luring Black's Rook away from the Pawn) RxR *4* P-Kt8(Q)ch, and White wins.

2 R-Kt4ch	K-R4
3 R-Kt4!	PxR
4 P-Kt7	

White wins, since his Pawn cannot be stopped.

NO. *232*

WHITE
*to play
and win*

VLK 1917

"THE Art of Exchanging Rooks," by Vlk (improbable name!).

> *1* K-Kt8   R-B3
> *2* R-B6

Daring Black to exchange, the consequence of which would be: *2* . . . RxR *3* PxR, P-B5 *4* P-B7, P-B6 *5* P-B8(Q), P-B7 *6* Q-QB5, and White wins.

> *2* . . .   P-B5

"Two can play at that game," as the fellow says. Now if White exchanges Rooks, this happens: *3* RxR, PxR *4* P-Kt6, P-B6 *5* P-Kt7, P-B7 *6* P-Kt8(Q), P-B8(Q), and the position is a draw.

> *3* R-R6ch

Once more putting the question to Black. If now *3* . . . RxR *4* PxR, P-B6 *5* P-R7, P-B7 *6* P-R8, and the Pawn becoming a Queen with check, wins for White.

> *3* . . .   K-Kt2
> *4* RxR

Now White exchanges, having forced Black's King to the Knight file.

> *4* . . .   PxR
> *5* P-Kt6   P-B6
> *6* P-Kt7   P-B7
> *7* P-Kt8(Q)ch

Queens with check, and White wins.

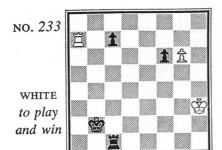

NO. 233

WHITE
to play
and win

EISENSTADT 1932

A SUDDEN sacrifice makes the process of winning this ending a quick and easy one.

> 1 R-Kt7ch   K-R6

Clearly if 1 . . . K-B6 2 RxPch, followed by exchanging Rooks and then pushing the Pawn, wins on the spot.

> 2 P-Kt7   R-KKt8
> 3 RxP

Threatens to win by 4 R-B3ch, K-Kt5 5 R-KKt3.

> 3 . . .   K-Kt5!

The best defense. If instead 3 . . . K-Kt7 4 R-K7, intending 5 R-K2ch followed by 6 R-KKt2, forces 4 . . . K-B8 when 5 R-K1ch, RxR 6 P-Kt8(Q) wins for White.

> 4 K-R4   R-Kt4

Prevents White's King from moving closer to his Pawn, to help it Queen. An attempt to Queen his own Pawn leads to this: 4 . . . P-B4 5 K-R5, P-B5 6 K-R6, P-B6 7 R-KB7, R-Kt6 8 K-R7, R-R3ch 9 K-Kt8, K-B5 10 K-B8, and White wins.

> 5 R-K7

Intends 6 R-K4ch followed by 7 R-KKt4.

> 5 . . .   K-B4

There is no comfort in 5 . . . K-B6 6 R-K3ch, K-Q5 7 R-KKt3, and White wins.

> 6 R-K5ch!   RxR

What else is there? If 6 . . . PxR 7 KxR wins, or if 6 . . . K-Q3 7 RxR, PxRch 8 KxP, and the game is over.

> 7 P-Kt8(Q)

White wins

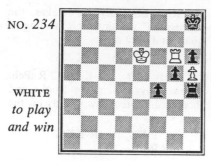

NO. 234

WHITE
*to play
and win*

WHITE is two Pawns behind, but his King and Rook are strongly placed. Black has two passed Pawns, but his King is confined to a corner, and faces great dangers.

1 K-B7

Threatens to win on the spot by 2 RxP mate.

1 . . .   RxP

If Black tries *1* . . . K-R2 instead, then *2* R-Kt7ch, K-R1 *3* K-Kt6, P-B6 (other moves are no better) *4* R-K7 forces mate.

2 R-Kt8ch	K-R2
3 R-Kt7ch	K-R1
4 K-Kt6	P-Kt5

To permit the Rook some freedom. Black must do something to counter White's threat of *5* R-Q7 followed by mate.

5 R-QR7	R-Kt4ch
6 KxP	P-Kt6

What choice is there? Black may not play *6* . . . R-Kt1, the penalty being *7* R-R7 mate. The Rook must stay on the Knight file, since moving it along the rank allows *7* R-R8ch and mate next.

7 KxR   P-Kt7

Or *7* . . . K-Kt1 (to give his King room) *8* KxP, and the other Pawn will fall.

8 R-R1

Stops the Pawn from Queening, and threatens to win by the simple, brutal *9* KxP.

8 . . .	P-B6
9 K-Kt6!	

White wins, as mate will be forced.

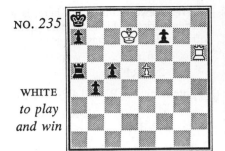

NO. 235

WHITE
to play
and win

HERBSTMANN

WHITE has only one Pawn to Black's four, but the strong position of his King suggests mating possibilities.

1 P-K6!

On the immediate *1* K-B7, Black defends by *1* . . . P-R3, and after *2* K-Kt6, R-Kt4ch *3* KxP, R-Kt2, he has nothing to fear.

1 . . .   PxP

But not *1* . . . R-R3 (attempting to pin the Pawn) as *2* PxP, RxR *3* P-B8(Q)ch wins.

2 K-B6   P-R3

If *2* . . . R-R3ch instead, *3* K-B7 forces a quick mate.

| *3* R-R8ch | K-R2 |
| *4* R-R7ch | K-R1 |

The alternative leads to a pretty finish: *4* . . . K-Kt1   *5* K-Kt6 (threatens mate) R-Kt4ch *6* KxP, and the Rook is trapped.

| *5* K-Kt6 | R-Kt4ch |
| *6* KxP | R-Kt1 |

The only square left—unfortunately.

7 R-R7 mate

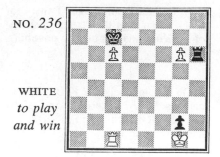

NO. *236*

WHITE
*to play
and win*

PROKES 1940

"THE Skewer," illustrated here, is a tactical trick which appears quite often in Rook endings.

1 P-Kt7	R-Kt3
2 R-R1	

Intending *3* R-R8 and *4* P-Kt8(Q).

2 . . .	K-Kt1
3 P-B7ch	

White offers a Pawn to draw the King away from the critical square.

3 . . .	KxP

Other King moves lead to this:
A] *3* . . . K-B1 *4* P-Kt8(Q)ch, RxQ *5* R-R8ch, and White wins the Rook.
B] *3* . . . K-Kt2 *4* P-B8(Q)ch, KxQ *5* P-Kt8(Q)ch, RxQ *6* R-R8ch, and White wins the Rook.

4 R-R8

One way or another, the Rook gets to this square. The threat now is Queening the Knight Pawn.

4 . . .   RxP

Black's King aːːRook are now in a straight line—in position to be skewered.

5 R-R7ch

Wins the Rook and the game.

NO. 237

WHITE
to play
and win

MORAVEC 1937

WHITE is a Pawn ahead, but what to do? If *1* P-Kt7, K-B3, and he makes no headway, or if *1* R-Kt7, K-B3, and after the exchange of Pawns, Black has no trouble drawing.

There is a win though, beginning with a brilliant move:

1 R-Q8ch!	KxR
2 P-Kt7	R-QKt5!

The Pawn must be stopped, and Black can be brilliant too.

3 KxR	P-B4ch

Now the position begins to look like a draw, as after *4* KxP, K-B2 *5* K-Kt5, KxP, and Black has nothing to fear from the Rook Pawn.

4 K-Kt5!	

White spurns the Pawn, and plays this, which is a killer.

4 . . .	K-B2
5 K-R6	

Threatens *6* K-R7 followed by Queening with check.

5 . . .	K-Kt1
6 K-Kt6	P-B5
7 P-R4	P-B6
8 P-R5	P-B7
9 P-R6	P-B8(Q)
10 P-R7 mate!	

Who would have thought that the Rook Pawn (hiding behind the King in the diagrammed position) would be the one to strike the final blow?

NO. *238*

WHITE
*to play
and win*

GABOR 1933

BLACK is subtly drawn into position to lose his Rook by the skewer attack.

1 P-Q5	R-QR1
2 P-Q6	K-B2
3 P-Q7	K-K2

There is nothing now in playing *4* P-Q8(Q)ch, as after *4* . . . RxQ *5* RxR, KxR   *6* P-R6, K-B2,   and Black overtakes the Rook Pawn.

4 P-R6	K-Q1
5 R-Q6	

Prevents Black's King from emerging, the consequence (after *5* . . . K-B2) being *6* P-Q8(Q)ch, RxQ *7* RxR, KxR *8* P-R7, and White wins.

5 . . .	R-Kt1

On *5* . . . R-R2 instead, *6* RxP, RxQP *7* R-Kt8ch, K-B2 (or *7* . . . K-K2 *8* R-Kt7ch) *8* P-R7 wins for White.

6 K-B3	R-Kt5

Purpose: to prevent White's King from advancing, and to get behind the Rook Pawn.

7 P-R7	R-QR5
8 RxP	

Clearing the way for *9* P-R8(Q)ch, RxQ *10* R-Kt8ch winning the Rook.

8 . . .	KxP

Or *8* . . . RxP *9* R-Kt8ch, KxP (forced) *10* R-Kt7ch, and the Rook falls.

9 R-Kt8

Threatens to Queen the Pawn next move.

9 . . .	RxP
10 R-Kt7ch	

White wins

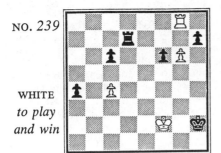

NO. *239*

WHITE
to play
and win

SELESNIEV 1914

1 R-KR8

PINS the Pawn and threatens a quick win by *2* RxPch, RxR *3* PxR.

1 . . .	R-Q7ch
2 K-B1	R-Q8ch

If instead *2* . . . R-KKt7 (getting behind the Pawn) *3* RxPch, K-Kt6 *4* P-Kt7, K-B6 *5* R-R3ch, R-Kt6 *6* RxRch, and White wins.

3 K-K2	R-KKt8

Keeps the dangerous Pawn under observation.

4 RxPch	K-Kt6
5 R-R1!	R-Kt7ch

Clearly, Black cannot afford *5* . . . RxR *6* P-Kt7, nor *5* . . . K-Kt7 *6* RxRch, in either case with a win for White.

6 K-K3	K-Kt5

Ready to meet *7* P-Kt7 with *7* . . . K-B4, uncovering the Rook.

7 R-R2!	R-Kt6ch

On *7* . . . R-Kt8 instead, the winning play is *8* K-B2, R-Kt6 *9* P-Kt2, forcing an exchange of Rooks.

8 K-B2	R-B6ch

Other moves allow the decisive *9* R-Kt2.

9 K-Kt1	R-KKt6ch

The alternative is *9* . . . R-K6 *10* P-Kt7, R-K1 *11* P-Kt8(Q)ch, RxQ *12* R-Kt2ch, and Black's Rook comes off the board.

10 R-Kt2

Forces an exchange of Rooks, after which nothing can stop the Knight Pawn.
White wins

NO. *240*

WHITE
*to play
and win*

LIBIURKIN 1949

THERE are several plausible ways to begin, but Black can refute them, viz:

A] *1* PxKt, RxP *2* P-Kt8(Q), RxQ, and White must take the draw by *3* RxP.

B] *1* P-Kt5, Kt-Q3 *2* P-R7, R-R5 *3* P-Kt6, Kt-B5ch, and Black's next move will be *4 . . .* KtxP with a draw as result.

The line of play that wins (and does so artistically) is this:

    1 P-R7   P-B8(Q)!

A necessary sacrifice if Black is to get behind the passed Pawn.

    2 RxQ   R-R7ch
    3 K-B1!   R-R7

The Rook Pawn looks like a goner.

    4 P-Kt5!   R-R8ch

Black does not take the Pawn immediately, as after *4 . . .* RxP *5* R-B6ch, K-Kt4 *6* R-QR6, RxR *7* PxR, White wins, the Knight being unable to prevent the Pawn from reaching the last square.

    5 K-B2!

White is generous, as *5 . . .* RxR is penalized at once by *6* P-R8(Q), and he wins.

♜ 254

    5 . . .   R-R7ch
    6 K-Kt1   RxP
    7 R-B6ch   K-Kt4

The point is that the King must move to the fourth rank (which he does) or the second. Should he choose the latter, say by *7 . . .* K-Kt2, then the play would run: *8* R-QR6, Kt-Q3 (attacks the Pawn) *9* RxRch, and capturing with check saves the Pawn and wins for White.

    8 R-QR6   Kt-Q3

Exchanging Rooks instead is hopeless, as *8 . . .* RxR *9* PxR, Kt-Q1 *10* P-R7, and Black is a move too late to catch the Pawn.

    9 RxR   KtxP
    10 R-R5

Pins the Knight (now we see why the King was forced to the fourth rank) and wins.

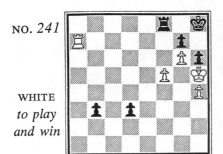

NO. *241*

WHITE
to play
and win

SELESNIEV 1919

1 P-B6!

AN ENERGETIC beginning. White threatens *2* PxPch winning a Rook.

   1 . . .   R-KKt1

Choice is limited: *1* . . . RxP instead allows *2* R-R8ch and mate next, while *1* . . . PxP *2* P-Kt7ch costs a Rook.

   2 R-KB7   P-Q7

Black must depend on his passed Pawns, since the alternatives *2* . . . PxP *3* R-R7 mate, or *2* . . . R-Q1 *3* RxP, P-Q7 *4* R-R7ch, K-Kt1 *5* P-B7ch, K-B1 *6* R-R8ch, K-K2 *7* RxR, KxR *8* P-B8(Q)ch, are not appetizing.

   3 PxPch   RxP
   4 KxP   P-Q8(Q)

This seems to offer a glimmer of hope. Certainly there is none in *4* . . . R-Kt1 *5* R-R7 mate, nor in *4* . . . RxR *5* PxR, and Black's King must wait for the *coup-de-grâce*.

   5 R-B8ch   R-Kt1
   6 P-Kt7 mate

NO. *242*

WHITE
to play
and win

BOTVINNIK 1956

FROM a game played in Moscow between Botvinnik and Najdorf.

By cleverly sacrificing a Pawn, White's King finds a good place to hide—right in the camp of the enemy!

1 P-K5	PxP
2 PxP	

With this idea: *3* R-Q7ch, RxR *4* P-K6ch, K-K2 *5* PxR, KxP *6* K-Kt6, and White captures the abandoned Pawns and wins.

2 . . .	K-K2
3 P-K6	R-R5

There is no fight in *3* . . . R-R3 *4* R-Q7ch, K-B1 *5* K-Kt6!, RxPch *6* K-R7, and Black's remaining Pawns will fall (*6* . . . R-K5 *7* RxP, R-K3 *8* R-Kt6).

4 P-Kt5!

A subtle sacrifice, the point of which we will see later.

4 . . .	PxP
5 R-Q7ch	K-B1
6 R-B7ch	K-Kt1
7 K-Kt6	

Getting in between the opponent's Pawns, the King safeguards himself against troublesome checks.

7 . . .	P-Kt5
8 P-R6!	

Threatens *9* P-R7ch, K-R1 *10* R-B8 mate.

8 . . .   PxP

Or *8* . . . R-R1 *9* PxP, P-Kt6 *10* P-K7, R-R3ch (*10* . . . P-Kt7 *11* R-B8ch and mate next) *11* R-B6, RxRch *12* KxR, and White mates in two more moves.

9 P-K7   R-R1

On *9* . . . R-R3ch *10* R-B6, R-R1 leads to the play that follows.

10 R-B6	R-K1
11 R-Q6	

White wins, there being no specific against the effects of *12* R-Q8, his next move.

The Queen

QUEEN endings abound in tactical brilliancies. There are wily combinations to do away with pieces, intrigues to waylay the Queen, and plots to get at the King.

The procedure to adopt with a Queen against a Pawn on the seventh is instructively shown in Lolli No. 243, Greco No. 244, Lolli No. 245, Salvioli No. 246, No. 247 and No. 248, Lolli No. 249 and Berger No. 250.

Lolli's No. 251 is an exhaustive study of Queen against Rook, while Rinck's No. 252 between the same opponents is in lighter vein.

Kantorovich No. 253 demonstrates that one Queen is as good as another—or even better! Cohn on the other hand points out in No. 254 that two Queens are not always superior to one.

Nos. 255, 256 and 257 are concerned with the problem of promoting a Pawn that stands on the brink of the Queening square, but for the moment is unable to move.

Rinck's No. 259 is a game-like Queen ending which shows the old master at his best.

In No. 260 by Zhek, White's attack is directed towards winning the Queen —until the very last move.

Typical Rinck, which is to say first-class, are No. 261 and No. 262, in each of which Queen and minor piece win neatly against the opposing Queen.

No. 263 and No. 273, by Richter and Gurvich respectively are endings which are sure to find their way into every chessplayer's private little notebook.

No. 265 came up in actual play, and was brilliantly won by Sormann.

Prokop's No. 266 is nothing less than a masterpiece. A quiet move by the King after a few vigorous checks leaves Black helpless to prevent mate or loss of his Queen.

In Kubbel's No. 267, artistic manipulation of the pieces enables Queen and Knight to overpower Black's King and Queen.

The Queen Pawn in Clausen's No. 269 undertakes a journey to the eighth square. Clever play renders all the obstacles in its path impotent.

Sparkling play by the combination of Queen and Knight highlights Erochin No. 270, while the ladder theme is represented by one of its most pleasing specimens in Troitzky's No. 272.

NO. *243*

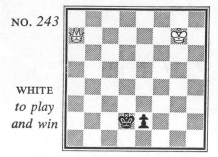

WHITE
to play
and win

LOLLI 1763

IN ENDINGS of Queen against a Pawn on the seventh rank, the method of winning shown here applies if the Pawn stands on the King, Queen, or Knight file. Should the Pawn occupy the Bishop or Rook file, different treatment is necessary, as we shall see in subsequent examples.

1 Q-B2

Pins the Pawn, and forces. . . .

1 . . .	K-Q8
2 Q-Q4ch	K-B7
3 Q-K3	K-Q8
4 Q-Q3ch	K-K8

Black has been forced to block his Pawn, giving White's King time to move one square closer. White keeps repeating this maneuver until his King is near enough either to help capture the Pawn or to assist in bringing about mate.

5 K-B6	K-B7
6 Q-Q2	K-B8
7 Q-B4ch	K-Kt7
8 Q-K3	K-B8
9 Q-B3ch	K-K8
10 K-K5	K-Q7
11 Q-B2	K-Q8
12 Q-Q4ch	K-B7
13 Q-K3	K-Q8
14 Q-Q3ch	K-K8
15 K-K4	K-B7
16 Q-B3ch	K-K8
17 K-Q3	K-Q8
18 QxPch	K-B8
19 Q-B2 mate	

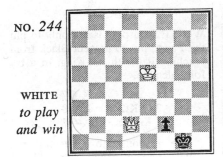

NO. *244*

WHITE
to play
and win

GRECO 1612

THE customary procedure against a Pawn on the seventh rank does not work if the Pawn occupies the Bishop or the Rook file. For instance, if *1* Q-Q4, K-Kt7 *2* Q-Kt4ch, K-R7 *3* Q-B3, K-Kt8 *4* Q-Kt3ch, K-R1!, and Black abandons the Pawn nonchalantly, since taking it allows a draw by stalemate.

White's winning chance in this and similar positions lies in his King being near enough (as it is here) to take part in a mating combination.

1 K-B4

Now Black's little trick of abandoning the Pawn does not work, as after *1* . . . K-R8 *2* Q-K2 (for Heaven's sake, not 2 K-Kt3, allowing *2* . . . P-B8(Kt)ch, and Black wins the Queen) K-Kt7 *3* K-Kt4, K-Kt8 (if 3 . . . K-R8 *4* Q-B1ch, K-R7 *5* QxPch) *4* K-Kt3, P-B8(Q) *5* Q-R2 mate.

1 . . .   P-B8(Q)ch
2 K-Kt3

The threat is *3* Q-R2 mate. If Black's Queen moves (say to QB5) to give the King room, then *3* Q-Kt2 is mate.

White wins

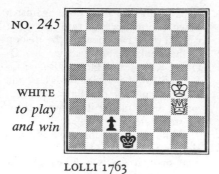

WHITE
to play
and win

LOLLI 1763

1 Q-QKt3

WHITE'S purpose is not only to pin the Pawn, but to prevent Black from reaching R8 with his King, in a try for stalemate.

1 . . .	K-Q7
2 Q-Kt2	K-Q8
3 K-B3!	K-Q7

The response to Queening the Pawn (and it would come like a flash) would be *4* Q-K2 mate.

4 K-B2	K-Q8

Clearly, on *4* . . . K-Q6 *5* K-K1 forces Black to give up his Pawn.

5 Q-Q4ch	K-B8
6 Q-QKt4	K-Q8
7 Q-K1 mate	

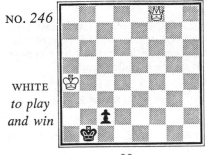

NO. *246*

WHITE
to play
and win

SALVIOLI 1887

1 Q-KB5

PINS the Pawn, and cuts down the choice of reasonable reply to two moves by the King.

1 . . .　　K-R8

Against *1* . . . K-Kt7, White proceeds *2* Q-B2, K-Kt8 *3* K-Kt3, P-B8(Kt)ch (or *3* . . . P-B8(Q), *4* Q-R2 mate) *4* K-R3, Kt-Q6 *5* Q-Q2 and mate next move.

2 K-Kt3!　　P-B8(Q)

Or *2* . . . P-B8(Kt)ch *3* K-R3, Kt-Q6 *4* Q-B1ch (side-stepping *4* QxKt, stalemate) and mate next move.

　　3 Q-QR5ch　　K-Kt8
　　4 Q-R2 mate

NO. 247

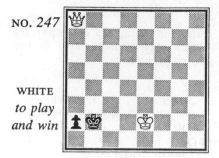

WHITE
*to play
and win*

SALVIOLI 1887

1 Q-Kt7ch   K-R8

BLACK threatens to stalemate himself. White can win this type of position only if his King is near enough to create a mating situation.

2 Q-K4   K-Kt7
3 Q-Q4ch   K-Kt8

Or 3 . . . K-Kt6 4 K-Q3, K-R6 5 K-B4, and Black will be mated next move.

4 Q-Q1ch   K-Kt7
5 Q-Q2ch   K-Kt8

Or 5 . . . K-R8 6 Q-B1 mate.

6 K-Q1!   P-R8(Q)

If 6 . . . P-R8(Kt) 7 Q-Kt4ch, K-R7 8 K-Q2, Kt-Kt6ch 9 K-B3, K-R8 (a Knight move instead allows 10 Q-Kt2 mate) 10 KxKt (definitely not 10 QxKt) K-Kt8 11 Q-K1 mate.

7 Q-B2 mate

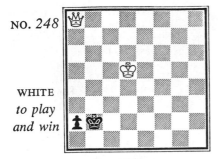

NO. *248*

WHITE
*to play
and win*

SALVIOLI 1887

WHITE wins because his King is close enough to assist in a mating operation. Were his King to stand on Q6 instead, there could be no win.

1 Q-R8ch	K-Kt8
2 Q-KR1ch	K-Kt7
3 Q-R2ch	K-Kt8
4 K-B4!	

This move and the next gain two tempos for White, while Black is busy Queening his Pawn.

4 . . .	P-R8(Q)
5 K-Kt3	

Threatens a mate which Black can only postpone by sacrificing his Queen.

White wins

NO. *249*

WHITE
to play
and win

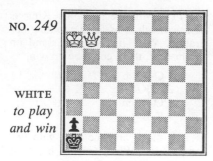

LOLLI 1763

ORDINARILY this would be a draw, with White's King so far away, and the usual procedure against a Pawn on the seventh rank ineffective. For instance, if *1* Q-K4, K-Kt7 *2* Q-Kt4ch, K-B7 *3* Q-R3, K-Kt8 *4* Q-Kt3ch, K-R8! Black has been forced to block his Pawn, but White cannot gain a move for his King to approach, since he must release the stalemate.

White wins this though with a little device which enables his King to come two squares closer. Back to the diagrammed position!

1 K-Kt6!

Lifts the stalemate by screening the Queen.

1 . . .	K-Kt7
2 K-R5 dis.ch	K-B8
3 Q-R1ch	K-Kt7
4 Q-Kt2ch	K-Kt8

Or *4* . . . K-Kt6 *5* Q-KKt7 followed by *6* Q-R1, winning easily.

5 K-R4	P-R8(Q)ch
6 K-Kt3	

And White forces mate (the position being an old friend by now).

NO. 250

WHITE
to play
and win

BERGER 1922

1 Q-Kt8ch	K-B7

IF *1* . . . K-R8 instead, *2* Q-Kt3, P-R6 *3* Q-B2, P-R7 *4* Q-B1 mate.

2 Q-R7	K-Kt6
3 Q-Q3ch	K-Kt7
4 Q-K4ch	K-Kt6

If *4* . . . K-B7 *5* Q-R1 wins, or if *4* . . . K-Kt8 *5* Q-Kt4ch, K-B7 *6* Q-R3, K-Kt8 *7* Q-Kt3ch, K-R8 *8* Q-B2 and mate next move.

5 K-B5	P-R6
6 K-Q4	P-R7
7 Q-R1	P-R8(Q)ch
8 QxQ	K-Kt7
9 Q-Kt2ch	K-Kt8

On *9* . . . K-Kt6 *10* Q-Kt7 followed by *11* Q-R1 is decisive.

10 K-K3	P-R8(Q)
11 Q-B2 mate	

NO. 251

WHITE
*to play
and win*

LOLLI 1763

THE safest place for the Rook, in endings of Queen against Rook, is close to his King. Once out in the open, the Rook is no match for the fleet-footed Queen.

In the diagrammed position, the Rook is in no danger. White's object therefore is to force the Rook away from the protection of the King, *to any other square* in fact, where it will be exposed to the threat of capture.

White accomplishes his object by playing three moves which bring about the position in the diagram, but *with Black to move.*

1 Q-Q4ch   K-R1

The King must move to the last rank, since *1* . . . K-R3 allows *2* Q-R4 mate.

2 Q-R8ch   K-R2

Again forced, the reply to *2* . . . R-Kt1 being *3* Q-R1 mate.

3 Q-Q8

Now White has the desired position, with Black to move.

Black, as we shall prove, has no moves that do not lose the Rook or expose him to mate.

♛ 266

If he moves the King:
3 . . . K-R3   *4* Q-R8ch, R-R2 *5* Q-QKt8, and Black will shortly be mated.

If he moves the Rook along the file:
A] *3* . . . R-Kt1 *4* Q-R5 mate
B] *3* . . . R-Kt3ch *4* QxRch, and mate next move
C] *3* . . . R-Kt4 *4* KxR
D] *3* . . . R-Kt5 *4* Q-R5ch, winning the Rook
E] *3* . . . R-Kt6   *4* Q-Q4ch, K-Kt1 (on *4* . . . K-R1 *5* Q-R4ch wins the Rook) *5* Q-B4ch, K-R1 (on *5* . . . K-B1 *6* Q-B8 is mate) *6* Q-R4ch, and White wins the Rook
F] *3* . . . R-Kt7 *4* Q-Q4ch, and White wins the Rook
G] *3* . . . R-Kt8   *4* Q-Q4ch, K-R1 (on *4* . . . K-R3 *5* Q-R4 is mate) *5* Q-R8ch, K-R2 (or *5* . . . R-Kt1 *6* Q-QR1 mate) *6* Q-R7ch, and Black loses his Rook

If he moves the Rook along the rank:
A] *3* . . . R-QB2 *4* QxRch wins
B] *3* . . . R-Q2 *4* QxRch wins
C] *3* . . . R-K2 *4* QxRch wins
D] *3* . . . R-KB2 *4* Q-Q4ch, K-R1 (if *4* . . . K-R3 *5* Q-R4 mate) *5* Q-R1ch, K-Kt1 (on *5* . . . R-R2 *6* Q-R8 is mate) *6* Q-Kt2ch, K-R1 (if *6* . . . K-B1 *7* Q-R8ch and mate next move, or if *6* . . . K-R2 *7* Q-R2ch wins the Rook) *7* Q-R2ch (attacks the Rook) R-R2 *8* Q-Kt8 mate
E] *3* . . . R-KKt2   *4* Q-Q4ch, and White wins the Rook
F] *3* . . . R-R2   *4* Q-Q4ch, K-Kt1 (if *4* . . . K-R1 *5* Q-R1ch, K-Kt1 *6* Q-Kt1ch wins the Rook) *5* Q-Kt4ch, K-R2 *6* Q-R4ch, K-Kt1 *7* Q-Kt3ch, K-R2 *8* Q-R2ch, K-Kt1 *9* Q-Kt8ch, and White wins the Rook
Q.E.D.
White wins

NO. 252

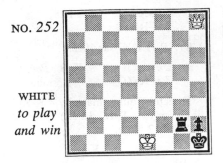

WHITE
*to play
and win*

RINCK 1917

THIS looks as though it might be a long, bitter fight. The win is easy and amusing though, the Queen zigzagging down to force a mate in twelve moves.

	1 Q-R8	K-Kt8

Black's replies need no comment —his moves are all compulsory.

2	Q-R7ch	K-R8
3	Q-Kt7	K-Kt8
4	Q-Kt6ch	K-R8
5	Q-B6	K-Kt8
6	Q-B5ch	K-R8
7	Q-Q5	K-Kt8
8	Q-Q4ch	K-R8
9	Q-K4	K-Kt8
10	Q-K3ch	K-R8
11	Q-KB3	K-Kt8
12	Q-B1 mate	

NO. 253

WHITE
*to play
and win*

KANTOROVICH 1952

1 R-R6ch   K-Kt8
2 R-R1ch!

A STARTLING sacrifice.

2 . . .   KxR
3 P-R8(Q)

Threatens quick mate by *4* K-Kt3 dis.ch (or by *4* K-B2 dis.ch) followed by *5* Q-Kt2 mate.

3 . . .   K-R7

This is what happens on other Black defenses:

A] *3* . . . Q-Q6ch *4* K-B2 dis.ch, K-R7 *5* Q-Kt2 mate

B] *3* . . . Q-B8ch *4* K-Kt3 dis.ch, K-Kt8 *5* Q-R7ch, K-R8 *6* Q-R7ch, K-Kt8 *7* Q-R2 mate

c] *3* . . . Q-KR5 *4* Q-R1ch, K-R7 *5* Q-Kt2ch, K-Kt8 *6* Q-Kt2 mate

D] *3* . . . Q-B7 *4* K-Kt3 dis.ch, K-Kt8 *5* Q-QR1ch, and mate next move

E] *3* . . . K-Kt8 *4* Q-R7ch, K-R8 *5* Q-R7ch, K-Kt8 *6* Q-Kt6ch, K-B8 (or *6* . . . K-R7 *7* Q-Kt2 mate) *7* Q-QKt1ch, Q-B8 *8* QxQ mate

4 Q-R8ch   K-Kt1
5 Q-Kt7ch   K-B1
6 Q-R1ch   Q-B8
7 QxQ mate

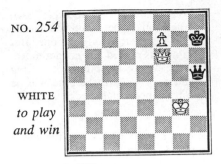

NO. *254*

WHITE
to play
and win

COHN 1929

THE natural impulse is to Queen the Pawn, and win with two Queens against one. This is what would happen:

1 P-B8(Q), Q-Kt5ch *2* K-B2 (if *2* KxQ stalemate) Q-K7ch *3* K-Kt3 (on *3* K-Kt1, Q-Kt7ch forces *4* KxQ and a draw by stalemate) Q-Kt5ch, and Black draws by perpetual check.

Another plausible try leads to this:

1 Q-K7, Q-Kt3ch *2* K-B4, Q-B3ch *3* QxQ, and Black draws by stalemate.

The win, and there is one, is by the pretty device of under-promotion, after which Black is helpless. This is the story:

    1 P-B8(Kt)ch!   K-Kt1
    2 Kt-K6

Threatens *3* Q-Kt7 mate.
        2 . . .   Q-B2
If *2* . . . Q-R2 instead *3* Q-B8 is mate.

    3 Q-Q8ch   K-R2
    4 Kt-Kt5ch

Wins Queen and game.

WHITE
to play
and win

HORWITZ AND KLING

IF WHITE could advance his Pawn another square he would win easily, having two Queens against one. But the Pawn is pinned and cannot move. Clearly, White must move his King —and to a square where he will be safe from perpetual check.

1 K-B8

Not *1* K-Q8, Q-B3 and the Pawn is pinned anew.

1 . . .   Q-Kt5ch

Checking at Kt1 or R1 instead allows *2* P-K8(Q) in reply.

2 K-Kt8   Q-Kt5ch
3 K-R8

The King is safe from checks here in spite of his apparently exposed position! If Black should try *3* . . . Q-R5ch or *3* . . . Q-R4ch, *4* Q-R2 in reply will force the Queens off the board, leaving the King Pawn as survivor and victor.

White wins

WHITE
to play
and win

HORWITZ AND KLING 1851

TO WIN this, White must promote his Pawn. He would then have the overwhelming advantage of two Queens against one.

Two problems must be solved: Advancing the Pawn (which is now pinned) and safeguarding his King from perpetual check (which would give Black a draw).

1 K-R7	Q-R8ch

If *1* . . . Q-Q2 instead (to renew the pin) *2* Q-K4ch, K-B4 *3* K-Kt8, and Black cannot pin the Pawn (*3* . . . Q-Q4 *4* QxQch wins for White) nor check advantageously (*3* . . . Q-Q1ch *4* P-B8(Q)ch).

2 K-Kt7!	Q-R8ch
3 K-Kt8	Q-R7
4 Q-Kt6ch	K-B6

The only move, since *4* . . . K-R5 or *4* . . . K-R6 allows *5* Q-R6ch with an exchange of Queens, while *4* . . . K-B5 *5* Q-K6ch loses the Queen outright.

5 K-Kt7!	Q-Kt7ch
6 Q-Kt6	Q-Kt2
7 K-Kt8	Q-Q4

Obviously *7* . . . Q-Kt1ch is useless after *8* P-B8(Q) in reply, while the pin by *7* . . . Q-Kt6 fails after *8* Q-Kt3ch, forcing the exchange of Queens.

8 K-R7	Q-R8ch

On *8* . . . Q-Q2 pinning the Pawn, *9* Q-Kt7ch cleverly unpins it.

9 Q-R6	Q-K5ch
10 K-R8	Q-K4ch
11 Q-Kt7	

Black must exchange Queens, and White wins

NO. *257*

WHITE
to play
and win

VAN VLIET 1888

WHITE'S win depends on Queening his Pawn. The manner in which the Pawn is freed from the pin (which now prevents its advance) is rather startling.

1 Q-Kt4

Immobilizes Black's King, and forces his Queen to move.

1 . . .   Q-R8

The Queen stays on the long diagonal to maintain the pin. There are other squares on this diagonal which the Queen could have chosen with the following results:

A] *1* . . . Q-Q4 *2* Q-R4ch, K-Kt3 *3* Q-Kt3ch!, QxQ *4* P-Kt8(Q)ch, and White wins the Queen

B] *1* . . . Q-KB6 *2* Q-R4ch, K-Kt3 *3* Q-Kt3ch, QxQ *4* P-Kt8(Q)ch, and White wins the Queen

C] *1* . . . Q-Kt7 *2* Q-R3ch, K-Kt3 (or Kt4) *3* Q-Kt2ch, QxQ *4* P-Kt8(Q)ch and White wins

2 Q-R3ch   K-Kt3
3 Q-Kt2ch   K-B4

What else is there? If
A] *3* . . . K-R3 (or R4) *4* Q-R2ch, K-Kt4 (or anywhere else on the Knight file) *5* Q-Kt1ch, QxQ *6* P-

Kt8(Q)ch, and White wins the Queen

B] *3* . . . K-B3 *4* P-Kt8(Q) and wins

C] *3* . . . K-B2 *4* Q-R2ch, QxQ *5* P-Kt8(Q)ch, and White wins the Queen

4 K-R7   Q-R2

Black has no check, so he clamps on a new pin.

5 Q-Kt6ch   K-Q4

On *5* . . . K-B5 instead, *6* K-R6 followed by Queening the Pawn wins.

6 K-R6

Leaves Black powerless to stop the Pawn's advance. If he tries *6* . . . Q-Q6ch, the response *7* Q-Kt5ch forces an exchange of Queens.

White wins

NO. 258

WHITE
to play
and win

HORWITZ AND KLING 1851

1 Q-Kt2ch	K-B1

IF BLACK plays *1* . . . K-R1 instead, then *2* Q-R8ch, Q-Kt1 *3* Q-R1ch and mate next move.

2 Q-R8ch	Q-K1
3 Q-Kt7	

Threatens to mate at Kt7.

3 . . .	Q-Q1

On *3* . . . Q-B2 *4* Q-B8ch, Q-K1 *5* P-Q7 is decisive, while *3* . . . Q-R5 is penalized by *4* Q-Kt7ch, K-K1 *5* Q-K7 mate.

4 K-Kt6	Q-K1ch
5 K-B6	Q-Q1ch
6 KxP	Q-K1ch

Running away to escape mate leads to this: *6* . . . K-Kt1 *7* Q-B7ch, K-R1 *8* Q-B6ch, and White wins.

7 Q-K7ch	QxQch
8 PxQch	K-K1
9 K-B6	

White wins

273

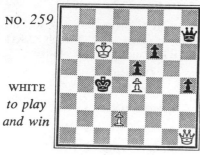

NO. 259

WHITE
*to play
and win*

RINCK 1906

1 Q-QKt1

A QUIET move, but it threatens to
win by *2* Q-Kt5ch, K-Q5 *3* Q-Q5
mate.

1 . . .   K-Q5
2 Q-Kt3!

Clearly indicating his intention—
3 Q-Q5 mate. There is more to
White's move though than this trans-
parent threat. Note that he lets Black
defend by capturing a Pawn with
check!

2 . . .   QxPch
3 K-Q6

Black must now guard against *4* Q-
B3 mate.

3 . . .   Q-QR1

The Queen moves away to give the
King a flight square. She must stay
on the long diagonal to prevent *4* Q-
Q5 mate, but was any square besides
QR1 available?

If *3 . . .* Q-Kt7 or *3 . . .* Q-R8
instead, *4* Q-B3ch, K-K5 *5* Q-B6ch,
and White wins the Queen.

4 Q-K3ch	K-B5
5 Q-B3ch	K-Kt4
6 Q-Kt3ch	K-R3

Obviously *6 . . .* K-R4 *7* Q-R3ch
costs the Queen.

7 Q-R4ch	K-Kt2
8 Q-Kt5ch	K-R2

Or *8 . . .* K-B1 *9* Q-Q7ch, K-Kt1
10 Q-B7 mate.

9 K-B7!

Appropriately enough, White ends
the combination as he began it—
with a quiet move. Black has no defense against the threat of mate.
White wins

NO. *260*

WHITE
to play
and win

ZHEK 1938

THERE is a twist in this ending
which may catch you by surprise.

1 Q-B1ch   P-B5

The only defense. The King may
not move to the Rook file, as the reply *2* Q-R1ch wins his Queen, while
on *1* . . . K-Kt3 *2* Q-Kt1ch, K-R3
3 Q-R2ch, K-Kt2 *4* Q-Kt3ch, K-R3
5 Q-R4ch, K-Kt2 *6* Q-Kt5ch, K-R2
7 K-B7!, and Black faces mate.

2 Q-Kt1ch   K-B4

Here too, moving to the Rook file
is fatal.

3 Q-Kt4ch	K-K4
4 Q-Kt5ch	K-Q5
5 Q-Kt1ch	K-K4

Forced, since *5* . . . K-B6 loses
the Queen after the reply *6* Q-R1ch.

6 Q-R1ch

Will White win the Queen?

6 . . .   P-Q5

No, he will not, but . .

7 QxRP

Mates the King!

WHITE
to play
and win

RINCK 1902

1 Q-B7ch   Q-B4

THE King must not move, since
1 . . . K-Kt5 allows *2* Kt-K5ch winning the Queen by a Knight fork,
while *1* . . . K-K5 *2* Q-Kt6ch wins
the Queen by the skewer attack.

     2 Q-B4ch   Q-K5
     3 Q-QB7ch   K-B4

On *3* . . . K-Kt5 *4* Q-Kt7ch leads
into the main line of play after
White's fifth move.

     4 Q-B7ch   K-Kt5
     5 Q-Kt7ch   K-B4

The only square left to the King.
If:

  A] *5* . . . K-R4 *6* Q-Kt5 mate
  B] *5* . . . K-R6 *6* Q-Kt3 mate
  C] *5* . . . K-B5 *6* Q-Kt5 mate

     6 Kt-Q4ch   K-B5
     7 Q-Kt3 mate

NO. *262*

WHITE
to play
and win

RINCK 1903

WHITE'S tactical play is artistic but no less incisive.

1 Q-Kt4ch   K-K4

The only flight square, *1* . . . K-Q6 costing the Queen after *2* Q-K2ch.

2 Q-Kt5ch   K-K5

Here if *2* . . . K-Q3 *3* Q-B6ch wins the Queen, while *2* . . . K-Q5 runs into *3* Q-K3 mate.

3 B-Kt6ch   K-Q5
4 Q-K3ch   K-Q4

Or *4* . . . K-B5 *5* Q-Q3ch, and White wins the Queen.

5 B-K4ch!

After this powerful move, Black can only decide in what manner his Queen will be lost. If he plays *5* . . . K-Q3 (or K3) *6* Q-R6ch wins the Queen on the rank. If he moves *5* . . . K-B5 *6* B-Q3ch wins the Queen on the diagonal, while *5* . . . K-K4 *6* B-Kt7ch wins the Queen by discovered attack.

White wins

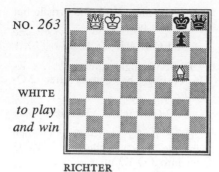

NO. *263*

WHITE
*to play
and win*

RICHTER

EVERY player from Grandmaster down, to whom I showed this ending picked *1* K-Q7 dis.ch as the first move in the solution. It does not win, though it would seem that the King should move in towards Black for the kill.

The winning line of play:

1 K-Kt7 dis.ch!	K-R2
2 Q-R2ch	K-Kt1
3 Q-R2ch	K-R2

Obviously, *3* . . . K-B1 instead is unsuitable, the reply *4* Q-R8ch costing Black his Queen.

4 Q-B7!

Decisive! Black is tied hand and foot. Neither King nor Pawn may move, while his Queen is restricted to one square. Note how White's first move by the King gave him control of three squares on the last rank.

4 . . .	Q-KKt1
5 Q-R5 mate!	

NO. *264*

WHITE
to play
and win

GUNST 1933

1 Q-B1

THREATENS a killing discovered attack, thus: *2* Kt-Q3 dis.ch, Q-Kt8 *3* Q-B6ch, Q-Kt7 *4* QxQ mate.

1 . . .   Q-Kt8

The only possible defense. Other tries lose as follows:

A] *1* . . . K-Kt7 *2* Kt-Q3ch
B] *1* . . . K-Kt8 *2* Kt-Q3 dis.ch
C] *1* . . . Q-B6ch *2* Kt-Q3 dis.ch
D] *1* . . . Q-R6ch *2* Kt-Q3 dis.ch

In all the above, White either wins the Queen or forces mate.

2 Q-B6ch	Q-Kt7
3 Kt-Kt3ch	K-Kt8
4 Q-B1ch	K-B7
5 Kt-R1ch!	K-Q7

On *5* . . . K-B6 instead, *6* Q-B6ch wins the Queen

    6 Q-B2ch   K-B6

Or *6* . . . K-B8 *7* Q-K1 mate.

    7 Q-B6ch

White wins the Queen and the game.

NO. *265*

WHITE
to play
and win

SORMANN 1908

SKILLFUL maneuvering of Queen and Knight brings about a problem-like mating position.

| 1 Q-Kt6ch | K-B5 |
| 2 Q-Q4ch | K-Kt6 |

If 2 . . . K-Kt4 instead, 3 Kt-R7ch forces the King away from his Queen.

3 Q-Q1ch	K-R6
4 Q-R1ch	K-Kt6
5 KtxPch	K-Kt5
6 Q-Q4ch	K-R6

Taking the Knight (or moving to Kt4) allows 7 Q-Kt6 mate.

| 7 Kt-B4ch | K-Kt6 |

The only move, 7 . . . K-R7 running into mate on the move, while 7 . . . K-Kt5 costs the Queen after 8 Kt-Kt6 dis.ch.

8 Kt-Q2ch	K-R6
9 Q-R1ch	K-Kt5
10 Q-Kt2ch	K-B4

Black of course avoids 10 . . . K-R4 11 Q-Kt6 mate.

| 11 Q-Kt6ch | K-Q4 |

12 Q-Q6 mate, and a pretty mate it is.

NO. *266*

WHITE
*to play
and win*

PROKOP 1944

1 Q-R1ch   K-Kt5

FORCED, as *1* . . . K-Kt6 loses the Queen by a Knight fork.

2 Q-Kt2ch   K-R5

Alternative moves by Black lead to this:

A] *2* . . . K-R4 *3* Q-R3ch, K-Kt3 (or *3* . . . K-Kt4 *4* Kt-Q4ch) *4* Q-R7ch, K-B3 (or Kt4) *5* Kt-Q4ch, and White wins the Queen.

B] *2* . . . K-B5 *3* Q-B3ch, K-Q4 (*3* . . . K-Kt4 *4* Kt-Q4ch wins) *4* Q-R5ch, K-K5 (on *4* . . . K-K3 *5* Kt-Q4ch wins) *5* Kt-Kt3ch wins the Queen

C] *2* . . . K-B4 *3* Q-R3ch, K-B5 (if *3* . . . K-B3 or Kt4 *4* Kt-Q4ch wins) *4* Q-B3ch, and White wins as in variation (B) above

3 Kt-B3ch	K-R4
4 Q-R3ch	K-Kt3
5 Q-Q6ch	K-R4
6 K-Kt8!!	

An amazing move. Quiet as it is, it leaves Black helpless. To begin with, his King has no moves, and his Queen has no checks.

6 . . .   P-R7

What else is there? If:

A] *6* . . . Q-B6 (unguarding his QB4 square) *7* Q-B5ch, K-R3 *8* Q-Kt5 mate

B] *6* . . . Q-B8 (unguarding his QB4 but still controlling QKt4) *7* Q-B5ch, K-R3 *8* Q-R7 mate

C] *6* . . . Q-KB7 (guarding squares QB4 and QR2) *7* Q-R3ch, K-Kt3 *8* Q-R7ch, and White mates next move.

7 Q-R3ch	K-Kt3
8 Q-R7ch	K-B3
9 Q-B7 mate	

NO. 267

WHITE
*to play
and win*

KUBBEL 1940

1 Kt-R2

THREATENS *2* Kt-Kt4—mate on the move.

| *1* . . . | K-K6 |
| *2* Kt-Kt4ch | K-B5 |

If *2* . . . K-K5 instead, *3* Kt-B6ch, K-B4 (moving to a Black square K4, K6 or B5 loses the Queen by a Knight fork) *4* Kt-Q7!, and White attacks the Queen while simultaneously threatening *5* Q-Kt4 mate.

3 Q-KB1ch   K-K5

Forced, as *3* . . . K-Kt4 runs into *4* Q-B6ch, K-R4 *5* Q-B5 mate.

4 Kt-B6ch   K-Q5

The only move, *4* . . . K-K4 losing the Queen by *5* Kt-Q7ch, and *4* . . . K-K6 by *5* KtxPch.

5 Q-Q1ch   K-B5

Again there is no choice, moving to a Black square being met by a Knight fork winning the Queen.

6 QxPch   K-B6

If *6* . . . K-Kt5 instead, *7* Q-R2! sets Black an impossible problem (the hardest kind to solve). If he moves his King (*7* . . . K-B6) then *8* Kt-Q5ch wins the Queen, while should he move his Queen, *8* Kt-Q5 mates the King.

7 Q-R8!

Threatens *8* Kt-Q5ch winning the Queen.

7 . . .   K-Q5

The King moves, since the Queen must stay put.

8 Kt-Q5

White wins the Queen.

282

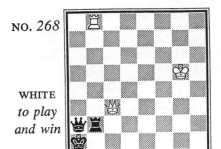

NO. 268

WHITE
to play
and win

HORWITZ 1889

PIECES are even, but Black's crowded position suggests the possibility of a White win.

1 K-R4!

The King must find a quiet place, away from annoying checks.

1 . . .   Q-R5ch

As good as there is, *1* . . . Q-Kt8 losing the Queen after *2* R-R8ch, and *1* . . . K-Kt8 *2* Q-K1ch leading into the main line of play.

2 K-Kt3   Q-R7

The Queen must return to protect the Rook, but not to B7 as then *3* R-R8ch, K-Kt8 *4* Q-K1ch, Q-B8 *5* R-R1ch, KxR *6* QxQch is too expensive.

3 Q-K1ch   R-Kt8

The alternative *3* . . . Q-Kt8 leads to *4* Q-R5ch, Q-R7 *5* Q-B3, K-Kt8 *6* Q-K1ch, and the procedure is the same as in the main line of play.

4 Q-K5ch   R-Kt7
5 Q-B3   K-Kt8

Forced, as *5* . . . Q-Kt8 *6* R-R8ch costs the Queen.

6 Q-K1ch   K-B7
7 R-B8ch   K-Q6

On *7* . . . K-Kt6 *8* Q-B3ch, K-R5 *9* R-R8ch wins the Queen.

8 R-B3ch

Begins a series of checks given by Rook and Queen alternately on the Black squares, which drives the unhappy King upward to his doom.

8 . . .   K-Q5
9 Q-K3ch   K-Q4
10 R-B5ch   K-Q3
11 Q-K5ch   K-Q2
12 R-B7ch   K-Q1
13 Q-K7 mate

WHITE
to play
and win

CLAUSEN

IT SEEMS almost incredible that the end of the winning combination finds White's modest little Pawn way up on the seventh rank, master of all it surveys.

1 P-Q4

Initiates a powerful threat: *2* Q-B2 mate.

| *1* . . . | K-B5 |
| *2* Q-R2ch | K-Kt4 |

Quick disaster follows *2* . . . K-Q6 when *3* Q-K2ch, K-B6 *4* Q-B2 mates the King.

3 Q-Kt3ch K-B3

The alternative is *3* . . . K-R4 when *4* Q-Kt4ch, K-R3 *5* Q-R4ch, K-Kt2 *6* Q-Kt5ch, K-R1 (or B1) *7* Q-R6ch, K-Kt1 *8* Q-R7ch, K-B1 *9* Q-R8 is mate.

4 B-K7! QxB

Other moves by the Queen allow White to mate by *5* P-Q5.

5 P-Q5ch	K-Q3
6 Q-Kt4ch	P-B4
7 PxP e.p.ch	K-K3
8 QxQch	KxQ
9 P-B7	

Nothing can stop the Pawn, who has led a charmed life, from becoming a Queen next move.
White wins

NO. *270*

WHITE
to play
and win

EROCHIN 1928

BLACK'S King and Queen are far apart, yet White manages to involve them in a combination resulting in loss of the Queen or worse.

    1 Kt-B2ch   K-R5

Not to R7 as *2* Q-R3 is mate.

    2 Q-Kt4ch   K-Kt4

The King avoids two pitfalls: *2* . . . K-Kt6 *3* Q-Kt4ch and mate next, and *2* . . . K-R4 *3* Q-Kt4 mate.

    3 Kt-Q4ch   K-Kt3

The only flight square. Moving to any other Black square permits a Knight fork impaling King and Queen, while returning to the fifth rank exposes the King to a discovered check by *4* Kt-K6, costing the Queen.

    4 Q-Kt6ch   K-Kt2

Black is given no choice. If *4* . . . K-B2 (or B4) *5* Kt-K6ch wins the Queen, and if *4* . . . K-R2 (or R4) *5* Kt-B6ch does the trick.

    5 Q-K4ch!   K-B1

If Black tries *5* . . . K-Kt3 instead, *6* Q-Kt1ch forces the King to one of the fatal Black squares.

    6 Q-R8ch   K-Q2
    7 Q-B6ch   K-K2
    8 Q-K6 mate!

NO. 271

WHITE
*to play
and win*

SOMOV-NASIMOVICH 1927

1 Q-R4ch   K-B4

ON *1* . . . K-B6 instead, *2* Q-R1ch, K-Q6 *3* Kt-K5ch, and Black must give up his Queen.

       2 Q-R7ch   K-Q4
       3 Kt-K3ch   K-K4
       4 Q-Kt7ch   K-B5!

The best chance. On *4* . . . Kt-B3 *5* K-Kt6 (to win the pinned Knight) Q-Q1 *6* Kt-B4ch, K-Q4 (leaves the Knight to its fate, but *6* . . . K-K3 runs into *7* Q-B7 mate) *7* QxKt, and White wins.

            5 Kt-Kt2ch!

But not the hasty *5* QxQ, and Black draws by stalemate.

       5 . . .   PxKt
       6 QxQ   P-Kt8(Q)

By ingenious play Black has replaced the Queen he lost with a new Queen, but White is prepared for even this contingency.

       7 Q-K3ch   K-K4

On *7* . . . K-Kt5 instead, *8* P-B3ch wins the Queen.

            8 P-B4ch

White wins the second Queen and the game.

NO. 272

WHITE
*to play
and win*

TROITZKY 1929

THE Queen wins this almost by herself, with a delightful series of zigzag checks.

	1 Q-B5ch	K-R1

The only move, since *1* . . . Q-Kt3 loses the Queen by *2* Kt-B8ch, and *1* . . . K-R3 exposes the King to mate in three, starting with *2* PxPch.

2 Q-K5ch	K-R2
3 Q-K4ch	K-R1
4 Q-Q4ch	K-R2
5 Q-Q3ch	K-R1
6 Q-B3ch	K-R2
7 Q-B2ch	K-R1
8 Q-Kt2ch	K-R2
9 Q-Kt1ch	K-R1

Now the Queen takes three giant steps for the denouement.

10 Q-KR1ch	Q-R2
11 Q-R1ch	K-Kt1
12 Q-R8ch	K-B2
13 KtxPch	

White wins the Queen and the game.

NO. *273*

WHITE
*to play
and win*

GURVICH 1927

A CAPTIVATING bit of endgame magic:

> *1* Kt-K4   Kt-Q6

Black avoids Queening with check, the reply *2* Kt-B2ch forcing him to give up his Queen at once.

> *2* Q-B2!   KtxQ

If instead *2* . . . P-Kt8(Q), pinning White's Queen, *3* Kt-Kt3ch, QxKt *4* QxQ wins for White.

> *3* Kt-Kt3ch!   K-Kt8
> *4* Kt-Kt5

Holds the King fast, and restricts Black to moves by one of the Knights.

> *4* . . .   Kt(R7)-Kt5

If the other Knight moves anywhere at all, the response is *5* Kt-R3 mate.

> *5* Kt-B3 mate

Variety of Pieces

BLACK'S KING in the Gorgiev No. 274 has a dismal future. He must decide the manner of his death—whether to be mated by a Knight or a Bishop.

Naiderashvilli's No. 275 is playful, and if not practical is none the less pleasing.

The awkward-looking Knights in Eisenstadt's No. 276 more than hold their own against the powerful Rook.

The play is exciting from first move to last in No. 278. The ending is a masterpiece of Korolkovian ingenuity.

The passed Pawns appear formidable in Troitzky's No. 280, but skillful play by Rook and Knight dissolves all the threats.

Rossolimo's 281 is unusually pretty, featuring as it does five zigzag checks by the Knight to force the King down from one end of the board to another.

In Isenegger's 282 and Topseyev's 283, Knight and Rook engage in a plot to capture the opponent's Rook. Both are fine studies, the latter especially being a delight. When a composer can create beauty from such scant material, he is a genuine artist.

In the Kakovin No. 284, winning a Rook is easy, but it must be captured at the right moment.

The finish is fine in Birnov's No. 285, leading as it does to the theme of Domination. The Bishop is attacked, and all the exits are barred!

In No. 286 and No. 287 by Fritz, threats are directed at the minor pieces, but the real object of White's attack is the King himself.

Black's Knight, in Gorgiev's No. 288, is driven into an awkward spot while fleeing from a bloodthirsty Rook. Unwillingly it involves the King, who becomes victim of as neat a mate as you would want to see.

Kasparyan's No. 290 shows Rook, Knight and Pawn pitted against a solitary Pawn—but that Pawn is poised on the seventh rank, on the brink of being crowned.

In Wotawa's No. 296, the setting (two Rooks against two connected Pawns on the seventh) is attractive— and so is the solution!

Rooks are sacrificed all over the board in No. 298, a lively ending by Gorgiev.

Skillful handling of the Rooks in Rinck's No. 299 enables White to exploit the adverse King's unfortunate position on the edge of the board.

In Wotawa's No. 300, White gives up one of his pieces, and then lets Black capture the remaining two *with check* —yet manages to win!

A fascinating variety of ideas!

NO. *274*

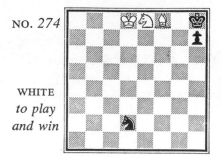

WHITE
*to play
and win*

GORGIEV 1938

THE position of Black's King indicates that mate is in the air, but will the mating piece be the Knight or the Bishop?

1 B-R6!

The plausible *1* Kt-B6 instead does not work, as after *1* . . . P-R4 *2* K-K7, Kt-B6 *3* K-B7, Kt-K4ch compels the King to leave, and sets aside the threat of mate.

1 . . .   Kt-K5

Black had no time to get his King into the open, his Knight being attacked, but the Knight might have moved to B6 instead with this result: *1* . . . Kt-B6 *2* K-K7, Kt-R5 *3* K-B7, Kt-B4 *4* K-B8, KtxB *5* Kt-Q6, and White's next move will be *6* Kt-B7 mate.

2 K-Q7!

This, and not K7 is the right square for the King. On *2* K-K7 instead, the reply *2* . . . K-Kt1 prevents White from making further progress.

Now if Black plays *2* . . . K-Kt1 *3* K-K7, Kt-Kt6 *4* Kt-B6ch, K-R1 *5* K-B7 forces mate.

2 . . .   Kt-B3ch

Hoping for *3* KtxKt and Black draws by stalemate.

3 K-K7   Kt-Kt1ch

If *3* . . . KtxKt instead, *4* K-B8!, Kt-Q3 *5* B-Kt7 is mate.

4 K-B8!   KtxB
5 Kt-Q6   Kt-B4
6 Kt-B7 mate

NO. 275

WHITE
to play
and win

NAIDERASHVILLI 1949

A BEAUTIFUL ending! White toys with his opponent (even forcing him to Queen a Pawn) while evolving a picturesque mate.

1 B-K3ch	K-Kt8
2 B-R6	P-Kt4
3 K-K7	P-Kt5
4 K-B6	P-Kt4
5 K-Kt5	K-B8
6 K-B5 dis.ch	K-Kt8
7 K-B4	K-B8
8 K-B3 dis.ch	K-Kt8
9 K-K3	K-B8
10 K-K2 dis.ch	K-Kt8
11 B-Q2	P-R4
12 K-Q1	P-R5
13 BxP	P-R6
14 B-Q5	P-R7
15 K-Q2	P-R8(Q)
16 BxQ	K-R7
17 B-Q5ch	K-Kt8
18 B-R3	P-Kt5
19 B-Kt3	PxB
20 B-Kt8	P-R7
21 B-R7 mate	

WHITE
to play
and win

EISENSTADT 1931

1 P-K7   R-R1

THE Pawn cannot be stopped by *1* . . . R-K4, as *2* Kt-B4ch wins the Rook.

2 Kt-K6

Intending *3* Kt-B8 next, cutting off the Rook.

2 . . .   R-K1

If *2* . . . R-QB1, White does not play *3* Kt-Q8 as *3* . . . R-B6ch *4* K-Kt2, RxKt draws, but *2* Kt-B4ch, K-R3 *3* Kt-Q8, which wins.

3 Kt-B7!

The move that does the trick. White must not be seduced by the attractive *3* Kt-B4ch, K-Kt4 *4* Kt-Q6ch, K-B3 *5* KtxR, when K-Q2, followed by *6* . . . KxP allows a draw (the two Knights alone being unable to force mate) nor by *3* Kt-B4ch, K-Kt4 *4* Kt-B7ch, K-B3 *5* KtxR, K-Q2, and again Black draws by capturing the Pawn.

3 . . .   RxP
4 Kt-B4 mate!

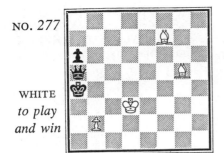

NO. 277

WHITE
to play
and win

RINCK 1914

GIVEN a chance, the Bishops can swoop down the diagonals, and come up with a Queen in their clutches.

    1 P-Kt3ch   K-Kt4

On *1* . . . K-Kt5, the skewer attack *2* B-Q2ch wins the Queen, while *1* . . . K-R6 is refuted by *2* B-B1ch, K-R7 *3* P-Kt4 dis.ch, and again White wins the Queen.

    2 B-K8ch   K-B4

Clearly, *2* . . . K-Kt3 loses the Queen at once by *3* B-Q8ch.

    3 P-Kt4ch!   QxP

The alternative is *3* . . . KxP *4* B-Q2ch.

    4 B-K7ch

White wins the Queen and the game.

293 ♔

NO. *278*

WHITE
to play
and win

KOROLKOV 1951

AN ASTONISHING ending, with all sorts of attack and counter-attack. Both sides indulge in surprise tactical play.

1 P-B7

White does not start with *1* B-Kt2, as the response would not be *1* . . . BxKt *2* P-B7dis.ch, and White wins, but simply *1* . . . RxP when *2* BxRch, K-R2 leaves nothing but a draw.

1 . . .   R-R3ch

Black loses after *1* . . . R-KB3 by *2* B-Kt2, and after *1* . . . R-Kt1 by *2* PxR(Q)ch, KxQ *3* Kt-K7ch followed by *4* KtxB.

2 B-R3!

Not *2* K-Kt1, BxKtch followed by *3* . . . K-Kt2, nor *2* K-Kt2, R-KB3, and White cannot pin the Rook.

| 2 . . . | RxBch |
| 3 K-Kt2 | R-R7ch! |

To which White must not play *4* KxR as *4* . . . B-K3ch wins the Pawn and draws.

| 4 K-B1! | R-R8ch |
| 5 K-Q2 | |

If *5* K-Kt2 instead, then *5* . . . R-

Kt8ch *6* K-B3, R-Kt6ch *7* K-Q4, R-Q6ch *8* KxR (on *8* K-K5, R-Q1 draws easily) BxKtch *9* K-Q4, K-Kt2, and Black has a draw.

5 . . .	R-R7ch
6 K-K3	R-R6ch
7 K-B4	R-R5ch
8 K-Kt5	

Bad for White would be *8* K-K5, R-R4ch followed by *9* . . . RxKt and Black wins, while *8* K-B3 is met by *8* . . . B-Kt2ch and *9* . . . R-R1.

| 8 . . . | R-Kt5ch! |
| 9 K-R6! | |

Best, the alternatives being:
A] *9* KxR, BxKtch *10* KxB, K-Kt2 *11* K-K6, K-B1 *12* K-B6, and Black is stalemated.
B] *9* K-R5, R-Kt1 *10* Kt-K7, R-B1 *11* Kt-Kt6ch, K-Kt2, and Black draws.

9 . . .   R-Kt1!

Cleverly avoiding *9* . . . R-Kt3ch *10* KxR, BxKtch *11* K-R6, and the Pawn will Queen.

10 Kt-K7

Threatens *11* PxR(Q) mate.
What does Black do now? If the Rook moves on the rank (say to B1 or Q1) *11* Kt-Kt6 is mate; if it moves on the file, the Pawn promotes to a Queen and forces mate.

10 . . .   B-K3

Ingenious to the last. If White plays *11* Kt-Kt6ch, then *11* . . . RxKtch *12* KxR, BxPch gives Black a draw.
But White has a last trump:

| 11 PxR(Q)ch | BxQ |
| 12 Kt-Kt6 mate! | |

WHITE
to play
and win

NAZANIAN 1938

WHITE seems to have a weak and somewhat scattered little army with which to put up a successful fight against the powerful Queen, but we shall see. . . .

1 Kt-Kt6ch   K-B2

If *1* . . . K-Q1 instead, 2 B-Kt5, QxB 3 P-B8(Q)ch, K-B2 4 Q-B8ch, KxKt (or *4* . . . K-Q3 5 Q-QB5ch, K-K4 6 P-Q6 dis.ch, K-B3 7 QxQch wins) 5 Q-B5ch, K-R3 6 Q-R5 mate.

2 P-B8(Q)!

The tempting 2 P-Q6ch fails after *2* . . . QxP (not *2* . . . KxP *3* B-B5ch and White wins) *3* B-B4 (expecting *3* . . . QxB *4* Kt-Q5ch) K-Q1! *4* BxQ, and Black draws by stalemate.

    2 . . .   QxQ
    3 P-Q6ch   K-B3

Other possibilities are:
A] *3* . . . QxP *4* B-B4, QxB *5* Kt-Q5ch, and White wins
B] *3* . . . K-Kt1 *4* Kt-Q7ch, and White wins the Queen
C] *3* . . . K-Q1 *4* B-Kt5ch, K-K1 *5* P-Q7ch, K-B2   *6* P-Q8(Q),   and White has a winning advantage.

    4 P-Kt5ch   KxP
    5 B-B5ch   KxB
    6 Kt-Q7ch

White wins the Queen and the game.

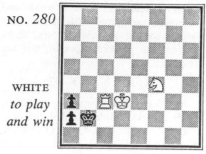

NO. *280*

WHITE
to play
and win

TROITZKY 1916

1 R-B2ch   K-Kt6

THE alternative *1* . . . K-Kt8 leads
to this: *2* Kt-K2, P-R8(Q) *3* Kt-
B3ch, QxKtch *4* KxQ, P-R7 *5* R-
Kt2ch, K-R1 *6* R-R2, K-Kt8 *7* R-R1
mate.

2 R-B1   P-R8(Q)!

The best chance. If instead *2* . . .
K-Kt7 *3* K-Q2, P-R8(Q) *4* Kt-Q3ch,
K-R7   *5* Kt-Kt4ch, K-Kt7   *6* RxQ,
KxR *7* K-B1, P-R7 *8* Kt-B2 mate.

3 RxQ   K-Kt7
4 R-KB1!

This is the key square for the
Rook, as will later be seen.

4 . . .   P-R7
5 K-B4!

Clears Q3 for the use of the Knight.

5 . . .   P-R8(Q)
6 Kt-Q3ch   K-R7
7 Kt-Kt4ch   K-Kt7
8 R-B2ch   K-Kt8

If *8* . . . K-R6 instead, *9* Kt-B2ch
wins the Queen, or if *8* . . . K-B8
9 Kt-R2ch, K-Kt8 (or *9* . . . K-Q8
10 R-B1ch) *10* K-Kt3, and Black is
lost.

9 K-Kt3

Black has no defense against the
threat of *10* R-B1 mate. Had the
Rook gone to KKt1 at the fourth
move, Black's saving move now
would be *9* . . . Q-R2, while had
the Rook moved to KR1, the defense
9 . . . Q-QR1 would prevent mate.
As it is. . . .
White wins

NO. *281*

WHITE
to play
and win

ROSSOLIMO 1928

BLACK has two threats which must be taken into account: *1* . . . P-R8(Q) and *1* . . . BxKt.

1 R-Kt8ch	K-Kt2

If *1* . . . K-Q2 *2* Kt-Kt8ch followed by *3* KxP wins.

2 Kt-B5ch	K-Kt3

Black must keep on attacking the Knight diagonally. Against *2* . . . K-B3 instead, White plays *3* R-B8ch followed by *4* KxP.

3 Kt-R4ch	K-Kt4

Here too if *3* . . . K-R4, the reply is *4* R-R8ch and *5* KxP.

4 Kt-B3ch	K-Kt5
5 Kt-R2ch	K-Kt6
6 Kt-B1ch	K-Kt7
7 KxP	KxKt
8 R-Kt1	

White pins the Bishop and wins.

NO. 282

WHITE
*to play
and win*

ISENEGGER 1949

| 1 Kt-K8ch | K-B1 |

OTHER moves lose the Rook: *1* . . . K-Q2 *2* R-Kt7ch, or *1* . . . K-Q1 *2* R-Kt8ch followed by *3* R-Kt7ch.

2 Kt-Q6ch	K-Q1
3 R-Kt8ch	K-Q2
4 R-Kt7ch	K-Q1

Hoping that White will grab the Rook without realizing that it leaves Black stalemated.

| 5 Kt-B7ch | K-B1 |

The alternative is interesting: *5* . . . K-K1 *6* K-K6 (threatens *7* R-Kt8 mate) K-B1 *7* K-B6, K-K1 *8* R-K7ch, K-B1 *9* R-Q7, K-Kt1 (or *9* . . . K-K1) *10* R-Q8 mate.

| 6 K-B6 | R-Kt2 |

The Rook must stay on the second rank. If for example, *6* . . . R-R5, then *7* Kt-Q6ch, K-Q1 *8* R-Q7 is mate.

7 Kt-Q6ch	K-Q1
8 R-Kt8ch	K-K2
9 Kt-B5ch	K-B3
10 KtxR	

White remains a Rook ahead, and wins.

NO. 283

WHITE
to play
and win

TOPSEYEV 1927

THE setting is simple, but there is a wealth of ideas in this remarkable ending.

1 R-R8ch	K-Q2

On *1* . . . K-K2 instead, the Knight fork *2* Kt-B6ch wins at once.

2 R-R7ch	K-Q3!

Angling for *3* RxR and stalemate.

3 Kt-B7ch	K-B2

Black avoids *3* . . . K-K3 when *4* Kt-Kt5ch wins the Rook, as well as *3* . . . K-K2 (or Q2) when *4* Kt-K5ch does likewise.

4 Kt-K5ch!	

White must not play *4* Kt-Q6ch, as Black has a defense in *4* . . . K-Q1, and his Rook is safe from capture.

4 . . .	K-Kt3!

But not *4* . . . K-Kt1 *5* Kt-B6ch, and the Rook is lost.

5 Kt-B4ch	K-R3
6 R-R6ch	K-Kt2!

On *6* . . . K-Kt4 instead, White finishes by *7* R-Kt6ch, K-R5 *8* K-B3 (threatens *9* R-Kt4 mate) R-QKt2 *9* Kt-Kt2ch (definitely not *9* RxR stalemate) K-R4 *10* RxR, and White wins.

7 Kt-Q6ch	K-Kt1

Here if *7* . . . K-R1 *8* R-R8 is mate, while should the King move to R3, Kt3 or B3, the reply *8* Kt-B8 (discovering check while attacking the Rook) wins for White.

8 R-R8ch	K-B2
9 Kt-Kt5ch	

White remains a Rook ahead, and wins.

299

NO. *284*

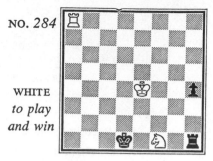

WHITE
*to play
and win*

KAKOVIN 1951

1 R-R1ch   K-K7

THE only move, *1* . . . K-B7 costing the Rook after *2* Kt-K3ch.

2 Kt-Kt3ch   PxKt
3 R-R2ch!

Brilliant! It's hard to resist *3* RxR, only to find there is no win after Black moves *3* . . . P-Kt7 in reply.

3 . . .   K-Q8
4 K-Q3   K-K8

If *4* . . . K-B8 *5* R-R1ch wins Rook and game.

5 K-K3

White insists on threatening mate.

5 . . .   K-B8

Black loses after *5* . . . K-Q8 by *6* R-R1ch followed by *7* RxR.

6 K-B3   K-Kt8
7 KxP   K-B8
8 R-R1ch

The move which began the attack —but this time it's decisive.

White wins the Rook and the game.

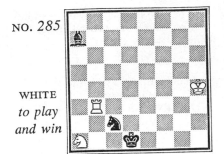

NO. 285

WHITE
to play
and win

BIRNOV 1946

WHITE wins a piece, but is forced to return it. Left with Rook against Bishop, a draw seems the likely result, but the weapon of "Domination" subdues the Bishop.

1 R-Kt1ch!

Forces Black into a pin which costs a piece.

1 . . .	K-Q7
2 R-Kt2	K-B8
3 RxKtch	K-Kt8
4 R-B4!	B-B7ch

If at once *4* . . . KxKt *5* R-R4ch wins the Bishop.

| *5* K-Kt4 | KxKt |
| *6* K-B3! | |

The Bishop now has no moves! The proof:

A] *6* . . . B-R5 *7* RxB
B] *6* . . . B-Kt6 *7* KxB
C] *6* . . . B-K8 *7* R-B1ch
D] *6* . . . B-Kt8 *7* R-B1ch
E] *6* . . . B-K6 *7* KxB
F] *6* . . . B-Q5 *7* RxB
G] *6* . . . B-B4 *7* RxB
H] *6* . . . B-Kt3   *7* R-R4ch, K-Kt7 *8* R-Kt4ch
I] *6* . . . B-R2 *7* R-R4ch

White wins—by Domination!

WHITE
to play
and win

FRITZ 1951

JUST when Black congratulates himself on having rescued his imperilled
Knights—disaster strikes!

1 R-K3ch   K-Q5

Should Black attack the Rook by
1 . . . K-B5 instead, then *2* Kt-
Kt2ch, K-Kt5 *3* KxKt wins easily.

2 R-KKt3   Kt-K5

Hoping with this attack on the
Rook to gain time to save his other
Knight.

3 R-QR3   Kt-Q4

Any other move by this Knight allows its immediate capture. At Q4 the
Knight is safe—but not the King.

4 Kt-B3 mate!

NO. *287*

WHITE
to play
and win

FRITZ 1951

WHITE threatens the minor pieces, but the real object of his attack is the King himself.

1 B-Kt3ch   K-K4

The King had choice of other squares, with these continuations:

A] *1* . . . K-Q3 (or B3) *2* R-Kt6ch winning the Knight

B] *1* . . . K-B4 *2* B-K6 (prevents the Knight from coming out) followed by *3* R-Kt6, winning the beast

C] *1* . . . K-Q5 *2* K-B2, B-B6 *3* R-Q1ch, and White wins the Bishop

D] *1* . . . K-K5 *2* R-Kt6, Kt-B4 *3* B-B2ch, K-K4 *4* R-Kt5, pinning and winning the Knight

| *2* K-B2 | B-Q5 |
| *3* R-Kt6 | Kt-B4 |

The Knight and Bishop have managed to save themselves, but in doing so betray their King. White's next move is. . . .

4 R-K6 mate!

NO. 288

WHITE
*to play
and win*

GORGIEV 1928

1 K-Kt4

BOTH of Black's pieces are now threatened. White could not play *1* RxB at once, as the reply *1* . . . Kt-Q5ch would cost his Rook.

1 . . .   Kt-Q5

Protecting the Bishop, but should the Bishop instead try to protect the Knight, this happens: *1* . . . B-Q4 *2* R-Q1, B-Kt1 *3* B-B4, BxB *4* KxB, Kt-R4ch *5* K-Kt5, Kt-Kt2 (or *5* . . . Kt-Kt6 *6* K-Kt4 winning the Knight) *6* K-Kt6, and the Knight is lost.

2 K-B3	B-K7
3 BxB	KtxBch
4 K-Q3	Kt-Kt6

The only square open to the Knight.

5 R-B3   Kt-R4

If *5* . . . Kt-R8 *6* K-K2, P-R4 *7* R-KR3 wins the Knight.

6 R-B5   Kt-Kt2

If instead *6* . . . Kt-Kt6 *7* R-KKt5, Kt-B8 (or *7* . . . Kt-R8 *8* K-K2, and the Knight is surrounded) *8* R-Kt2, and White's next move *9* K-K2 attacks and wins the Knight.

7 R-B8 mate!

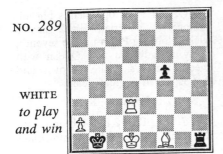

NO. *289*

WHITE
*to play
and win*

FRITZ 1953

1 P-R3!

SURPRISING, but it is more important to retain the Pawn (a potential
Queen!) than to save the Bishop.
Had White played *1* R-KB3 instead,
the continuation *1* . . . KxP *2* RxP
leaves him a piece ahead, but with no
win in sight.

| *1* . . . | RxBch |
| *2* K-K2 | R-B5 |

Forced; if *2* . . . R-R8 instead,
3 R-Q1ch, RxR *4* KxR, and White
wins, his Pawn being beyond pursuit,
while Black's can never get through.
Or if *2* . . . K-B7 *3* R-Q2ch!, K-B6
4 KxR, KxR *5* P-R4, and White wins
easily.

| *3* R-Kt3ch | K-B7 |
| *4* R-Kt4! | RxR |

No better is *4* . . . R-K5ch
5 RxR, PxR *6* P-R4, and White wins.

5 PxR

White wins, his Pawn having apparently been destined from the start
to be crowned.

WHITE
to play
and win

KASPARYAN 1936

TO OFFSET his opponent's big advantage in material, Black has a wicked-looking Pawn on the seventh, ready to advance and Queen with check. But it's White's move, and that is worth a great deal.

1 P-R5ch   K-R3

If *1* . . . KxP *2* R-R7ch and *3* R-R1, while *1* . . . K-B3 is immediate suicide by *2* R-B7 mate.

2 Kt-B7ch   KxP

If instead *2* . . . K-Kt2 *3* Kt-Kt5ch, K-Kt1 (or *3* . . . K-B1 *4* R-B7ch, K-K1 *5* K-K3, and the Pawn is lost) *4* R-K8ch, K-Kt2 *5* P-R6ch, K-Kt3 (*5* . . . KxP *6* R-R8ch and *7* R-R1 or *5* . . . K-B3 *6* R-K6 mate) *6* K-Kt4, P-B8(Q) *7* R-K6ch, Q-B3 *8* RxQch, KxR *9* K-R5!, and Black is helpless to stop the Pawn.

3 R-K5ch   K-R5

If *3* . . . K-Kt3 *4* R-Kt5ch, KxKt (*4* . . . K-R2 *5* R-R5ch and *6* R-R1) *5* R-B5ch, K-Kt3 *6* K-Kt4, and the Pawn is stopped dead in its tracks.

4 Kt-Kt5!

Lets Black Queen with check!

4 . . .   P-B8(Q)ch

Black can be coy and play *4* . . . K-R4 instead, when the right procedure is *5* Kt-K4 dis.ch, K-R5 *6* Kt-Q2 (but not *6* KtxP stalemate) and White wins.

5 Kt-B3ch	K-R6
6 R-R5ch	K-Kt7
7 R-R2 mate	

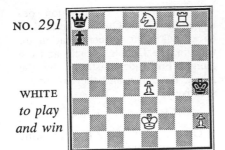

NO. *291*

WHITE
*to play
and win*

PLATOV 1914

NO LONG-DRAWN out battle this.
White disposes of his opponent with
four vigorous moves.

1 R-R8ch   K-Kt4

The alternative is *1* . . . K-Kt5,
when *2* Kt-B6ch wins the Queen by
discovered attack.

2 Kt-Q6   Q-B3

Now the Queen is held to one
move, the capture *2* . . . QxR being
met by *3* Kt-B7ch winning the Queen.

3 Kt-B7ch   K-B5

What else is there? If *3* . . . K-
Kt3 (or B3) *4* R-R6ch wins the
Queen, or if *3* . . . K-Kt5 *4* Kt-K5ch
does likewise.

4 R-R4 mate!

A problem-like mating position

NO. 292

WHITE
*to play
and win*

HORWITZ AND KLING 1851

WHITE plays a combination designed to win the Queen. The tactical tricks making up the combination are the Pin, the Double Attack, and the Knight Fork, demonstrated by the Rook, the Pawn and the Knight respectively.

1 R-R4ch	K-K4

On *1* . . . K-B4 *2* R-R5ch wins the Queen at once.

2 R-R5	P-B4

If *2* . . . QxR instead, *3* Kt-B6ch wins the Queen.

3 RxP	QxR
4 P-Q4ch	KxP

Or *4* . . . QxP *5* Kt-B6ch, attacking King and Queen.

5 Kt-K6ch

White wins the Queen and the game.

NO. 293

WHITE
*to play
and win*

BRON 1927

DESPITE her great mobility, the Queen is caught and subdued by the Knight and Rook working together in perfect harmony.

1 R-B8   Q-R6

If *1* . . . QxR (or *1* . . . Q-B2) 2 Kt-Q6ch wins the Queen.

2 Kt-Q4ch   K-Kt3

The only flight square, as moving to the Rook file loses by *3* R-R8ch.

3 R-Kt8ch   K-B4

The alternatives *3* . . . K-B2 or *3* . . . K-R2 let King and Queen fall into the Knight's clutches by *4* Kt-Kt5ch.

4 R-Kt5ch   K-Q3
5 R-Q5ch   K-K2

Here too *5* . . . K-B2 is met by 6 Kt-Kt5ch.

6 R-QR5!

Shifting the attack to the Queen.

6 . . .   QxR

It is either this, or *6* . . . Q-Q3 when 7 Kt-B5ch wins the Queen.

7 Kt-B6ch

White wins the Queen and the game.

NO. 294

WHITE
to play
and win

DAINIEKO 1951

1 P-Kt7!

WHITE begins with a powerful threat: *2* R-R8, pinning the Queen.

1 . . .   K-B2

The best defense, *1* . . . BxP coming to grief after *2* R-R8, K-B2 (if *2* . . . K-K2 simply *3* RxQ wins) *3* BxB, QxP (on *3* . . . QxB *4* P-Kt8(Q) wins) *4* R-B8 mate, while if *1* . . . QxKtP *2* P-Q7 dis.ch, K-B2 *3* P-Q8(Kt)ch, and King and Queen are impaled.

2 R-R8	QxKtP
3 R-B8ch!	KxR
4 P-Q7 dis.ch	K-B2

Unpins the Pawn, which can now advance.

5 P-Q8(Kt)ch!

Definitely not *5* P-Q8(Q), when Black wins by *5* . . . Q-Kt8ch *6* K-R8, Q-KR8 mate.

5 . . .   K-K1
6 KtxQ

White wins

NO. 295

WHITE
*to play
and win*

BRON 1946

CHESS can never fail to be exciting as long as the lesser force outwits the greater.

    1 R-R5ch   K-K3!

Best, as *1* . . . P-B4 allows the brutal continuation *2* RxPch, QxR *3* BxQ, KxB, and White wins an easy Pawn ending, while *1* . . . K-Q5 *2* P-K3ch is of course unthinkable.

    2 B-Kt3ch   P-Q4
    3 RxP

Threatens to discover check, and win the Queen. If for example, Black plays *3* . . . QxKtP *4* RxP dis.ch wins for White.

    3 . . .   QxBP

To which White can not reply *4* R-KB5 dis.ch, as Black simply captures by *4* . . . KxR.

    4 P-Q4!

Now the idea is to continue with *5* R-K5ch, K-Q3 *6* R-K6 mate.

    4 . . .   P-B4

Clears a flight square for the King at B3.

    5 P-K4   QxKtP

If instead *5* . . . PxP *6* R-Q8ch, K-B3 (or B4) *7* R-B8ch and White wins the Queen.

Despite the fact that Black's Queen is out of danger (even to the point that she threatens the Bishop) White engineers a sparkling finale.

    6 R-Q6 dble.ch!   KxR
    7 P-K5ch   K-B3
    8 P-Q5 mate!

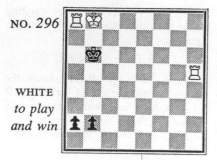

NO. 296

WHITE
*to play
and win*

WOTAWA 1952

ONE'S first impression is that White should be happy to draw against two such menacing Pawns on the seventh. But White has a win—and a pretty one it is.

1 R(R5)-QR5

Threatens to win by *2* R(R8)-R6 mate.

  1 . . .   K-B3
    2 K-B8

Renews the mate threat.

  2 . . .   K-Q3
    3 K-Q8   K-K3

If the King returns, then this happens: *3* . . . K-B3 *4* R-B8ch, K-Kt2 (on *4* . . . K-Kt3 *5* RxP, P-Kt8(Q) *6* R-Kt8ch wins the Queen) *5* R-Kt5ch, K-R2 (or *5* . . . K-R3 *6* RxP, P-R8(Q) *7* R-R8 mate) *6* K-B7 (threatens *7* R-R5 mate) P-R8(Q) *7* R-Kt7ch, K-R3 *8* R-R8 mate.

Another possibility is *3* . . . K-B3 *4* R-B8ch, K-Q3 *5* R(R5)-B5, K-K3 *6* K-K8, K-B3 *7* R(B8)-B6ch, K-Kt2 *8* R-Kt5ch, K-R2 *9* K-B7, P-Kt8(Q) *10* R-R5 mate.

  4 R(R8)-R6ch   K-B2
  5 R-B5ch   K-Kt2
  6 R-Kt5ch   K-B2

Here if *6* . . . K-R2 *7* RxP, P-Kt8(Q) *8* R-R2 mate.

  7 R(Kt5)-Kt6   P-Kt8(Q)
  8 R(R6)-B6 mate

NO. 297

WHITE
*to play
and win*

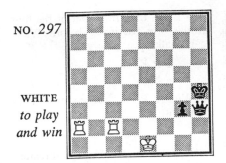

PLATOV 1927

WHITE'S every move must be a hammer blow, or else the Queen will wrest the attack from him.

1 R-R4ch	K-Kt4
2 R-B5ch	K-B3
3 R-R6ch	K-K2

The King must come closer to the Rooks, as *3* . . . K-B2 instead is fatal after *4* R-B7ch followed by *5* R-R8ch.

4 R-B7ch	K-Q1
5 R(B7)-KR7	

Attacks the Queen, and also threatens *6* R(R6)-R8 mate.

5 . . .	Q-Kt7

If instead *5* . . . QxR *6* R-R8ch, K-B2 *7* R-R7ch wins the Queen.

6 R(R6)-R8ch	QxR
7 R-R8ch	

White wins the Queen and the game.

NO. 298

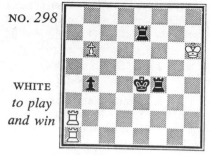

WHITE
*to play
and win*

GORGIEV 1930

NO LESS than three out of the four Rooks are sacrificed before White can chalk up a victory.

    1 R-K1ch   K-B4
    2 RxR

Wins a Rook, but it's only for a moment.

    2 . . .   K-B3

Attacks the Rook while threatening mate on the move.

    3 R-B7ch!   KxR
    4 P-Kt7   R-B3ch

So that the Rook can gain time to get behind the Pawn.

    5 K-R7   R-QKt3

The alternative *5* . . . R-B4 (threatening mate) succumbs to *6* R-KB2!, RxR *7* P-Kt8(Q), and Black has no mate at R7, since White's Queen controls that square.

    6 R-R7

Now Black must guard against *7* P-Kt8(Q) dis.ch, followed by *8* QxR.

    6 . . .   K-K3

If the King moves to the first rank instead, say by *6* . . . K-K1, then simply *7* R-R8ch followed by Queening the Pawn wins for White.

    7 R-R6!

Pins the Black Rook, thereby removing its pressure on the Pawn.

    7 . . .   RxR
    8 P-Kt8(Q)

White wins

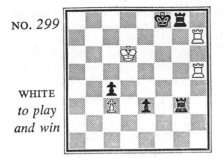

NO. 299

WHITE
to play
and win

RINCK 1922

KNIGHTS were never more agile than these Rooks, who drive the King out into the open and weave a mating net around him.

1 R-B5ch	K-K1
2 R-K7ch	K-Q1
3 R-Q7ch	K-B1

Black has no chance after *3 . . .* K-K1, when *4* R-QR5, R(Kt6)-Kt3ch *5* K-B7 leaves him helpless to avert the mate at R8.

| 4 R-B5ch | K-Kt1 |
| 5 R-Kt5ch | K-R1 |

If *5 . . .* K-B1 instead, *6* R-B7ch, K-Q1 *7* R-Kt8 mate.

6 K-B7

Threatens *7* R-R5 mate.

6 . . .   R(Kt6)-Kt4

On *6 . . .* R(Kt1)-Kt4 instead, White mates in three, beginning with *7* R-Q8ch.

7 R-Q8ch   K-R2

Or *7 . . .* RxR *8* RxR, and Black must give up his remaining Rook to prevent mate.

8 R-Kt7ch	K-R3
9 R-Q6ch	K-R4
10 R-R7ch	K-Kt4
11 R-Kt6ch	K-B4
12 R-R5 mate	

NO. *300*

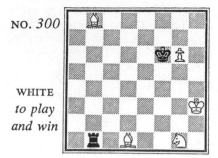

WHITE
to play
and win

WOTAWA 1916

WITH his pieces so widely scattered, and threatened with capture as well, how can White hope to win?

Strangely enough, though all his pieces are removed by capture, White does manage to force a win.

1 B-K5ch!   KxB

On *1 . . .* KxP instead, the reply 2 B-B2ch wins the Rook.

2 P-Kt7   R-Kt1
3 B-Kt3!

Threatens to Queen the Pawn next move.

3 . . .   RxBch

This looks good, as the Bishop is captured with check.

4 Kt-B3ch!

Now Black is in check, and has no time to bring his Rook back to Kt1.

4 . . .   RxKtch
5 K-Kt2!

The Rook has been lured to this square by two successive sacrifices, and can no longer stop the Pawn from Queening.

White wins

INDEX OF COMPOSERS

(The numbers refer to the diagrams)

317

About the Author

Irving Chernev is a chess master who has taken part in state and United States Championship tournaments. Known as "The Believe It or Not Man" of the chess world, Chernev combines his encyclopedic knowledge with a seemingly artless and effortless style of writing. He presents his material with the flair of a born _raconteur,_ his real purpose being, he says, to entertain. And with the instinct of the born teacher, he knows that spontaneity and a humorous approach are the most effective ways of leavening the learning process.

Chernev loves chess. His desire to write books originated with the very deep affection he had for the game. It seemed the most natural thing in the world to pass on his delight in chess to other people. He writes only about what gives him pleasure, and he writes about it with an ardor and enthusiasm that are infectious.

Chernev is the co-author of _An Invitation to Chess_ (the #1 best seller in chess books), author of the remarkable _Logical Chess, Move by Move_ (probably the most instructive chess book ever written), _Combinations: The Heart of Chess, Chessboard Magic!, The Bright Side of Chess, 1000 Best Short Games of Chess_ and many other distinguished and much-loved books.

A CATALOGUE OF SELECTED DOVER BOOKS
IN ALL FIELDS OF INTEREST

A CATALOGUE OF SELECTED DOVER BOOKS
IN ALL FIELDS OF INTEREST

AMERICA'S OLD MASTERS, James T. Flexner. Four men emerged unexpectedly from provincial 18th century America to leadership in European art: Benjamin West, J. S. Copley, C. R. Peale, Gilbert Stuart. Brilliant coverage of lives and contributions. Revised, 1967 edition. 69 plates. 365pp. of text.
21806-6 Paperbound $3.00

FIRST FLOWERS OF OUR WILDERNESS: AMERICAN PAINTING, THE COLONIAL PERIOD, James T. Flexner. Painters, and regional painting traditions from earliest Colonial times up to the emergence of Copley, West and Peale Sr., Foster, Gustavus Hesselius, Feke, John Smibert and many anonymous painters in the primitive manner. Engaging presentation, with 162 illustrations. xxii + 368pp.
22180-6 Paperbound $3.50

THE LIGHT OF DISTANT SKIES: AMERICAN PAINTING, 1760-1835, James T. Flexner. The great generation of early American painters goes to Europe to learn and to teach: West, Copley, Gilbert Stuart and others. Allston, Trumbull, Morse; also contemporary American painters—primitives, derivatives, academics—who remained in America. 102 illustrations. xiii + 306pp.
22179-2 Paperbound $3.50

A HISTORY OF THE RISE AND PROGRESS OF THE ARTS OF DESIGN IN THE UNITED STATES, William Dunlap. Much the richest mine of information on early American painters, sculptors, architects, engravers, miniaturists, etc. The only source of information for scores of artists, the major primary source for many others. Unabridged reprint of rare original 1834 edition, with new introduction by James T. Flexner, and 394 new illustrations. Edited by Rita Weiss. 6⅜ x 9⅝.
21695-0, 21696-9, 21697-7 Three volumes, Paperbound $13.50

EPOCHS OF CHINESE AND JAPANESE ART, Ernest F. Fenollosa. From primitive Chinese art to the 20th century, thorough history, explanation of every important art period and form, including Japanese woodcuts; main stress on China and Japan, but Tibet, Korea also included. Still unexcelled for its detailed, rich coverage of cultural background, aesthetic elements, diffusion studies, particularly of the historical period. 2nd, 1913 edition. 242 illustrations. lii + 439pp. of text.
20364-6, 20365-4 Two volumes, Paperbound $6.00

THE GENTLE ART OF MAKING ENEMIES, James A. M. Whistler. Greatest wit of his day deflates Oscar Wilde, Ruskin, Swinburne; strikes back at inane critics, exhibitions, art journalism; aesthetics of impressionist revolution in most striking form. Highly readable classic by great painter. Reproduction of edition designed by Whistler. Introduction by Alfred Werner. xxxvi + 334pp.
21875-9 Paperbound $2.50

VISUAL ILLUSIONS: THEIR CAUSES, CHARACTERISTICS, AND APPLICATIONS, Matthew Luckiesh. Thorough description and discussion of optical illusion, geometric and perspective, particularly; size and shape distortions, illusions of color, of motion; natural illusions; use of illusion in art and magic, industry, etc. Most useful today with op art, also for classical art. Scores of effects illustrated. Introduction by William H. Ittleson. 100 illustrations. xxi + 252pp.

21530-X Paperbound $2.00

A HANDBOOK OF ANATOMY FOR ART STUDENTS, Arthur Thomson. Thorough, virtually exhaustive coverage of skeletal structure, musculature, etc. Full text, supplemented by anatomical diagrams and drawings and by photographs of undraped figures. Unique in its comparison of male and female forms, pointing out differences of contour, texture, form. 211 figures, 40 drawings, 86 photographs. xx + 459pp. 5⅜ x 8⅜.

21163-0 Paperbound $3.50

150 MASTERPIECES OF DRAWING, Selected by Anthony Toney. Full page reproductions of drawings from the early 16th to the end of the 18th century, all beautifully reproduced: Rembrandt, Michelangelo, Dürer, Fragonard, Urs, Graf, Wouwerman, many others. First-rate browsing book, model book for artists. xviii + 150pp. 8⅜ x 11¼.

21032-4 Paperbound $2.50

THE LATER WORK OF AUBREY BEARDSLEY, Aubrey Beardsley. Exotic, erotic, ironic masterpieces in full maturity: Comedy Ballet, Venus and Tannhauser, Pierrot, Lysistrata, Rape of the Lock, Savoy material, Ali Baba, Volpone, etc. This material revolutionized the art world, and is still powerful, fresh, brilliant. With *The Early Work*, all Beardsley's finest work. 174 plates, 2 in color. xiv + 176pp. 8⅛ x 11.

21817-1 Paperbound $3.00

DRAWINGS OF REMBRANDT, Rembrandt van Rijn. Complete reproduction of fabulously rare edition by Lippmann and Hofstede de Groot, completely reedited, updated, improved by Prof. Seymour Slive, Fogg Museum. Portraits, Biblical sketches, landscapes, Oriental types, nudes, episodes from classical mythology—All Rembrandt's fertile genius. Also selection of drawings by his pupils and followers. "Stunning volumes," *Saturday Review*. 550 illustrations. lxxviii + 552pp. 9⅛ x 12¼.

21485-0, 21486-9 Two volumes, Paperbound $10.00

THE DISASTERS OF WAR, Francisco Goya. One of the masterpieces of Western civilization—83 etchings that record Goya's shattering, bitter reaction to the Napoleonic war that swept through Spain after the insurrection of 1808 and to war in general. Reprint of the first edition, with three additional plates from Boston's Museum of Fine Arts. All plates facsimile size. Introduction by Philip Hofer, Fogg Museum. v + 97pp. 9⅜ x 8¼.

21872-4 Paperbound $2.00

GRAPHIC WORKS OF ODILON REDON. Largest collection of Redon's graphic works ever assembled: 172 lithographs, 28 etchings and engravings, 9 drawings. These include some of his most famous works. All the plates from *Odilon Redon: oeuvre graphique complet,* plus additional plates. New introduction and caption translations by Alfred Werner. 209 illustrations. xxvii + 209pp. 9⅛ x 12¼.

21966-8 Paperbound $4.00

DESIGN BY ACCIDENT; A BOOK OF "ACCIDENTAL EFFECTS" FOR ARTISTS AND DESIGNERS, James F. O'Brien. Create your own unique, striking, imaginative effects by "controlled accident" interaction of materials: paints and lacquers, oil and water based paints, splatter, crackling materials, shatter, similar items. Everything you do will be different; first book on this limitless art, so useful to both fine artist and commercial artist. Full instructions. 192 plates showing "accidents," 8 in color. viii + 215pp. 8⅜ x 11¼. 21942-9 Paperbound $3.50

THE BOOK OF SIGNS, Rudolf Koch. Famed German type designer draws 493 beautiful symbols: religious, mystical, alchemical, imperial, property marks, runes, etc. Remarkable fusion of traditional and modern. Good for suggestions of timelessness, smartness, modernity. Text. vi + 104pp. 6⅛ x 9¼. 20162-7 Paperbound $1.25

HISTORY OF INDIAN AND INDONESIAN ART, Ananda K. Coomaraswamy. An unabridged republication of one of the finest books by a great scholar in Eastern art. Rich in descriptive material, history, social backgrounds; Sunga reliefs, Rajput paintings, Gupta temples, Burmese frescoes, textiles, jewelry, sculpture, etc. 400 photos. viii + 423pp. 6⅜ x 9¾. 21436-2 Paperbound $5.00

PRIMITIVE ART, Franz Boas. America's foremost anthropologist surveys textiles, ceramics, woodcarving, basketry, metalwork, etc.; patterns, technology, creation of symbols, style origins. All areas of world, but very full on Northwest Coast Indians. More than 350 illustrations of baskets, boxes, totem poles, weapons, etc. 378 pp. 20025-6 Paperbound $3.00

THE GENTLEMAN AND CABINET MAKER'S DIRECTOR, Thomas Chippendale. Full reprint (third edition, 1762) of most influential furniture book of all time, by master cabinetmaker. 200 plates, illustrating chairs, sofas, mirrors, tables, cabinets, plus 24 photographs of surviving pieces. Biographical introduction by N. Bienenstock. vi + 249pp. 9⅞ x 12¾. 21601-2 Paperbound $4.00

AMERICAN ANTIQUE FURNITURE, Edgar G. Miller, Jr. The basic coverage of all American furniture before 1840. Individual chapters cover type of furniture—clocks, tables, sideboards, etc.—chronologically, with inexhaustible wealth of data. More than 2100 photographs, all identified, commented on. Essential to all early American collectors. Introduction by H. E. Keyes. vi + 1106pp. 7⅞ x 10¾. 21599-7, 21600-4 Two volumes, Paperbound $11.00

PENNSYLVANIA DUTCH AMERICAN FOLK ART, Henry J. Kauffman. 279 photos, 28 drawings of tulipware, Fraktur script, painted tinware, toys, flowered furniture, quilts, samplers, hex signs, house interiors, etc. Full descriptive text. Excellent for tourist, rewarding for designer, collector. Map. 146pp. 7⅞ x 10¾. 21205-X Paperbound $2.50

EARLY NEW ENGLAND GRAVESTONE RUBBINGS, Edmund V. Gillon, Jr. 43 photographs, 226 carefully reproduced rubbings show heavily symbolic, sometimes macabre early gravestones, up to early 19th century. Remarkable early American primitive art, occasionally strikingly beautiful; always powerful. Text. xxvi + 207pp. 8⅜ x 11¼. 21380-3 Paperbound $3.50

ALPHABETS AND ORNAMENTS, Ernst Lehner. Well-known pictorial source for decorative alphabets, script examples, cartouches, frames, decorative title pages, calligraphic initials, borders, similar material. 14th to 19th century, mostly European. Useful in almost any graphic arts designing, varied styles. 750 illustrations. 256pp. 7 x 10.   21905-4 Paperbound $4.00

PAINTING: A CREATIVE APPROACH, Norman Colquhoun. For the beginner simple guide provides an instructive approach to painting: major stumbling blocks for beginner; overcoming them, technical points; paints and pigments; oil painting; watercolor and other media and color. New section on "plastic" paints. Glossary. Formerly *Paint Your Own Pictures*. 221pp.   22000-1 Paperbound $1.75

THE ENJOYMENT AND USE OF COLOR, Walter Sargent. Explanation of the relations between colors themselves and between colors in nature and art, including hundreds of little-known facts about color values, intensities, effects of high and low illumination, complementary colors. Many practical hints for painters, references to great masters. 7 color plates, 29 illustrations. x + 274pp.
20944-X Paperbound $2.75

THE NOTEBOOKS OF LEONARDO DA VINCI, compiled and edited by Jean Paul Richter. 1566 extracts from original manuscripts reveal the full range of Leonardo's versatile genius: all his writings on painting, sculpture, architecture, anatomy, astronomy, geography, topography, physiology, mining, music, etc., in both Italian and English, with 186 plates of manuscript pages and more than 500 additional drawings. Includes studies for the Last Supper, the lost Sforza monument, and other works. Total of xlvii + 866pp. 7⅞ x 10¾.
22572-0, 22573-9 Two volumes, Paperbound $10.00

MONTGOMERY WARD CATALOGUE OF 1895. Tea gowns, yards of flannel and pillow-case lace, stereoscopes, books of gospel hymns, the New Improved Singer Sewing Machine, side saddles, milk skimmers, straight-edged razors, high-button shoes, spittoons, and on and on . . . listing some 25,000 items, practically all illustrated. Essential to the shoppers of the 1890's, it is our truest record of the spirit of the period. Unaltered reprint of Issue No. 57, Spring and Summer 1895. Introduction by Boris Emmet. Innumerable illustrations. xiii + 624pp. 8½ x 11⅝.
22377-9 Paperbound $6.95

THE CRYSTAL PALACE EXHIBITION ILLUSTRATED CATALOGUE (LONDON, 1851). One of the wonders of the modern world—the Crystal Palace Exhibition in which all the nations of the civilized world exhibited their achievements in the arts and sciences—presented in an equally important illustrated catalogue. More than 1700 items pictured with accompanying text—ceramics, textiles, cast-iron work, carpets, pianos, sleds, razors, wall-papers, billiard tables, beehives, silverware and hundreds of other artifacts—represent the focal point of Victorian culture in the Western World. Probably the largest collection of Victorian decorative art ever assembled—indispensable for antiquarians and designers. Unabridged republication of the Art-Journal Catalogue of the Great Exhibition of 1851, with all terminal essays. New introduction by John Gloag, F.S.A. xxxiv + 426pp. 9 x 12.
22503-8 Paperbound $4.50

A HISTORY OF COSTUME, Carl Köhler. Definitive history, based on surviving pieces of clothing primarily, and paintings, statues, etc. secondarily. Highly readable text, supplemented by 594 illustrations of costumes of the ancient Mediterranean peoples, Greece and Rome, the Teutonic prehistoric period; costumes of the Middle Ages, Renaissance, Baroque, 18th and 19th centuries. Clear, measured patterns are provided for many clothing articles. Approach is practical throughout. Enlarged by Emma von Sichart. 464pp.   21030-8 Paperbound $3.50

ORIENTAL RUGS, ANTIQUE AND MODERN, Walter A. Hawley. A complete and authoritative treatise on the Oriental rug—where they are made, by whom and how, designs and symbols, characteristics in detail of the six major groups, how to distinguish them and how to buy them. Detailed technical data is provided on periods, weaves, warps, wefts, textures, sides, ends and knots, although no technical background is required for an understanding. 11 color plates, 80 halftones, 4 maps. vi + 320pp. 6⅛ x 9⅛.   22366-3 Paperbound $5.00

TEN BOOKS ON ARCHITECTURE, Vitruvius. By any standards the most important book on architecture ever written. Early Roman discussion of aesthetics of building, construction methods, orders, sites, and every other aspect of architecture has inspired, instructed architecture for about 2,000 years. Stands behind Palladio, Michelangelo, Bramante, Wren, countless others. Definitive Morris H. Morgan translation. 68 illustrations. xii + 331pp.   20645-9 Paperbound $3.00

THE FOUR BOOKS OF ARCHITECTURE, Andrea Palladio. Translated into every major Western European language in the two centuries following its publication in 1570, this has been one of the most influential books in the history of architecture. Complete reprint of the 1738 Isaac Ware edition. New introduction by Adolf Placzek, Columbia Univ. 216 plates. xxii + 110pp. of text. 9½ x 12¾.
21308-0 Clothbound $10.00

STICKS AND STONES: A STUDY OF AMERICAN ARCHITECTURE AND CIVILIZATION, Lewis Mumford.One of the great classics of American cultural history. American architecture from the medieval-inspired earliest forms to the early 20th century; evolution of structure and style, and reciprocal influences on environment. 21 photographic illustrations. 238pp.   20202-X Paperbound $2.00

THE AMERICAN BUILDER'S COMPANION, Asher Benjamin. The most widely used early 19th century architectural style and source book, for colonial up into Greek Revival periods. Extensive development of geometry of carpentering, construction of sashes, frames, doors, stairs; plans and elevations of domestic and other buildings. Hundreds of thousands of houses were built according to this book, now invaluable to historians, architects, restorers, etc. 1827 edition. 59 plates. 114pp. 7⅞ x 10¾.
22236-5 Paperbound $3.50

DUTCH HOUSES IN THE HUDSON VALLEY BEFORE 1776, Helen Wilkinson Reynolds. The standard survey of the Dutch colonial house and outbuildings, with constructional features, decoration, and local history associated with individual homesteads. Introduction by Franklin D. Roosevelt. Map. 150 illustrations. 469pp. 6⅝ x 9¼.   21469-9 Paperbound $4.00

THE ARCHITECTURE OF COUNTRY HOUSES, Andrew J. Downing. Together with Vaux's *Villas and Cottages* this is the basic book for Hudson River Gothic architecture of the middle Victorian period. Full, sound discussions of general aspects of housing, architecture, style, decoration, furnishing, together with scores of detailed house plans, illustrations of specific buildings, accompanied by full text. Perhaps the most influential single American architectural book. 1850 edition. Introduction by J. Stewart Johnson. 321 figures, 34 architectural designs. xvi + 560pp.
22003-6 Paperbound $4.00

LOST EXAMPLES OF COLONIAL ARCHITECTURE, John Mead Howells. Full-page photographs of buildings that have disappeared or been so altered as to be denatured, including many designed by major early American architects. 245 plates. xvii + 248pp. 7⅞ x 10¾. 21143-6 Paperbound $3.50

DOMESTIC ARCHITECTURE OF THE AMERICAN COLONIES AND OF THE EARLY REPUBLIC, Fiske Kimball. Foremost architect and restorer of Williamsburg and Monticello covers nearly 200 homes between 1620-1825. Architectural details, construction, style features, special fixtures, floor plans, etc. Generally considered finest work in its area. 219 illustrations of houses, doorways, windows, capital mantels. xx + 314pp. 7⅞ x 10¾. 21743-4 Paperbound $4.00

EARLY AMERICAN ROOMS: 1650-1858, edited by Russell Hawes Kettell. Tour of 12 rooms, each representative of a different era in American history and each furnished, decorated, designed and occupied in the style of the era. 72 plans and elevations, 8-page color section, etc., show fabrics, wall papers, arrangements, etc. Full descriptive text. xvii + 200pp. of text. 8⅜ x 11¼.
21633-0 Paperbound $5.00

THE FITZWILLIAM VIRGINAL BOOK, edited by J. Fuller Maitland and W. B. Squire. Full modern printing of famous early 17th-century ms. volume of 300 works by Morley, Byrd, Bull, Gibbons, etc. For piano or other modern keyboard instrument; easy to read format. xxxvi + 938pp. 8⅜ x 11.
21068-5, 21069-3 Two volumes, Paperbound $10.00

KEYBOARD MUSIC, Johann Sebastian Bach. Bach Gesellschaft edition. A rich selection of Bach's masterpieces for the harpsichord: the six English Suites, six French Suites, the six Partitas (Clavierübung part I), the Goldberg Variations (Clavierübung part IV), the fifteen Two-Part Inventions and the fifteen Three-Part Sinfonias. Clearly reproduced on large sheets with ample margins; eminently playable. vi + 312pp. 8⅛ x 11. 22360-4 Paperbound $5.00

THE MUSIC OF BACH: AN INTRODUCTION, Charles Sanford Terry. A fine, nontechnical introduction to Bach's music, both instrumental and vocal. Covers organ music, chamber music, passion music, other types. Analyzes themes, developments, innovations. x + 114pp. 21075-8 Paperbound $1.25

BEETHOVEN AND HIS NINE SYMPHONIES, Sir George Grove. Noted British musicologist provides best history, analysis, commentary on symphonies. Very thorough, rigorously accurate; necessary to both advanced student and amateur music lover. 436 musical passages. vii + 407 pp. 20334-4 Paperbound $2.75

JOHANN SEBASTIAN BACH, Philipp Spitta. One of the great classics of musicology, this definitive analysis of Bach's music (and life) has never been surpassed. Lucid, nontechnical analyses of hundreds of pieces (30 pages devoted to St. Matthew Passion, 26 to B Minor Mass). Also includes major analysis of 18th-century music. 450 musical examples. 40-page musical supplement. Total of xx + 1799pp.
(EUK) 22278-0, 22279-9 Two volumes, Clothbound $17.50

MOZART AND HIS PIANO CONCERTOS, Cuthbert Girdlestone. The only full-length study of an important area of Mozart's creativity. Provides detailed analyses of all 23 concertos, traces inspirational sources. 417 musical examples. Second edition. 509pp.
21271-8 Paperbound $3.50

THE PERFECT WAGNERITE: A COMMENTARY ON THE NIBLUNG'S RING, George Bernard Shaw. Brilliant and still relevant criticism in remarkable essays on Wagner's Ring cycle, Shaw's ideas on political and social ideology behind the plots, role of Leitmotifs, vocal requisites, etc. Prefaces. xxi + 136pp.
(USO) 21707-8 Paperbound $1.50

DON GIOVANNI, W. A. Mozart. Complete libretto, modern English translation; biographies of composer and librettist; accounts of early performances and critical reaction. Lavishly illustrated. All the material you need to understand and appreciate this great work. Dover Opera Guide and Libretto Series; translated and introduced by Ellen Bleiler. 92 illustrations. 209pp.
21134-7 Paperbound $2.00

HIGH FIDELITY SYSTEMS: A LAYMAN'S GUIDE, Roy F. Allison. All the basic information you need for setting up your own audio system: high fidelity and stereo record players, tape records, F.M. Connections, adjusting tone arm, cartridge, checking needle alignment, positioning speakers, phasing speakers, adjusting hums, trouble-shooting, maintenance, and similar topics. Enlarged 1965 edition. More than 50 charts, diagrams, photos. iv + 91pp. 21514-8 Paperbound $1.25

REPRODUCTION OF SOUND, Edgar Villchur. Thorough coverage for laymen of high fidelity systems, reproducing systems in general, needles, amplifiers, preamps, loudspeakers, feedback, explaining physical background. "A rare talent for making technicalities vividly comprehensible," R. Darrell, High Fidelity. 69 figures. iv + 92pp. 21515-6 Paperbound $1.25

HEAR ME TALKIN' TO YA: THE STORY OF JAZZ AS TOLD BY THE MEN WHO MADE IT, Nat Shapiro and Nat Hentoff. Louis Armstrong, Fats Waller, Jo Jones, Clarence Williams, Billy Holiday, Duke Ellington, Jelly Roll Morton and dozens of other jazz greats tell how it was in Chicago's South Side, New Orleans, depression Harlem and the modern West Coast as jazz was born and grew. xvi + 429pp.
21726-4 Paperbound $2.50

FABLES OF AESOP, translated by Sir Roger L'Estrange. A reproduction of the very rare 1931 Paris edition; a selection of the most interesting fables, together with 50 imaginative drawings by Alexander Calder. v + 128pp. 6½x9¼.
21780-9 Paperbound $1.50

AGAINST THE GRAIN (A REBOURS), Joris K. Huysmans. Filled with weird images, evidences of a bizarre imagination, exotic experiments with hallucinatory drugs, rich tastes and smells and the diversions of its sybarite hero Duc Jean des Esseintes, this classic novel pushed 19th-century literary decadence to its limits. Full unabridged edition. Do not confuse this with abridged editions generally sold. Introduction by Havelock Ellis. xlix + 206pp. 22190-3 Paperbound $2.00

VARIORUM SHAKESPEARE: HAMLET. Edited by Horace H. Furness; a landmark of American scholarship. Exhaustive footnotes and appendices treat all doubtful words and phrases, as well as suggested critical emendations throughout the play's history. First volume contains editor's own text, collated with all Quartos and Folios. Second volume contains full first Quarto, translations of Shakespeare's sources (Belleforest, and Saxo Grammaticus), Der Bestrafte Brudermord, and many essays on critical and historical points of interest by major authorities of past and present. Includes details of staging and costuming over the years. By far the best edition available for serious students of Shakespeare. Total of xx + 905pp. 21004-9, 21005-7, 2 volumes, Paperbound $7.00

A LIFE OF WILLIAM SHAKESPEARE, Sir Sidney Lee. This is the standard life of Shakespeare, summarizing everything known about Shakespeare and his plays. Incredibly rich in material, broad in coverage, clear and judicious, it has served thousands as the best introduction to Shakespeare. 1931 edition. 9 plates. xxix + 792pp. (USO) 21967-4 Paperbound $3.75

MASTERS OF THE DRAMA, John Gassner. Most comprehensive history of the drama in print, covering every tradition from Greeks to modern Europe and America, including India, Far East, etc. Covers more than 800 dramatists, 2000 plays, with biographical material, plot summaries, theatre history, criticism, etc. "Best of its kind in English," New Republic. 77 illustrations. xxii + 890pp. 20100-7 Clothbound $8.50

THE EVOLUTION OF THE ENGLISH LANGUAGE, George McKnight. The growth of English, from the 14th century to the present. Unusual, non-technical account presents basic information in very interesting form: sound shifts, change in grammar and syntax, vocabulary growth, similar topics. Abundantly illustrated with quotations. Formerly Modern English in the Making. xii + 590pp. 21932-1 Paperbound $3.50

AN ETYMOLOGICAL DICTIONARY OF MODERN ENGLISH, Ernest Weekley. Fullest, richest work of its sort, by foremost British lexicographer. Detailed word histories, including many colloquial and archaic words; extensive quotations. Do not confuse this with the Concise Etymological Dictionary, which is much abridged. Total of xxvii + 830pp. 6½ x 9¼. 21873-2, 21874-0 Two volumes, Paperbound $6.00

FLATLAND: A ROMANCE OF MANY DIMENSIONS, E. A. Abbott. Classic of science-fiction explores ramifications of life in a two-dimensional world, and what happens when a three-dimensional being intrudes. Amusing reading, but also useful as introduction to thought about hyperspace. Introduction by Banesh Hoffmann. 16 illustrations. xx + 103pp. 20001-9 Paperbound $1.00

POEMS OF ANNE BRADSTREET, edited with an introduction by Robert Hutchinson. A new selection of poems by America's first poet and perhaps the first significant woman poet in the English language. 48 poems display her development in works of considerable variety—love poems, domestic poems, religious meditations, formal elegies, "quaternions," etc. Notes, bibliography. viii + 222pp.

22160-1 Paperbound $2.50

THREE GOTHIC NOVELS: THE CASTLE OF OTRANTO BY HORACE WALPOLE; VATHEK BY WILLIAM BECKFORD; THE VAMPYRE BY JOHN POLIDORI, WITH FRAGMENT OF A NOVEL BY LORD BYRON, edited by E. F. Bleiler. The first Gothic novel, by Walpole; the finest Oriental tale in English, by Beckford; powerful Romantic supernatural story in versions by Polidori and Byron. All extremely important in history of literature; all still exciting, packed with supernatural thrills, ghosts, haunted castles, magic, etc. xl + 291pp.

21232-7 Paperbound $2.50

THE BEST TALES OF HOFFMANN, E. T. A. Hoffmann. 10 of Hoffmann's most important stories, in modern re-editings of standard translations: Nutcracker and the King of Mice, Signor Formica, Automata, The Sandman, Rath Krespel, The Golden Flowerpot, Master Martin the Cooper, The Mines of Falun, The King's Betrothed, A New Year's Eve Adventure. 7 illustrations by Hoffmann. Edited by E. F. Bleiler. xxxix + 419pp.

21793-0 Paperbound $3.00

GHOST AND HORROR STORIES OF AMBROSE BIERCE, Ambrose Bierce. 23 strikingly modern stories of the horrors latent in the human mind: The Eyes of the Panther, The Damned Thing, An Occurrence at Owl Creek Bridge, An Inhabitant of Carcosa, etc., plus the dream-essay, Visions of the Night. Edited by E. F. Bleiler. xxii + 199pp.

20767-6 Paperbound $1.50

BEST GHOST STORIES OF J. S. LEFANU, J. Sheridan LeFanu. Finest stories by Victorian master often considered greatest supernatural writer of all. Carmilla, Green Tea, The Haunted Baronet, The Familiar, and 12 others. Most never before available in the U. S. A. Edited by E. F. Bleiler. 8 illustrations from Victorian publications. xvii + 467pp.

20415-4 Paperbound $3.00

MATHEMATICAL FOUNDATIONS OF INFORMATION THEORY, A. I. Khinchin. Comprehensive introduction to work of Shannon, McMillan, Feinstein and Khinchin, placing these investigations on a rigorous mathematical basis. Covers entropy concept in probability theory, uniqueness theorem, Shannon's inequality, ergodic sources, the E property, martingale concept, noise, Feinstein's fundamental lemma, Shanon's first and second theorems. Translated by R. A. Silverman and M. D. Friedman. iii + 120pp.

60434-9 Paperbound $1.75

SEVEN SCIENCE FICTION NOVELS, H. G. Wells. The standard collection of the great novels. Complete, unabridged. *First Men in the Moon, Island of Dr. Moreau, War of the Worlds, Food of the Gods, Invisible Man, Time Machine, In the Days of the Comet.* Not only science fiction fans, but every educated person owes it to himself to read these novels. 1015pp.

(USO) 20264-X Clothbound $5.00

LAST AND FIRST MEN AND STAR MAKER, TWO SCIENCE FICTION NOVELS, Olaf Stapledon. Greatest future histories in science fiction. In the first, human intelligence is the "hero," through strange paths of evolution, interplanetary invasions, incredible technologies, near extinctions and reemergences. Star Maker describes the quest of a band of star rovers for intelligence itself, through time and space: weird inhuman civilizations, crustacean minds, symbiotic worlds, etc. Complete, unabridged. v + 438pp. (USO) 21962-3 Paperbound $2.50

THREE PROPHETIC NOVELS, H. G. WELLS. Stages of a consistently planned future for mankind. *When the Sleeper Wakes,* and *A Story of the Days to Come,* anticipate *Brave New World* and *1984,* in the 21st Century; *The Time Machine,* only complete version in print, shows farther future and the end of mankind. All show Wells's greatest gifts as storyteller and novelist. Edited by E. F. Bleiler. x + 335pp. (USO) 20605-X Paperbound $2.50

THE DEVIL'S DICTIONARY, Ambrose Bierce. America's own Oscar Wilde— Ambrose Bierce—offers his barbed iconoclastic wisdom in over 1,000 definitions hailed by H. L. Mencken as "some of the most gorgeous witticisms in the English language." 145pp. 20487-1 Paperbound $1.25

MAX AND MORITZ, Wilhelm Busch. Great children's classic, father of comic strip, of two bad boys, Max and Moritz. Also Ker and Plunk (Plisch und Plumm), Cat and Mouse, Deceitful Henry, Ice-Peter, The Boy and the Pipe, and five other pieces. Original German, with English translation. Edited by H. Arthur Klein; translations by various hands and H. Arthur Klein. vi + 216pp. 20181-3 Paperbound $2.00

PIGS IS PIGS AND OTHER FAVORITES, Ellis Parker Butler. The title story is one of the best humor short stories, as Mike Flannery obfuscates biology and English. Also included, That Pup of Murchison's, The Great American Pie Company, and Perkins of Portland. 14 illustrations. v + 109pp. 21532-6 Paperbound $1.25

THE PETERKIN PAPERS, Lucretia P. Hale. It takes genius to be as stupidly mad as the Peterkins, as they decide to become wise, celebrate the "Fourth," keep a cow, and otherwise strain the resources of the Lady from Philadelphia. Basic book of American humor. 153 illustrations. 219pp. 20794-3 Paperbound $1.50

PERRAULT'S FAIRY TALES, translated by A. E. Johnson and S. R. Littlewood, with 34 full-page illustrations by Gustave Doré. All the original Perrault stories— Cinderella, Sleeping Beauty, Bluebeard, Little Red Riding Hood, Puss in Boots, Tom Thumb, etc.—with their witty verse morals and the magnificent illustrations of Doré. One of the five or six great books of European fairy tales. viii + 117pp. 8⅛ x 11. 22311-6 Paperbound $2.00

OLD HUNGARIAN FAIRY TALES, Baroness Orczy. Favorites translated and adapted by author of the *Scarlet Pimpernel.* Eight fairy tales include "The Suitors of Princess Fire-Fly," "The Twin Hunchbacks," "Mr. Cuttlefish's Love Story," and "The Enchanted Cat." This little volume of magic and adventure will captivate children as it has for generations. 90 drawings by Montagu Barstow. 96pp. 22293-4 Paperbound $1.95

THE RED FAIRY BOOK, Andrew Lang. Lang's color fairy books have long been children's favorites. This volume includes Rapunzel, Jack and the Bean-stalk and 35 other stories, familiar and unfamiliar. 4 plates, 93 illustrations x + 367pp.
21673-X Paperbound $2.50

THE BLUE FAIRY BOOK, Andrew Lang. Lang's tales come from all countries and all times. Here are 37 tales from Grimm, the Arabian Nights, Greek Mythology, and other fascinating sources. 8 plates, 130 illustrations. xi + 390pp.
21437-0 Paperbound $2.50

HOUSEHOLD STORIES BY THE BROTHERS GRIMM. Classic English-language edition of the well-known tales — Rumpelstiltskin, Snow White, Hansel and Gretel, The Twelve Brothers, Faithful John, Rapunzel, Tom Thumb (52 stories in all). Translated into simple, straightforward English by Lucy Crane. Ornamented with head-pieces, vignettes, elaborate decorative initials and a dozen full-page illustrations by Walter Crane. x + 269pp.
21080-4 Paperbound $2.00

THE MERRY ADVENTURES OF ROBIN HOOD, Howard Pyle. The finest modern versions of the traditional ballads and tales about the great English outlaw. Howard Pyle's complete prose version, with every word, every illustration of the first edition. Do not confuse this facsimile of the original (1883) with modern editions that change text or illustrations. 23 plates plus many page decorations. xxii + 296pp.
22043-5 Paperbound $2.50

THE STORY OF KING ARTHUR AND HIS KNIGHTS, Howard Pyle. The finest children's version of the life of King Arthur; brilliantly retold by Pyle, with 48 of his most imaginative illustrations. xviii + 313pp. 6⅛ x 9¼.
21445-1 Paperbound $2.50

THE WONDERFUL WIZARD OF OZ, L. Frank Baum. America's finest children's book in facsimile of first edition with all Denslow illustrations in full color. The edition a child should have. Introduction by Martin Gardner. 23 color plates, scores of drawings. iv + 267pp.
20691-2 Paperbound $2.50

THE MARVELOUS LAND OF OZ, L. Frank Baum. The second Oz book, every bit as imaginative as the Wizard. The hero is a boy named Tip, but the Scarecrow and the Tin Woodman are back, as is the Oz magic. 16 color plates, 120 drawings by John R. Neill. 287pp.
20692-0 Paperbound $2.50

THE MAGICAL MONARCH OF MO, L. Frank Baum. Remarkable adventures in a land even stranger than Oz. The best of Baum's books not in the Oz series. 15 color plates and dozens of drawings by Frank Verbeck. xviii + 237pp.
21892-9 Paperbound $2.25

THE BAD CHILD'S BOOK OF BEASTS, MORE BEASTS FOR WORSE CHILDREN, A MORAL ALPHABET, Hilaire Belloc. Three complete humor classics in one volume. Be kind to the frog, and do not call him names . . . and 28 other whimsical animals. Familiar favorites and some not so well known. Illustrated by Basil Blackwell. 156pp.
(USO) 20749-8 Paperbound $1.50

EAST O' THE SUN AND WEST O' THE MOON, George W. Dasent. Considered the best of all translations of these Norwegian folk tales, this collection has been enjoyed by generations of children (and folklorists too). Includes True and Untrue, Why the Sea is Salt, East O' the Sun and West O' the Moon, Why the Bear is Stumpy-Tailed, Boots and the Troll, The Cock and the Hen, Rich Peter the Pedlar, and 52 more. The only edition with all 59 tales. 77 illustrations by Erik Werenskiold and Theodor Kittelsen. xv + 418pp.   22521-6 Paperbound $3.50

GOOPS AND HOW TO BE THEM, Gelett Burgess. Classic of tongue-in-cheek humor, masquerading as etiquette book. 87 verses, twice as many cartoons, show mischievous Goops as they demonstrate to children virtues of table manners, neatness, courtesy, etc. Favorite for generations. viii + 88pp. $6\frac{1}{2}$ x $9\frac{1}{4}$.
22233-0 Paperbound $1.25

ALICE'S ADVENTURES UNDER GROUND, Lewis Carroll. The first version, quite different from the final *Alice in Wonderland,* printed out by Carroll himself with his own illustrations. Complete facsimile of the "million dollar" manuscript Carroll gave to Alice Liddell in 1864. Introduction by Martin Gardner. viii + 96pp. Title and dedication pages in color.   21482-6 Paperbound $1.25

THE BROWNIES, THEIR BOOK, Palmer Cox. Small as mice, cunning as foxes, exuberant and full of mischief, the Brownies go to the zoo, toy shop, seashore, circus, etc., in 24 verse adventures and 266 illustrations. Long a favorite, since their first appearance in St. Nicholas Magazine. xi + 144pp. $6\frac{5}{8}$ x $9\frac{1}{4}$.
21265-3 Paperbound $1.75

SONGS OF CHILDHOOD, Walter De La Mare. Published (under the pseudonym Walter Ramal) when De La Mare was only 29, this charming collection has long been a favorite children's book. A facsimile of the first edition in paper, the 47 poems capture the simplicity of the nursery rhyme and the ballad, including such lyrics as I Met Eve, Tartary, The Silver Penny. vii + 106pp. (USO) 21972-0 Paperbound
$1.25

THE COMPLETE NONSENSE OF EDWARD LEAR, Edward Lear. The finest 19th-century humorist-cartoonist in full: all nonsense limericks, zany alphabets, Owl and Pussycat, songs, nonsense botany, and more than 500 illustrations by Lear himself. Edited by Holbrook Jackson. xxix + 287pp.   (USO) 20167-8 Paperbound $2.00

BILLY WHISKERS: THE AUTOBIOGRAPHY OF A GOAT, Frances Trego Montgomery. A favorite of children since the early 20th century, here are the escapades of that rambunctious, irresistible and mischievous goat—Billy Whiskers. Much in the spirit of *Peck's Bad Boy,* this is a book that children never tire of reading or hearing. All the original familiar illustrations by W. H. Fry are included: 6 color plates, 18 black and white drawings. 159pp.   22345-0 Paperbound $2.00

MOTHER GOOSE MELODIES. Faithful republication of the fabulously rare Munroe and Francis "copyright 1833" Boston edition—the most important Mother Goose collection, usually referred to as the "original." Familiar rhymes plus many rare ones, with wonderful old woodcut illustrations. Edited by E. F. Bleiler. 128pp. $4\frac{1}{2}$ x $6\frac{3}{8}$.   22577-1 Paperbound $1.00

TWO LITTLE SAVAGES; BEING THE ADVENTURES OF TWO BOYS WHO LIVED AS INDIANS AND WHAT THEY LEARNED, Ernest Thompson Seton. Great classic of nature and boyhood provides a vast range of woodlore in most palatable form, a genuinely entertaining story. Two farm boys build a teepee in woods and live in it for a month, working out Indian solutions to living problems, star lore, birds and animals, plants, etc. 293 illustrations. vii + 286pp.

20985-7 Paperbound $2.50

PETER PIPER'S PRACTICAL PRINCIPLES OF PLAIN & PERFECT PRONUNCIATION. Alliterative jingles and tongue-twisters of surprising charm, that made their first appearance in America about 1830. Republished in full with the spirited woodcut illustrations from this earliest American edition. 32pp. 4½ x 6⅜.

22560-7 Paperbound $1.00

SCIENCE EXPERIMENTS AND AMUSEMENTS FOR CHILDREN, Charles Vivian. 73 easy experiments, requiring only materials found at home or easily available, such as candles, coins, steel wool, etc.; illustrate basic phenomena like vacuum, simple chemical reaction, etc. All safe. Modern, well-planned. Formerly *Science Games for Children.* 102 photos, numerous drawings. 96pp. 6⅛ x 9¼.

21856-2 Paperbound $1.25

AN INTRODUCTION TO CHESS MOVES AND TACTICS SIMPLY EXPLAINED, Leonard Barden. Informal intermediate introduction, quite strong in explaining reasons for moves. Covers basic material, tactics, important openings, traps, positional play in middle game, end game. Attempts to isolate patterns and recurrent configurations. Formerly *Chess.* 58 figures. 102pp. (USO) 21210-6 Paperbound $1.25

LASKER'S MANUAL OF CHESS, Dr. Emanuel Lasker. Lasker was not only one of the five great World Champions, he was also one of the ablest expositors, theorists, and analysts. In many ways, his Manual, permeated with his philosophy of battle, filled with keen insights, is one of the greatest works ever written on chess. Filled with analyzed games by the great players. A single-volume library that will profit almost any chess player, beginner or master. 308 diagrams. xli x 349pp.

20640-8 Paperbound $2.75

THE MASTER BOOK OF MATHEMATICAL RECREATIONS, Fred Schuh. In opinion of many the finest work ever prepared on mathematical puzzles, stunts, recreations; exhaustively thorough explanations of mathematics involved, analysis of effects, citation of puzzles and games. Mathematics involved is elementary. Translated by F. Göbel. 194 figures. xxiv + 430pp.

22134-2 Paperbound $3.00

MATHEMATICS, MAGIC AND MYSTERY, Martin Gardner. Puzzle editor for Scientific American explains mathematics behind various mystifying tricks: card tricks, stage "mind reading," coin and match tricks, counting out games, geometric dissections, etc. Probability sets, theory of numbers clearly explained. Also provides more than 400 tricks, guaranteed to work, that you can do. 135 illustrations. xii + 176pp.

20335-2 Paperbound $1.50

MATHEMATICAL PUZZLES FOR BEGINNERS AND ENTHUSIASTS, Geoffrey Mott-Smith. 189 puzzles from easy to difficult—involving arithmetic, logic, algebra, properties of digits, probability, etc.—for enjoyment and mental stimulus. Explanation of mathematical principles behind the puzzles. 135 illustrations. viii + 248pp.
20198-8 Paperbound $1.75

PAPER FOLDING FOR BEGINNERS, William D. Murray and Francis J. Rigney. Easiest book on the market, clearest instructions on making interesting, beautiful origami. Sail boats, cups, roosters, frogs that move legs, bonbon boxes, standing birds, etc. 40 projects; more than 275 diagrams and photographs. 94pp.
20713-7 Paperbound $1.00

TRICKS AND GAMES ON THE POOL TABLE, Fred Herrmann. 79 tricks and games— some solitaires, some for two or more players, some competitive games—to entertain you between formal games. Mystifying shots and throws, unusual caroms, tricks involving such props as cork, coins, a hat, etc. Formerly *Fun on the Pool Table*. 77 figures. 95pp.
21814-7 Paperbound $1.00

HAND SHADOWS TO BE THROWN UPON THE WALL: A SERIES OF NOVEL AND AMUSING FIGURES FORMED BY THE HAND, Henry Bursill. Delightful picturebook from great-grandfather's day shows how to make 18 different hand shadows: a bird that flies, duck that quacks, dog that wags his tail, camel, goose, deer, boy, turtle, etc. Only book of its sort. vi + 33pp. 6½ x 9¼. 21779-5 Paperbound $1.00

WHITTLING AND WOODCARVING, E. J. Tangerman. 18th printing of best book on market. "If you can cut a potato you can carve" toys and puzzles, chains, chessmen, caricatures, masks, frames, woodcut blocks, surface patterns, much more. Information on tools, woods, techniques. Also goes into serious wood sculpture from Middle Ages to present, East and West. 464 photos, figures. x + 293pp.
20965-2 Paperbound $2.00

HISTORY OF PHILOSOPHY, Julián Marias. Possibly the clearest, most easily followed, best planned, most useful one-volume history of philosophy on the market; neither skimpy nor overfull. Full details on system of every major philosopher and dozens of less important thinkers from pre-Socratics up to Existentialism and later. Strong on many European figures usually omitted. Has gone through dozens of editions in Europe. 1966 edition, translated by Stanley Appelbaum and Clarence Strowbridge. xviii + 505pp.
21739-6 Paperbound $3.50

YOGA: A SCIENTIFIC EVALUATION, Kovoor T. Behanan. Scientific but non-technical study of physiological results of yoga exercises; done under auspices of Yale U. Relations to Indian thought, to psychoanalysis, etc. 16 photos. xxiii + 270pp.
20505-3 Paperbound $2.50

Prices subject to change without notice.
Available at your book dealer or write for free catalogue to Dept. GI, Dover Publications, Inc., 180 Varick St., N. Y., N. Y. 10014. Dover publishes more than 150 books each year on science, elementary and advanced mathematics, biology, music, art, literary history, social sciences and other areas.